CHOICE AND PUBLIC POLICY

Also by Peter Taylor-Gooby

DEPENDENCY CULTURE (*with Hartley Dean*)

EUROPEAN WELFARE FUTURES (*with Vic George and Giuliano Bonoli*)

EUROPEAN WELFARE POLICY: Squaring the Welfare Circle (*with Vic George*)

FROM BUTSKELLISM TO THE NEW RIGHT

MARKETS AND MANAGERS (*with Robyn Lawson*)

POLITICAL PHILOSOPHY AND SOCIAL WELFARE (*with Raymond Plant and Harry Lesser*)

PUBLIC OPINION, IDEOLOGY AND THE WELFARE STATE

SOCIAL CHANGE, SOCIAL WELFARE AND SOCIAL SCIENCE

SOCIAL THEORY AND SOCIAL WELFARE (*with Jen Dale*)

THE PRIVATE PROVISION OF PUBLIC WELFARE (*with Elim Papadakis*)

Choice and Public Policy

The Limits to Welfare Markets

Edited by

Peter Taylor-Gooby
Professor of Social Policy
University of Kent at Canterbury

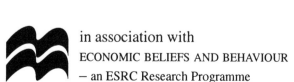

in association with
ECONOMIC BELIEFS AND BEHAVIOUR
– an ESRC Research Programme

First published in Great Britain 1998 by
MACMILLAN PRESS LTD
Houndmills, Basingstoke, Hampshire RG21 6XS and London
Companies and representatives throughout the world

A catalogue record for this book is available from the British Library.

ISBN 0–333–67820–6 hardcover
ISBN 0–333–73131–X paperback

First published in the United States of America 1998 by
ST. MARTIN'S PRESS, INC.,
Scholarly and Reference Division,
175 Fifth Avenue, New York, N.Y. 10010

ISBN 0–312–21262–3

Library of Congress Cataloging-in-Publication Data
Choice and public policy : the limits to welfare markets / Peter
Taylor-Gooby [editor].
p. cm.
Papers of a UK government research project carried out from 1994
to 1998.
Includes bibliographical references and index.
ISBN 0–312–21262–3 (cloth)
1. Social choice—Great Britain.   2. Public welfare—Contracting
out—Great Britain.   3. Privatization—Great Britain.   4. Great
Britain—Social policy.   I. Taylor-Gooby, Peter.
HB846.8.C48 1998
361.6'5'0941—dc21   97–38762
                                                                        CIP

This book is printed on paper suitable for recycling and made from fully managed and
sustained forest sources.

10   9   8   7   6   5   4   3   2   1
07   06   05   04   03   02   01   00   99   98

Printed and bound in Great Britain by
Antony Rowe Ltd, Chippenham, Wiltshire

Contents

vi   *Contents*

List of Tables

List of Figures

Preface

This book arises from the research programme into *Economic Beliefs and Behaviour* in which the UK government's Economic and Social Research Council invested £1.5 million between 1994 and 1998. Recent developments in social science call into question the traditional model of economic behaviour which understands choice as governed by the rational assessment of alternative means to achieve an individual's goals. A growing body of work in psychology, sociology, social anthropology and economics demonstrates that pressure from social groups, cultural values, changing perceptions of individual interests, messages received from the media and many other factors affect the choices people make in the real world.

At the practical level, the programme examines how people's beliefs, values and cultural attitudes relate to their actions as employers, managers or workers and their choices as consumers, as taxpayers and as investors. Many factors currently focus the attention of policy-makers on market behaviour and market choice. These include: the growing flexibility of labour markets, the expansion of world markets and the increased awareness of international competition, the shift towards the privatisation of state services and the fact that many people have more money to spend and more choices to make, while some do not. Choices are at once more complex and more decisive in their impact, both at the individual level and the level of the firm or the nation.

The 14 projects included in the programme range from studies of economic choice in everyday life, for example in ethical investment as against investment driven by the traditional balance of return and security, the decisions people make in planning to finance their social care in old age and the process of buying and selling owner-occupied housing, to carefully controlled laboratory experiments concerned with consistency in choice under uncertainty and the question of what makes a particular alternative salient, and to theoretical work on the parallels between the development and sustenance of social norms and genetic evolution. A full list of projects and publications is given in the Appendix.

The central theme in the research is that choice is a social process, not the outcome of a rational and individual calculus comparing the costs and benefits of alternatives. Choices are not made in terms of the relative utilities of a particular range of options, but are influenced by cultural expectations and preconceptions, by norms prevalent in society and by experience and learning from the experience of others. Expectations about the role of government, kinship obligation and individual responsibility derived from the experience of living in a welfare state play a strong role in influencing views on social security fraud or willingness to pay taxes for better education, health and social care; ideas about wage-determination are influenced by notions of equity and desert as well as market price; in markets and quasi-markets in public services, the willingness of budget-holders to develop innovations and take risks is influenced by assumptions about the proper role of public sector professionals; ethical investment is as much expressive of individual values as it is part of a coherent rational strategy to deny funds to particular firms.

At the theoretical level, the work of the programme shows that economic behaviour cannot be understood as simply deliberative, rational and instrumental. Cultural values matter, social context matters and experience matters as influences on how people choose. At the practical level, any approach to policy-making that assumes that individuals will behave as active consumers or as service entrepreneurs in a welfare market runs the risk of disappointment. The new directions in public policy that stress privatisation and the role of markets are based on a flawed approach to behaviour.

These points are developed in more detail in the following chapters. The new public policy opens up the way to a radical restructuring of the balance of the state and individual and family responsibility. The research programme indicates that an understanding of the impact of the new policies cannot be derived *a priori* from the axioms of rational choice theory but requires an analysis that takes seriously the point that economic choice is a social process and involves examination of the operation of policies in concrete situations.

This book has involved contributions and influences too numerous to acknowledge adequately. The encouragement of the Steering Committee – Ruth Byrne, Bill Callaghan, Chris Downs, John Hey (who attended the meetings of the book's contributors), Anthea Tinker, Bob Tyrrell, Janette Weir and the chair, George Wright – the support of the ESRC staff involved with the programme, particularly our programme officers, Lindsey Fidler, Andrew Lester, Alex Monckton, Mohammed Quraishi, Phil Sooben, Ed Weir, and of course the commitment of the 76 academic investigators, co-applicants, research fellows, officers and assistants, and their technicians and support staff who carried out the work in 26 university departments and research institutes were all essential ingredients. Ms Patricia Smith, the administrator, ensured the smooth running of the programme. We owe a special debt to the respondents to our seemingly irrelevant, perplexing and sometimes, we hope, intriguing investigations, who number, taken together, in excess of 7200 people in Britain and the US.

PETER TAYLOR-GOOBY

Notes on the Contributors

Jane Beattie worked as a Lecturer in Experimental Psychology in the School of Biological Sciences at the University of Sussex, after having taught in the Graduate School of Business at the University of Chicago. Her research interests centred on the psychology of decision-making, applied to diverse real-life contexts. Tragically, she died during the spring of 1997.

Lindsay Brook is a Research Director at Social and Community Planning Research, co-Director of the British Social Attitudes survey series since 1985 and editor of the annual BSA Reports. He is also a member of the Centre for Research into Elections and Social Trends, an ESRC Research Centre linking SCPR and Nuffield College Oxford, the aim of which is to increase understanding of long-term political, social and economic change.

Harriet Clarke is a Research Associate at the Nuffield Community Care Studies Unit, University of Leicester. Since 1994 she has worked with Gillian Parker researching attitudes and behaviour towards financial provision for care in old age. She is currently involved in research exploring the support needs of disabled parents.

Hartley Dean is Reader in Social Policy at the University of Luton. His main research interests are in social security, inequality and citizenship. His publications include *Poverty, Riches and Social Citizenship* (with M. Melrose), *Welfare, Law and Citizenship* and *Dependency Culture* (with P. Taylor-Gooby).

Julie Dickinson is a Lecturer in Organisational Psychology at Birkbeck College. She has published several articles on people's explanations of pay differentials. She is interested in the development of economic knowledge and common sense justifications for socio-economic inequality.

Helga Dittmar is a Lecturer in Psychology in the School of Social Sciences at the University of Sussex. Her most recent book is *The Social Psychology of Material Possessions* (1992) and her research interests include the links between self and material possessions, economic socialisation, impulsive and compulsive shopping and adolescent body image.

Christine Ennew is Professor of Marketing in the School of Management and Finance at the University of Nottingham. Her research interests lie in the area of marketing and include public and financial services. She has published in a variety of journals including *British Journal of Management, European Journal of Marketing* and *Journal of Marketing Management.*

Teresa Feighan was a researcher in the Department of Economics at the University of Nottingham from 1994 to 1996. She is now carrying out research in Ireland.

John Hall is a Senior Research Economist at the Institute for Fiscal Studies. His research interests include local government finance and attitudes towards taxation and public spending. Recent publications include *Who Pays Business Rates?* with Stephen Bond, Kevin Denny and William McCluskey.

Alan Lewis is Reader in Psychology and Director of the Centre for Economic Psychology at Bath University and edits *the Journal of Economic Psychology.* His articles have appeared in economics, social science and psychology journals. Recent publications include *The New Economic Mind: The Social Psychology of Economic Behaviour* with P. Webley and A. Furnham.

Craig Mackenzie is Research Officer in the School of Social Sciences at Bath University. His main research interest is business ethics and ethical investment. He is author of *The Shareholder Action Handbook* and editor of the *Ethical Business* Website.

Ruth Madigan is a Senior Lecturer in the Department of Sociology at the University of Glasgow. Her teaching and research interests lie in Urban Sociology and Methods of Social Research. Recent publications include *House Beautiful: Style and Consumption in the Home* with Moira Munro.

Clodagh Memery is a researcher in the Centre for Housing Research at the University of Glasgow. Her interests lie in survey research.

Hilary Metcalf is Head of Employment Studies at the Policy Studies Institute. She has published widely on employment disadvantage for women, older workers, young people, the long-term unemployed and homeless people. Her publications include 'Hidden Unemployment and the Labour Market' in *Understanding Unemployment* edited by Ethnie McLaughlin.

Tariq Modood is a Programme Director at the Policy Studies Institute. His many publications include (co-author) *Ethnic Minorities in Britain: Diversity and Disadvantage, Church, State and Religious Minorities, Debating Cultural Hybridity* and *The Politics of Multiculturalism in the New Europe*.

Moira Munro is Professor of Planning and Housing at Heriot Watt University. She is an economist with research interests in the operation of the housing market, housing finance and gender and the meaning of the home. She edits *Housing Studies* and is author of *Housing Finance* (1991) and a wide range of journal articles.

Gillian Parker is Nuffield Professor of Community Care at the University of Leicester and Director of the Nuffield Community Care Studies Unit. Her publications include *With This Body: Caring and Disability in Marriage, Different Types of Care, Different Types of Carer* (with Dorothy Lawton), and *With Due Care and Attention: a Review of Research on Informal Care*. Her current research interests include informal care and disability, population forecasting for long-term care needs and finance for long-term care.

Ian Preston is Lecturer in Economics at University College London and a Research Fellow of the Institute for Fiscal Studies. His research interests are in the field of applied public microeconomics and include consumer demand, income distribution, local government funding and attitudes to public spending. His publications include articles in the *Economic Journal*, the *Journal of Public Economics*, the *European Economic Review* and *Applied Statistics* and the *The Measurement of Household Welfare* (with R.Blundell and I.Walker). He is an editor of *Fiscal Studies*.

Lucia Sell-Trujillo is currently completing her PhD on instrumentalisation of acquaintances. Her research interests are social representations in work environments, childhood mythology, institutionalisation of normative structures and the understanding of networks and social support systems.

Peter Taylor-Gooby is Professor of Social Policy at the University of Kent. His main research interests lie in understanding the relationship between values, attitudes and choice and in European social policy. Among his recent publications are *European Welfare Policy* (with Vic George) and *Social Change, Social Welfare and Social Science*.

Satnam Virdee is a Fellow in the Ethnic Equality Group at PSI, where he has worked since 1992. He is an industrial sociologist. His main research interests lie in the analysis of the changing position of ethnic minorities in class relations in contemporary Britain. His publications include 'Black Self-Organisation in Trade Unions' in *Sociological Review* and (as co-author) *Ethnic Minorities in Britain: Diversity and Disadvantage*.

Paul Webley is Reader in Economic Psychology at the University of Exeter. His main research interests are in personal financial management, rule breaking and children's economic behaviour. He is the co-author of *The Individual in the Economy* (with S.E.G. Lea and R.M. Tarpy), *Tax Evasion: An Experimental Approach* (with H.S.J. Robben, H. Elffers and D.J. Hessing), *Children's Saving* (with E.J. Sonuga-Barke) and *The New Economic Mind* (with A. Lewis and A. Furnham).

David Whynes is Reader in Health Economics at the University of Nottingham. His main research interests are in policy evaluation in health care and in the economics of the welfare state. He is author of a number books on economic aspects of health care and public policy including *Current Issues in the Economics of Welfare* (with Nick Barnes).

Adrian Winnett is Lecturer in Economics at Bath University. His main interests are natural resource and environmental economics and the role of financial markets in promoting environmentally sensitive management. He has specialist regional interests in South East Asia and European transitional economies.

1 Choice and the Policy Agenda

Peter Taylor-Gooby

At the end of the 1990s, individual choice has moved to the top of the policy agenda. Many people have higher disposable incomes, working and family life are more flexible and governments wish to reduce state intervention and extend the role of markets. For some, cutbacks in public services, unemployment, benefit constraint and lower pay reduce the scope of palatable choice. Recent developments in social science have called the dominant framework in understanding economic decisions – in work, saving and spending – into question. This book reviews evidence from a range of settings on how far it is reasonable to see market choice as simply reflecting what people want. In this chapter we discuss the main reasons why choice has ascended the political agenda and review some recent developments in understanding how people make decisions.

The particular interest of this book lies in the fact that the political ideology that has been dominant in the most far-reaching policy reform programme of the post-war period in Western Europe, the market reforms of the late 1980s and 1990s in the UK, is based on a specific understanding of choice and behaviour and of economic and social change. This ideology claims that the substitution of a market-based system for state intervention and government planning offers the best way to meet the challenges posed by current developments. The main part of the book consists of chapters exploring practical economic decision-making in a wide range of areas relevant to policy. In the concluding chapter we use this evidence to evaluate the strengths and weaknesses of the most influential strand directing public policy reform in the UK.

Three factors are of particular importance in the salience of economic choice – shifts in the circumstances of individual life, wider economic and social changes and ideological commitments at the political level.

1

ECONOMIC CHOICES IN EVERYDAY LIFE

The economic decisions people make are now of greater personal significance. There are a number of reasons for this. For most groups in the population, real incomes have risen over the post-war period. Many individuals as consumers have a higher disposable income and thus a greater capacity for choice. Some do not, and for them choices are particularly straitened. Recent policies which shift the tax burden from direct to indirect taxation reinforce this trend. The declining role of public services in areas ranging from pension provision to health and social care, education, social housing and transport leads people to consider different options more frequently in areas where they were unlikely to do so in the past. As the more or less universal state services (which offered little choice but acted as a safety-net) decline in significance, the outcome of unsuccessful choices in areas like planning for retirement or house purchase can be more damaging, especially for more vulnerable groups. Thus choice often involves a greater element of risk.

People also experience a greater range of economic choices as producers. Changes in the labour market coupled with government policies designed to enhance flexibility have created a situation where some individuals are likely to have more varied employment over their working life and thus be exposed to a greater range of choices in work. The increase in self-employment and small business combined with the greater importance attached to innovation and enterprise mean that more people are taking entrepreneurial decisions.

Rising incomes (for some) have led to an increase in savings, and a wider range of investment opportunities have become available at the same time as private investment for old age and health and social care has become more important. The proportion of the population who invest in private housing has risen. For all these reasons many people are now faced with a greater range of choices in shopping, saving, working life and investment. Some, excluded from the expansion of choice, face a particular disadvantage.

ECONOMIC AND SOCIAL CHANGE

Many commentators have suggested that, as a result of the social and economic changes of recent years, the Keynesian apparatus of economic management is no longer capable of nourishing national success. These arguments support the tendency for government to curtail direct intervention and service provision in a number of areas and reinforce the acceptance of liberal free market ideology.

The most significant changes discussed from this perspective are in three areas: shifts in the international economic structure; new styles of economic organisation and management; and changing patterns of social need.

The Changing International Political Economy

At the first level a number of developments have reduced the control of government over key features of the national economy. Up to the late 1960s capital markets were largely national and exchange rates were loosely pegged to the dollar. The rise in importance of other national currencies (particularly the yen and the mark), the expansion of resources available for currency speculation resulting particularly from the oil-price hike of the 1970s and the slackening of exchange controls have created a massive international currency market (Michie, 1994; Hutton, 1995, ch. 3). The confidence of speculators has become essential in maintaining a stable international trading position and this confidence may be affected by perceptions of internal policy. Thus the declining value of the franc in the early 1980s led France to abandon its experiment in strong Keynesian economic management and introduce welfare cuts and a programme of denationalisation (Streeck, 1995, p. 389). In 1992, currency instability forced Italy and the UK to leave the European Monetary System and effectively to devalue. Fears about the operation of international capital markets thus act as a constraint on national policy.

The expansion of international trade, the dissolution of the political barriers imposed by the communist/capitalist split and the growing role of new capitalist countries also influence policy. Governments in relatively high-waged European economies are concerned about the impact of international competition. Much of the debate has concerned newly-industrialised Asian economies. Available evidence indicates that Asian exports make up a relatively small proportion of European imports, but have succeeded in capturing from Europe much of the growth in developing markets elsewhere in Asia and in Africa (UN, 1994, tables A.15 and A.16). The proportion of European and US trade made up of low-cost Southern imports is estimated to have doubled between the late 1970s and the early

1990s (Wood, 1994; Esping-Andersen, 1995, pp. 256–61). The formerly state socialist nations of Central and Eastern Europe are strong competitors for West European investment and trade.

The third factor diminishing national economic control is the growth in multi-national companies and political institutions alongside the freer international markets. Multi-national corporations have expanded very rapidly over the past fifteen years (Carnoy *et al*, 1993, p. 49). One recent estimate is that about two-fifths of the jobs created by British-origin multi-nationals are abroad (Marginson, 1994, p. 64). Nations which wish to attract or retain investment from such companies experience competitive pressures in relation to state policies in the areas mentioned above. The importance of political institutions such as the EU with its Single European Market and the recently established North American Free Trade Association is at present hard to judge. The EU has had an impact on UK policy making in respect of equal opportunities, health and safety, agricultural and fisheries policy and employment law, although the country initially opted out from the social chapter. How far the EU will develop beyond an economic association remains unclear. Some writers argue that its role in economic policy-making already constitutes it as a kind of multi-tiered federal state (Leibfried and Pierson, 1995) while others believe that 'it is difficult to see how a close union can be achieved unless new or complementary institutions for delivery of social protection are devised' (Begg and Nectoux, 1995, p. 300).

New Styles of Economic Organisation

The changes at the economic level all imply a reduction in the capacity of the nation state to control affairs in its own territory. This reinforces the position of those who advocate the reduction of intervention in markets. A second issue concerns changes in the character of work in industrial societies. This has political as well as social and economic implications.

The main development is a shift from manufacturing to service sector employment compounded in recent years by the decline of the manufacturing sector in the UK. Manufacturing sector employment peaked in 1966 at 45 per cent of the labour force and has since declined to 18 per cent (Department of Employment, 1995, Table S1.2). In part the shift is due to the introduction of new technology displacing workers, in part to the decline of the manufacturing sector in this country. In 1951, manufacturing accounted for 39 per cent of the UK GDP; by 1995 its contribution had fallen to 22 per cent (CSO, 1954, Table 290; 1995, Table 14.7)

The declining significance of manufacturing employment is associated with a new complexity in social relations. The industrial system provided an obvious basis for the division of the population into social classes. This in turn provided both the motor (in class politics) and the object (in redistributive welfare) for the distinctively European contribution to social integration – the Keynesian welfare state. Changes in patterns of work generate a more complex politics in which consumption patterns (Dunleavy and Husbands, 1985, pp. 18–25) or different bases for social division (Jones et al, 1991, pp. 189–94) carry greater significance. This social change is linked to changes in management practices. The new information technology opens up the possibility of co-ordinating the activities of enterprises without the need for direct chains of command, so that industrial firms no longer find it desirable to establish control over all aspects of their operation from raw materials to after-sales service by bureaucratic management (Kanter, 1985, pp. 42–58 – see Handy's influential analysis of the shift from 'employment organisations' to 'contractual organisations' 1984, p. 80). The opportunities for interlinkages between smaller operations which do not need to be directly owned by one combine multiply. Piore and Sabel regard such industrial communities of interacting producers as the model of future industrial organisation. They argue that such structures permit 'flexible specialisation' and are both more open to innovation and more able to cope with the shocks of changes in markets and manufacturing processes which the greater openness of international trade makes more frequent (1984, pp. 5–6).

The trend to more decentralisation and flexibility in management structures and in the organisation of enterprises has been reflected in developments in the public sector. The new welfare state managerialism emphasises the use of markets to co-ordinate the activities of a multiplicity of public and sometimes private or voluntary service providers. Typically, government agencies set prices for services and operate a system of quality regulation, but do not administer services directly (Flynn, 1995, pp. 126–39; Taylor-Gooby and Lawson, 1993, pp. 133–6).

The social and political changes associated with a restructuring of economic activity lead to demands for a more open and flexible organisation of patterns of work and provide the techniques that make it possible. Some commentators have combined these arguments with new theories about cultural change into a universal account of the transition to a post-Fordist social structure. If Fordism was characterised by a correspondence between 'mass production, mass consumption, modernist cultural forms and mass public provision of welfare, then post-Fordism is characterised by an emerging coalition between flexible production, differentiated and segmented consumption patterns, post-modernist cultural forms and a restructured welfare state' (Burrows and Loader, 1994, p. 1). Mass production was predicated on mass consumption. The welfare state handled the resulting patterns of class conflict. A more flexible production system less securely located in the firm control of a Keynesian welfare state is linked to the increasing diversity of consumption patterns discussed earlier, and is reflected in a more mixed and decentralised welfare system.

Jessop argues that the key concerns of the state must now be the securing of success in more open international markets and the guarantee of labour market flexibility and of a free rein for innovation. He characterises the resulting system as a Schumpeterian Workfare State: 'it marks a clear break with the Keynesian Welfare State as domestic full employment is deprioritised in favour of international competitiveness, and redistributive welfare rights take second place to a productivist re-ordering of social policy' (1994, p. 24). The nation state which directed the Keynesian system retains its legal status and powers, but loses its effective capacity to exert authority. It is 'hollowed out' by a combination of technological change, growing internationalisation and the regionalisation of economies. As capital markets and (in some fields) markets in goods and services become more international, economies must respond to pressures which are not under the control of the nation state. New technologies assist this process, allowing for the integration of production processes of which the component parts are widely separated and for the swifter exchange of information. Under these circumstances, the previous pattern of national regulation of mass production and consumption cannot be sustained.

The applicability of the model to the UK is widely contested. It is pointed out that mass-production and mass-consumption remains dominant in much of the economy and that international patterns of trade are complex (Pinch, 1994; Warde, 1994). However real changes in production processes have taken place as a result of the introduction of new technology and for other reasons, international capital shifts must be seen as of fundamental importance since the forced UK devaluation and exit from the EMS in 1992 and it is clear that concern about international competition is a key constraint under which economic policy must operate.

New Patterns of Social Need

The third factor identified as relevant to the increasing salience of choice is the changing pattern of social need. The most important factors here are the ageing of the population, the changes in family structure, particularly the growing numbers of one-parent families, the increased numbers of un- and sub-employed people and, some would add, the increased uncertainty of modern social life. Unemployment has fallen from over ten per cent in the early 1990s but remains high at about eight per cent in 1996. About seven per cent of the workforce are in temporary and twenty-five per cent in part-time jobs (ONS, 1997, pp. 84, 78 and 76). These changes imply increased spending commitments in future years although the impact of population ageing is not so great in the UK as in other countries, due to its relatively low level of health spending and of state benefits and its comparatively favourable age-structure (Oxley and Martin, 1991, pp. 168–72, EU, 1995, p. 114).

There has been considerable debate about the sustainability of current levels of state provision. The UK government has argued consistently for retrenchment and for the substitution of private markets for state provision. For example the Green Paper on social security reform states bluntly that 'there are few who would say that the commitments [of the existing pension scheme] can be met' (DHSS, 1985, page 21; see also DHSS, 1989, para 1.4 on the costs of health and social care). However, recent EU estimates indicate that, if unemployment in EU countries were to return to the level of the early 1970s and the upward trend in labour force participation on the part of women were to continue, the problem of financing pensions and other services for those aged 65 or over would be resolved in most European countries. If unemployment remains at current levels of over 10 per cent then 'the difficulties of achieving the necessary transfer from those below 65 to those above will be acute and the pressure radically to reform pension systems could prove irresistible' (EU, 1996, p. 43).

Changes in the international context of government have created a climate in which privatisation and the expansion of market systems are encouraged. Innovation in management and a restructuring of work have provided further opportunities for the development of such approaches. Social changes have put additional pressures on traditional state-run welfare systems and public policies and have fuelled demands for more private provision. At the level of the organisation of industry and of state provision the extended use of markets directs attention towards entrepreneurship and decentralised patterns of public policy. All these factors extend the scope for individual economic choice and place greater emphasis on the economic decisions people make.

THE POLITICS OF CHOICE IN THE UK

The most striking manifestation of the changed terms of international trade – the oil crisis of the mid-1970s – hit the UK economy particularly hard. The UK was the first major industrial national to apply for an IMF loan (in 1976). It experienced negative growth in 1980 and 1981 and took until 1983 to recover the lost ground (OECD, 1995, Table A.1). When the Conservative party came to power in 1979 it had a large majority, a radical programme and circumstances which convinced voters that thorough-going reform was necessary.

The reforms contained three elements relevant to economic choice: a radical pruning back of the interventionist and service-providing activities of government; the expansion of individual consumer choice and the enhancement of labour market flexibility. The Labour party, which was elected to government in 1997, committed itself to pursue Conservative spending constraints for at least two years and in effect accepted many of the presumptions of the Conservatives about the use of markets and the stronger role of individual choice in public policy (Labour Party, 1997, p. 13). The result is that the relevance of market choice to many of the issues examined in chapters two to ten of this book is not seriously contested in British politics. We will review these issues in turn.

Retrenchment

The Conservative government succeeded in reducing service spending as a percentage of GDP over the period between 1979 and the late 1980s, but was unable to control rises in the 1990s which brought expenditure back to a level just above that of 17 years ago by 1996 (Treasury, 1996, Table 1.4). Lower debt interest payments and the practice of accounting privatisation proceeds as negative expenditure reduce the 1996 spending level to slightly below that of 1979. The main areas to experience spending cuts were: social housing, trade and industrial support and more recently defence. The greatest difficulty in containing spending arose in the large welfare state areas – health, social care and cash benefits. Since spending was only contained at or slightly below previous levels through the most rigorous constraints of the post-war period, the limited success of the government reveals the difficulty of redirecting state activity.

The government also pursued a vigorous programme of deregulation across a wide range of areas. This included the abolition of the wages council system in 1993, the deregulation of a number of business areas, including bus transport and telecommunications, and the relaxation of controls such as rent controls and restrictions on working hours. Deregulation was linked to a programme of denationalisation of most of state-owned industry including the major state power, water and sewage utilities, road and rail transport, airlines and telephones.

Consumer Choice

The main elements in the new consumerism were the rising disposable incomes for considerable groups in the population that characterised much of the post-war period; the policies designed to cut back on direct taxation which enhanced spending power; the expansion in available credit; and the restructuring of public services which was intended to give a wider range of choice to citizens.

Over the period from the 1971 to 1995 personal disposable income rose by 82 per cent, taking inflation into account. Incomes also grew more unequal, with the gap between the lower and upper quartiles widening by just over a half again (ONS, 1997, pp. 81, 90). Direct taxation was cut back especially for higher income groups. However, indirect and local taxes and insurance contributions were increased with the result that the tax burden was redistributed downwards rather than reduced (Hansard, WA, vol 272 cols 339–50, 26 February 1996).

The increased incomes of those who enjoyed them tended to be directed to consumption rather than investment, and in this they were assisted by the expansion in available credit, much of it secured on housing. Over the period of income growth noted above, personal savings declined from about 14 per cent in the late 1970s to ten per cent by the early 1990s and are predicted to fall to nine per cent (OECD, 1996, Table A.26).

Changes in the public sector provided a different perspective on consumer choice. Reforms in education, health and personal social services were designed to decentralise state services. National administrative structures were broken up into smaller agencies, comprising schools, hospital trusts, fund-holding GP practices and a range of other care and service providers. Private and voluntary agencies could also supply services in health and social care and in pre-school education. Individuals (or professionals working on their behalf) selected the services they wanted (and to which they could gain access) and government agencies paid at a negotiated rate. Thus direct administration was replaced by a system of consumer-driven quasi-market choice.

Labour Market Flexibility

The aims of the British Government's Employment Department are 'to support economic growth by promoting a competitive, efficient and flexible labour market' (Employment Department Group, 1995, p. 8). The main reforms in support of these policies have been the weakening of trade unions and the relaxation of laws regulating employment and wages. Strike votes must be by secret ballot, pickets are no longer immune from civil actions, picketing is restricted, the closed shop is abolished and strikers' benefit entitlements have been reduced (Marsh, 1992, p. 34). Trade union membership declined from 52 to 27 per cent of the labour force between 1979 and 1995 (ONS, 1997, p. 83). Unemployment benefits have been cut back and made subject to increasingly stringent tests of availability to work, culminating in the replacement of National Insurance benefit by the Jobseekers' Allowance in 1996. Claimants must specify a minimum wage level which is acceptable to the authorities. The UK negotiated an opt-out clause from the Social Chapter of the Maastricht Treaty which extends majority voting to issues of health and safety at work, equal opportunities, protection for pensioners and the unemployed, consultation and other matters.

By 1994, the UK had no regulation of working time or wage levels, no legal protection for those hired under fixed term contracts and no right to representation at the workplace. It scored zero – lowest among EU and EFTA countries and alongside the US – in a composite index of labour market standards, covering regulation of working time, minimum wages, employment protection, employee representation and fixed-term contracts (OECD, 1994, Table 4.8, p. 154).

Political Ideology in the UK

The Conservative free market experiment of the 1980s and 1990s in the UK was directed by a clear ideology. Its execution was complicated by the high levels of demand for social spending and the weakness of economic growth for much of the period, which undermined attempts to reduce spending significantly, and by the importance of directing some policies to benefit electorally significant groups. Market-centred approaches had considerable impact on British political life, and influenced the approaches of opposition groups.

The UK Labour party underwent a protracted policy review after four consecutive election defeats leading to its longest period in opposition since the first world war. The outcome is further removed from the traditional Labour stance of state intervention in the economy, full employment, a key role for trade unions, nationalisation, high levels of public spending, a redistributive taxation regime and directly-provided public services than it is from current Conservative policies. The key differences between Labour and Conservative policies are that Labour endorses a more thoroughgoing training and employment policy, approves the social chapter of the Maastricht Treaty and is more firmly committed to membership of the EU. Both parties are determined to restrain public spending and taxation, to limit the role of state intervention and direct public service provision and to stress the responsibility of individuals for their lives through such measures as welfare-to-work schemes and an expanded role for private insurance-based pensions. Crucial areas in which the party has conceded a shift in the direction of the market are in the approval of the purchase of council housing, the extension of consumer choice between schools and the retention of an internal market within the NHS. Choice is high on the policy agenda for the 1997 Labour government.

Both main parties have responded to the changed circumstances of the past two decades by pursuing policies which imply a greater role for markets, although obvious differences remain. In this sense, the liberalism of the 1980s can be said to have changed the face of British politics. The issues of choice which this book examines will remain central to debate, whoever governs.

NEW APPROACHES TO ECONOMIC BEHAVIOUR

Developments in three areas are relevant. These concern the techniques that people often use to deal with complexity or with uncertainty when making choices, the theories of rationality that have guided the dominant tradition in economic thought in this field and arguments about the structure of norms and values derived from sociological work.

The Human Limitations of Choice

Work in this area centres on the psychological concepts of cognition, participation and motivation and often pursues an experimental method. A number of writers have argued that there is a close analogy between the problems people face when making judgements of physical qualities, such as size and distance, and those which apply to the more abstract assessments involved in economic choice. In both areas 'people rely on a limited number of heuristic principles which reduce complex tasks ... to simpler judgemental operations. ... These heuristics are quite useful, but sometimes they lead to severe and systematic errors' (Tversky and Kahneman, 1974, p. 1124). We receive less immediate feedback from abstract than from physical errors, and are less likely to develop mechanisms to correct them.

Common heuristics, that can sometimes be subject to error are the use of stereotypes to judge the likelihood that an instance falls into a category or the ease with which instances can be brought to mind to estimate the likelihood of an event. *Anchor points,* from which people start out when making a judgement, are particularly important. Individuals often choose as if overly attached to the status quo. Their current position becomes endowed, as it were, with a particular charm, so that they are reluctant to exchange it for something of apparently greater value. *Loss aversion* – whereby individuals seem to experience greater unhappiness at losses than happiness at equivalent gains – is influenced by the reference point from which loss or gain is estimated (Thaler, 1992, pp. 64–78). 'Money illusion' whereby people experience difficulty in making allowance for inflation in discussing wages and prices (Shafir, Tversky and Diamond, 1994) may be the result of anchoring in terms of number of currency units rather than their value. Personality and motivation may also be significant in relation to choices over time. For example, people are typically more reluctant to spend money from a savings account than from a current account, although strict rationality would imply that all resources are equivalent. One explanation refers to the categorisation of resources into notionally separate *mental accounts*. Savings schemes are mechanisms through which people compensate psychological weaknesses in carrying out a rational saving decision by precommitting themselves. As Shefrim and Thaler put it, balancing 'immediate gratification against long-term benefits entail a conflict that is not present in a choice between a white shirt and a blue one' (1988, p. 611).

This work does not suggest that the rational approach to choice is fundamentally flawed, but that the perspective must be modified to take account of human limitations. Since we are all aware of these problems, the use of rules of thumb and other heuristics is entirely rational. One solution is to argue that 'mind is the scarce resource'. Rationality may be understood in terms of the application of mental energy where it produces the highest return (Simon, 1978, p. 14). The outcome of these arguments is a *bounded rationality* in which choice is understood as influenced by our limited capacities.

The point may be made with greater or lesser force. In a recent review of studies of rationality (1993, quoted in Hutton, 1995, p. 230) Kahnemann argues that 'the maintenance of coherent beliefs and preferences is too demanding a task for limited minds. Maximising the experienced utility of a stream of future outcomes can only be harder'. The notion of rational choice may be too perfect for the world in which we live. This may overstate the point. After all people often succeed in making sensible choices. However, the issues discussed above must be taken into account. Status quo bias implies that individuals will be reluctant to respond to new opportunities. The point is particularly relevant at a time of rapid change, when public services are withdrawn and individuals are increasingly expected to take responsibility for organising savings and insurance schemes for their future needs in areas like health care and pensions. Similarly loss aversion may imply that losers at a time of rapid social change feel their losses more keenly than winners their gains (Pierson, 1996, p. 18)

Rationality and Consistent Preferences

Developments in theoretical understanding of choice also raise
questions about how we understand economic decision-making. The
traditional economic theory of choice typically understands behaviour as revealing preferences which are understood as existing independently from the choices which express them. The content of
preferences is not itself the concern of the theory – what people
value is their own business – but choices must be consistent. Thus
stable preferences form the basis of rational economic choice, and
are revealed in actions.

This approach implies that secure rational choices are not influenced by extraneous factors to do with the context in which a choice
is made, but should be based on consistent deliberation between
available options as ways of achieving preferences. However, there
is considerable empirical evidence that the context in which economic decisions are set (their 'framing') may influence preferences
(see, for example, Thaler, 1980). Tversky and Kahneman (1979,
1981) argue that the effect is analogous to the way in which perspective influences perceptions of scale in the physical world, so
that illusion again influences choice.

Such arguments have led to a number of different theoretical
approaches to understanding choice. Kahneman and Tversky develop *prospect theory*. This approach combines arguments about loss
aversion, anchor points and framing. It suggests that people estimate anticipated future losses and gains in relation to some current reference point, that they are more upset at losses than happy
at gains, and that their dissatisfaction or pleasure is less at losses
and gains of the same absolute magnitude if they are apprehended
as part of a greater amount – the difference between 1100 and
1000 is seen as less than the difference between 100 and 0. This
explains phenomena such as the Allais paradox, in which most people
are swayed by a small probability of a negative outcome to reject
an otherwise attractive gamble, but irrationally accept a similar option
in a second gamble, when the small additional probability of a
negative outcome is masked by much larger probabilities of negative outcomes in both the options presented (Hargeaves-Heap *et al.*,
1992, pp. 37–9).

Other perceptual and cognitive explanations focus on the role of
regret at possible losses causing individuals to prefer uncertainties
where the possibility of experiencing distress at losing what they

might have had if things had turned out differently is minimised (Loomes and Sugden, 1982). Thus they may be reluctant to pursue a course of action as a result of anticipated distress at missing a glittering prize and simply gaining a perfectly respectable one, and may choose instead a more cautious option where the possibilities for such regret are reduced.

These explanations of apparent irrationalities in behaviour identified in experimental settings are reinforced by concerns arising at a more abstract theoretical level. In an article which provides a concise summary of the debate, Sugden takes as his starting point Savage's axioms of the rational foundations of economic choice (1954). He is able to show that there are serious problems with the notion that preferences must always be complete and consistent. The simplest way of making the point is the observation that it is easy to imagine rational individuals saying that they don't quite know where their preferences lie when offered a choice between a large prize with a low probability and an assured modest prize (1991, p. 758). People make such choices in practice, in careers or saving for example, but in most cases the process of choosing is more complex than the operation of reason on clear pre-existing preferences.

Arguments derived from rationality are similarly empty in providing accounts of social behaviour. A large number of situations exist – in everyday life and in experiments – in which people seem to be able to co-ordinate behaviour to mutual advantage, when it is difficult to see how they can achieve this on the basis of strict rationality. How can we trust others to co-operate when it sometimes serves their interest best not to do so? At one level, voluntary blood donorship or honesty box sales schemes often work. People don't invariably steal milk from neighbours' doorsteps when they could get away with it. This phenomenon is often discussed in terms of the rather artificial example of the 'prisoner's dilemma'. Two prisoners, held in separate cells face a choice between turning state evidence or keeping quiet. If both refuse to speak, they will receive a light sentence. If one confesses, that one goes free and the other receives a long term. If both confess, they get a medium sentence. Rationality suggests confession – the options then are a medium sentence (if the other also confesses) and going free. The best outcome for both (keeping quiet and getting a short sentence) is unattainable through the individual exercise of reason, since each will reason that it makes sense for the other to confess and ensure that the non-confessor receives the heavy sentence.

In practical experiments based on this and similar problems it is possible to establish conditions of co-operation, where people achieve the best mutual outcome (Thaler, 1992, p. 20; Bethwaite and Tompkinson, 1996, pp. 269–71; Sugden, 1991, p. 775). Such co-operation is fragile. Defection by one party speedily leads the other to defect also. In one well-known experiment, the best choice strategy in terms of achieving the optimum outcome in a repeated prisoner's dilemma game was simply to imitate the behaviour of the co-player in the previous round. Altruism bred altruism and *vice versa* (Axelrod, 1984). Evidence from other choice games, such as the Ultimatum Game and the Dictator Game (Guth and Tiertz, 1990; Camerer and Thaler, 1995; Hoffman et al, 1994; Sugden, 1991, p. 775) points to similar conclusions. People are not programmed to operate as automatic instrumental rationalists, but are capable of responding to circumstances and to the behaviour they perceive in others.

Such findings imply that there are limits to the usefulness of principles of rationality and consistency in explaining how people choose. One argument suggests that choices are not simply the expression of pre-existing preferences, but are developed and constructed in the process of making them. This point pays attention to the evidence noted above of the way in which the context of choice ('framing') influences outcomes. Social framing may be added to perceptual framing in the influences on choice. This has implications for our understanding of choice and also for the theoretical underpinning of economics if that discipline is to provide a satisfactory theory of economic behaviour. Sugden concludes: 'there was a time when . . . the job of the economic theorist seemed to be one of drawing out the often complex implications of a fairly simple and uncontroversial set of axioms. But it is becoming clear that these foundations are less secure than we thought, and that they need to be examined and perhaps rebuilt' (1991, p. 783).

The implications of these points for current changes in public policy are that it is difficult to read off the impact of the shift towards a greater reliance on market choice from pre-existing theory. Situational factors in the context of choice may play a role in affecting how options are understood which may lead to unexpected outcomes. More broadly, if choices are seen as influenced by context, the institutional structure may play an active role in affecting outcomes. This point is relevant to debates such as those about the expansion of consumerism and competition in the NHS and through greater choice in education. Structural reforms may change patterns of commitment to neighbourhood schools, increase demands on doctors and affect the service-ethic of professionals.

The Social Context of Choice

The point that choices are made in a social context has long been a central theme of sociological argument at the most abstract level. The most influential recent restatement of the approach is found in the work of Giddens who argues that sociological understanding involves a 'double hermeneutic'. On the one hand 'the social world, unlike the natural world, has to be grasped as a skilled accomplishment of active human subjects . . . Generating descriptions of social conduct depends upon . . . penetrating the frames of meaning which lay actors themselves draw upon . . .' (1976, p. 154). On the other 'the realm of human agency is bounded. Men produce society, but . . . not under conditions of their own choosing . . . structures are constituted through action and reciprocally . . . action is constituted structurally' (1976, p. 161). A full understanding of choice requires apprehension of the choosers' own understanding of their actions, observation of the operation of social structures and institutions in constraining actions and an awareness of how the former rests on the latter and how actions reproduce or modify future institutional constraints. There are clear echoes of the distinction found in Weber and Dilthey between sociological explanation that is 'adequate at the level of meaning' (*Verstehen*) and 'at the causal level of human regularity' (*Erklären* – see Giddens, 1976, pp. 55–6).

In practice few sociological analyses measure up to such demanding requirements. For our purposes the salient point is that the context which influences actions must include the understanding of that context by members of society – as Giddens terms it social action is 'reflexive'. Hollis makes a similar point in an ingenious critique of utility-maximising accounts of rationality which rests on Weberian arguments and claims that the rational choice notion of action can never give us more than a 'bargain-hunter' or a 'throughput mechanism notion of choice' (1987, pp. 146–7). Crucially, such approaches cannot account for the possibility of creativity and self-development through choice, which may modify our preferences, or for more general plans of life. It is difficult to see how to choose (from the standpoint of utility-maximisation) between a short merry life and industry and prudent investment for a distant prosperous old age – the choices are likely to influence the kind of person you

become and the people you mix with and condition the development of your preferences and the satisfaction you ultimately gain
(see Hargreaves-Heap *et al.*, 1992, pp. 76–9). Such choices depend
upon current preferences and social context, but they also influence the development of social context which is a conditioning factor
in the development of future preferences.

On the larger scale, the notion of rationality itself seems subject
to variation in different social settings. In his account of the pervasive spread of rationality throughout social, cultural and economic
life in Western society in *The Sociology of Religion*, Weber argues
that it is 'only in the West' that such an approach has attained 'its
present dominant place in our culture' (1930, pp. 15–16). Other
sociologists have also understood social arrangements typified by
the dominance of rational calculative approaches as one among
several possible formations. For example, Gellner describes rational-
scientific, fundamentalist and post-modern orientations to social
choice as providing the distinguishing characteristics of different
kinds of society, typified by reliance on means-end deliberation,
adherence to normative structures and the critical erosion of the
value of all the possible goals that could provide the ends for rational
means (see for example Gellner, 1992, p. 1).

When we descend from the general level of the social construction of rationality to examine the issues involved in developing an
account of choice that is applicable to the specific problems identified by researchers such as Thaler or Sugden and which combines
insights from different disciplinary approaches, we immediately
encounter difficulties. The puzzles of instrumental rationality have
led some of those involved in the debate to treat the findings and
methods of psychologists, sociologists and social anthropologists as
discrete and portable elements that can be detached from each
other and recombined with traditional economic theories to overcome the obstacles these confront. Thus prospect theory is seen as
importing psychological theories of cognition and evaluation to set
the operation of rational choice based on consistent preferences in
a particular context that resolves the apparent irregularities. Lunt
argues that Shefrim and Thaler's mental accounts 'separate money
into liquid and non-liquid assets in a way that mirrors the hemi-
spheric separation of the human brain into a planner and a doer . . .
the argument takes broad conceptions from psychological theory
to bridge gaps between the assumptions of macro-economic theory
and observed economic behaviour' (1996, p. 278). The point is that

the problems encountered by traditional theories of rationality are not appropriately treated as simple 'anomalies', requiring a modification of theory to accommodate them, but point to fundamental issues in economic choice. This leads to the study of choice as a variety of human social behaviour, and a strong emphasis on empirical analysis of the way choices are actually made in everyday life. Whether a suitably modified instrumental rationality can in fact deal with these difficulties or whether a more fundamental rethinking is necessary is at present unclear.

A different route to a similar position is provided by the influential *socio-economics* associated with Etzioni. This approach draws on psychoanalysis as well as social science. Etzioni (1988) identifies two fundamentally opposed approaches to human nature – the rational, self-interested, utility-maximising paradigm, and the irrational, amoral and impulsive individual encountered in psychoanalysis. He offers an alternative approach to moral decision-making – the individual is seen as influenced in addition by normative commitments and affective involvements, which guide the use of information in making decisions. Such commitments and involvements frame choices and are affected by individual membership of social groups. This approach has attracted interest and debate because it situates rational choice within the context of social meanings, and points out that such meanings do not simply furnish external goals for the operation of rationality, but influence and are influenced by behaviour directed to those goals. For example, pursuit of career success in order to become a respected member of the community may stultify itself if the instrumentally rational means of self-advancement are erosive of the features of the community that made prominence in it desirable in the first place – as the banker Bulstrode discovers in *Middlemarch*. 'Balance between the selection of means according to their instrumental merits and sustaining the goal commitment' is a fundamental limitation on rational behaviour (Etzioni, 1968, p. 258).

Etzioni's application of his approach to community and family life through a 'communitarian' politics (1993) may seem highly speculative but the idea that a socio-economic paradigm, which includes a role for the social influences of both morality and affection alongside rationality in decision-making, has led to the rapid development of socio-economics as an inter-disciplinary approach to choice. The *Society for the Advancement of Socio-Economics*, expanded rapidly to over 10,000 academic members, mainly in the

United States, within four years of being founded in 1989 and acts as a focus for research. Its organising secretary wrote in the foreword to a collection of essays from its first conference: 'general features of the field can be discerned ... with regard to such core concerns as the moral underpinnings of economic behaviour; the complex nature of rationality, self-interest, motivation and preference formation; the importance of organisational culture, political institutions and other elements of social structure as mediators of economic activity of both individuals and business firms ... there is as yet no overarching socio-economic framework that specifies *a priori* how intellectual inquiry should proceed' (Coughlin, 1991, p. 5).

The expanding interest in building linkages between economics, psychology, sociology and other social sciences, together with the absence of agreement on how this might best be done, generate a fruitful field for research. The nine studies contained in this book have been selected to illustrate particular issues in the understanding of economic choice in the context of current developments in public policy which make choices particularly salient in certain areas. In content, the studies range from analyses of the different cultural and practical context of entrepreneurship among different British Asian communities to studies of the expectations and attitudes that influence people in making decisions about how to finance care for themselves and their dependents in old age, should it be needed, the issues shaping choices between ethical, green and profit-maximising personal investment, the detail of the process of housing choice, what influences family doctors to take on the role of quasi-independent 'fund-holders' in the British NHS, attitudes to the role of government and the private sector in providing welfare services and to paying the taxes necessary to support state provision, the ideas about citizenship of those involved in benefit fraud, and the beliefs about the fairness of differentials that underlie wage negotiations. As regards method, the studies for the most part combine large-scale structured questionnaire surveys with more detailed discursive interviewing of smaller groups among the main sample, although some confine themselves to one or other method. The advantage of a combined approach is that it enables the research to pursue the statistical analysis of behaviour in the aggregate with the individual exploration of the way in which choices are understood by individuals who make them. This enables the link between social context and the way in which an individual understands the relevance of that context to be examined.

The main points to emerge from the research are both negative and positive. On the negative side, as much previous work has shown, it is difficult to give convincing accounts of the choices encountered in the individual studies in terms of the traditional model of rational, utility-maximising actor. On the positive side, the role played by social context – in particular normative commitment and group membership in framing and influencing social choices – is real but complex and appears to be particular to specific studies. For example, work on British Asian entrepreneurs emphasises the role of religion in influencing Britons of Pakistani origin whose culture is permeated with Islamic beliefs to accept very high levels of risk and low returns on the grounds that the favour of God will lead their business to eventually prosper. Weberian analysis of the role of Calvinism in fostering the high levels of accumulation and investment necessary to the take-off of capitalism in Europe provides an analogy, but there is little evidence in the other studies of a comparable impact from cultural values in producing behaviour that might appear irrational from a traditional standpoint.

The diversity of interpretation reflects the experience of other research in this field and the absence of a dominant and comprehensive paradigm. One feature to emerge across several of the studies is the role of social norms in relation to the reciprocal commitments between individual and government that make up citizenship. Here the violation of expectations about the choices that are conveniently available to people is clearly important. For example the expectation that social care would be available to meet the needs of frail elderly relatives or of individuals themselves colours views on the appropriate role for individual and for government responsibility in this sector. Similarly, those involved in social security benefit fraud often report a powerful sense of betrayal in the realisation that it is virtually impossible to live at current benefit levels, so that the exploitation of opportunities to get extra money from whatever source becomes a normal feature of life. The experience of problems in access to the NHS, especially long waiting lists, appears to have a major effect on views about state and private welfare provision precisely because it contradicts the expectation that health care will be available when it is needed.

The implication for an approach that relies on a shift towards market choice is that social context and in particular the beliefs and assumptions previously current in the field influence the choices that people make and how they think about and evaluate the range of choices on offer. The direction of choice cannot simply be read off from a snapshot assessment of the options currently available. The influence of social context must be understood not only in terms of existing norms, but in how those norms operate over time and how they are reinforced or contradicted by experience. Approaches such as prospect theory could usefully expand the crucial importance of reference to anchor points to include the assumptions that individuals have about their entitlements, obligations and opportunities in society as such a yardstick and one that was normative rather than cognitive in origin. If this argument is pursued and if losses tend to bulk larger than gains as prospect theory implies, apparent reductions in standards in public policy should create more dissatisfaction that was achieved by the corresponding improvements in other areas or in an individual's tax position. Retrenchment wins few friends. Similarly, any move that seeks to transfer responsibility for meeting social needs away from government and towards the individual cannot assume that individual behaviour will re-orientate itself immediately in response to new incentives. For example, policies designed to change welfare professionals into service entrepreneurs may take time to achieve their effects.

We return to these issues in the concluding chapter.

CONCLUSION

In this chapter we have reviewed the main reasons why economic choice has come to occupy a central position on the agendas of public policy and of social science in recent years. People are faced with more choices in their everyday lives. Social and economic changes ensure that the importance of getting choices right for people's happiness and welfare will not diminish. The social structures developed to reduce such risks – the Keynesian welfare state and the apparatus of trade union politics and social service support that surrounded it – are growing less powerful. The main political parties emphasise individual choice, opportunity and consumerism in their programmes.

As practical politics moves towards the advocacy of a greater degree of market freedom, theoretical developments in social science are increasingly questioning the relevance of the neo-classical tradition of rational choice as a route to achieve the greatest satisfaction for the most people. Such an approach may fail to take into account the ways in which we actually arrive at the decisions that govern our lives and may ignore the influence of the wider social context of values surrounding work, family, saving and spending. Empirical studies are essential to understanding how choices are made in practice. Policies based on misleading theory may produce results that are unanticipated and upsetting.

The following nine chapters analyse the way in which people make concrete choices in matters that are of considerable importance in their lives. We draw out the implications for public policy and for the theories which underpin it in the final chapter.

2 Paying for Long-Term Care in the UK: Policy, Theory and Evidence

Gillian Parker and Harriet Clarke

INTRODUCTION

Questions about who should provide and pay for long-term care for older people have moved up the policy agenda in the UK over the last 15 years. Concern is often justified, particularly by politicians, as a wise response to the ageing of the population. However, as this process of ageing has been taking place since the turn of the 20th century, why should concern manifest itself now? It can, perhaps, be understood by referring to other social, economic and political changes which have taken place over a shorter period but which, in combination, have opened up the space for a discussion about who 'should' provide and pay for care.

The first set of changes relates to the family. Smaller overall family size and the increasing numbers of people who have no children at all have raised anxieties about the ability of the 'family' to provide in the future the informal care that it supplies at present. At the same time, some feel that increased divorce and remarriage and the more complex family forms that result may 'blur' lines of responsibility for older generations.

The second change is increased labour market participation amongst married women, which is seen as a threat to traditional sources of unpaid care for older people. Thirdly, there is the increased affluence of some older people, which has fuelled the perception that most older people are now in a position to pay for services that might otherwise have been provided for them.

The fourth change, and one which has had the power to harness the other three and create the debate, is the renewed ideological emphasis in politics on individual responsibility for welfare (Gordon, 1988; Klein and Millar, 1995). Until recently this has concentrated on pension provision, with a period of change in policy which has

24

reduced the coverage of the SERPS system and encouraged increasing levels of personal and occupational pension provision as alternatives. More recently, however, the 'self-provision' debate has moved beyond financial support for old age into care support.

The Griffiths Report concluded that 'central government should look in detail at a range of options for encouraging individuals to take responsibility for planning for their future [care] needs' (Griffiths, 1988, para.6.63). What in the past was a 'cash or care' argument is turning into a cash for care debate, with the cash increasingly being provided via private means. Support for this appears to transcend political divisions; the Commission on Social Justice report (1994) argued that 'it is not feasible to extend the founding principle of the NHS – that treatment should be free at the point of use – to the comprehensive provision of care and help with everyday activities... responsibility should start with the individual' (p. 299).

Some see the change in community care funding arrangements implemented in 1993 as an incentive for older people 'with above average means... to make their own provision against the risk of needing long-term care' (Laing and Buisson, 1993, p. 8). It is difficult to know quite what is meant here because, as we explain later, the state has never paid for the social (rather than health) care of older people with 'above average means'. However, publicity about people using their own resources to fund residential and nursing home care, before they seek state support, has raised the issue on the political agenda. The Department of Health has raised the capital limits below which state funding is available, in response to anxieties about older people having to sell their homes to pay for care. It has also issued consultation and policy documents on the ways in which private insurance and state support for care might interact to protect capital (DoH, 1996, 1997).

The insurance industry, meanwhile, has dipped its toes in the water with a few long-term care policies. However, it remains loathe to develop such products wholesale until it has a clearer view of the Government's intentions and the likely reaction of the public at large.

In this uncertain policy environment, we carried out the research described here to discover what the population at large really did feel about paying for their own care in old age and what, if anything, they had done about planning for it. The material presented draws on only a small part of the analysis carried out. We have concentrated on two themes that cut across many of the projects reported in this book: notions of justice and fairness in relation to economic choice and decision making in uncertainty.

THE RESEARCH

The research was in two stages.

Stage One

We carried out a nationally representative sample survey of men and women aged between 25 and 70 years in England and Wales. The Social and Community Planning Research field force carried out structured interviews in late 1995. The main focus was on people's attitudes and beliefs about responsibility for providing and paying for care in old age. The interview included questions about the balance between the state and the individual for financing care and about respondents' views of private insurance for long-term care, as well as their beliefs about the 'best way' in which care should be funded. Beliefs about family responsibility were explored using the vignette technique developed by Finch and Mason (1993) while other questions covered home ownership and the role of housing equity in the finance of care, beliefs about saving, inheritance and paying for care, and respondents' understanding of the current costs of different forms of private care. Basic socio-economic data were collected, along with more detailed information about respondents' personal experiences of chronic ill-health or disability, of providing informal care and about their and their households' financial circumstances.

Nine hundred and fifty-seven people were interviewed – a response rate of 70 per cent. Weighting to compensate for non-response gave an effective sample size of 950.

Stage Two

In stage two we returned to a sub-sample of respondents to investigate their actual and planned behaviour for securing care in older age. We sampled them on the basis of the views they had expressed in stage one; those who were consistently 'pro-state', those who were consistently 'pro-individual', those who expressed consistent views about shared responsibility (the 'mixed economy' group), and those whose views were inconsistent. We sampled 140 people for this stage and 102 were interviewed by the SCPR field force in June 1996. The second stage interview was structured but included a higher proportion of open-ended questions than in the first stage. It established the extent to which, if at all, respondents had made financial plans for care in old age, should they need it, and explored in more detail their views about personal responsibility for care of elderly parents.

JUSTICE AND FAIRNESS

Notions of justice and fairness loomed large in the beliefs of our respondents about who 'should' be responsible for the care of older people. However, these notions were not always consistent with one another.

Who Should Pay for the Care of Older People?

There was a broad consensus in the first stage about who should be responsible for paying for or providing support for elderly people in a range of situations. There was very limited support, under any circumstances, for individuals having to pay for care entirely themselves. The majority felt that the state should be responsible, either for all old people or for those that could not afford to pay for care. As the degree of assistance rose, so did support for state involvement; thus 29 per cent felt that the state should pay for all those who needed residential or nursing home care. However, the majority (just over two-thirds) supported means testing in some form – whether for help with cooking or shopping, with washing or dressing, or with the costs of residential or nursing home care. This finding stands in contrast to surveys of attitudes towards health care where there is still overwhelming support for a service free at the point of delivery for all, regardless of income (Jowell, Curtice, Brook and Ahrendt, 1994).

While there was enthusiasm for some form of state support for care, only a minority of the sample were prepared to pay more than they do currently to ensure this. Just over a third of the sample (38 per cent) had said that in some or all circumstances the state should support all older people, regardless of financial circumstances. This group were asked if this would still be their view if this level of support required increases of £100 and £500 per year for the 'average' tax payer. Six per cent shifted their view at £100, suggesting that some 31 per cent of the population sampled would still support state-financed care for all older people at this cost. Of course, as we know from other studies in the programme, people's desire for tax payers to make increased contributions rarely includes themselves (see chapter 5).

There was no greater enthusiasm in the first stage sample for paying for care through insurance. While most felt that people should be able to buy insurance if they wished (78 per cent), there was limited support for compulsory insurance, either for the population at large (15 per cent) or for those in paid work (24 per cent). Among those who approved of compulsory insurance for people in work, most felt that it should be a shared responsibility between individuals and their employer, or the employer's responsibility alone.

In the second stage half the respondents thought that it would be a good idea for insurance, paid for by contributions over a working life, to be widely available to those who wanted it. However, few would contemplate taking out insurance. We gave respondents a broad idea of how much a policy might cost someone their age and subsequently asked whether they would consider purchasing long-term care insurance at the moment. Only six of the 102 people interviewed in the second stage said that they would. Cost was seen as a major stumbling block, even among those who were in the 'pro-individual' group.

The first stage sample were also reluctant to dip into their own pockets through using capital. The sale of houses to pay for care, whether to raise additional income by 'trading down' and investing the released capital, or because state-funded assistance with the costs of residential or nursing home care takes into account the value of property, has been a key issue in recent debate about paying for care in old age. We explored this in the first stage by using a series of vignettes in which respondents were asked to imagine an elderly couple who needed help with everyday tasks such as dressing, cooking and cleaning. The couple were said to have no income to spare but to own a home which, in the three vignettes, was valued variously at £100,000, £50,000 and £25,000. Respondents were asked to choose between a number of options the couple might use to obtain help.

We found that people discriminated on the basis of wealth. With a house valued at £100,000 only 55 per cent felt that the state should provide care, compared with 69 and 78 per cent respectively when the house was worth £50,000 and £25,000. Although selling the house in order to finance residential care, or borrowing against it to finance domiciliary care, were given as explicit options, relatively few supported using housing capital in these ways. Support for using capital increased as the value of the house did, but even when it was worth £100,000, only a quarter (27 per cent) of respondents supported this approach.

Why Should the State Pay?

Our analysis shows that attitudes about whether and to what extent the state should be involved in paying for care are, as one would expect, largely related to political affiliation (Parker and Clarke, 1997). Despite this, however, the sense that emerges from the material is of confused or generally unformed views about how to pay for care. On the one hand there is majority support for the state's involvement, but with the view that help should be means-tested. On the other hand, there is a reluctance to use available means – and particularly the capital held in housing – to fund care, either prospectively or currently. Some reasons for this confusion came through in both stages.

Mistaken beliefs about past and current provision
First, people have inaccurate perceptions about the current funding arrangements for care. For example, some believe that the financial support system for residential and nursing home care for older people has changed and that what was previously provided by the state is no longer available. They are wrong in this. Since the 1948 National Assistance Act, people requiring the support of the state for long-term social care in residential settings have had to demonstrate that their means were below a given level. Otherwise they are required to contribute towards the cost of care. Until the final implementation of the 1990 NHS and Community Care Act in 1993, this rule applied whether the care was provided and paid for by the local authority or whether it was provided in the independent sector and paid for by the social security system (Baldwin, 1994). In April 1993 social security funding for new entrants to residential or nursing home care was withdrawn and resources

transferred to local authority social services departments (SSDs). People seeking state assistance with long-term care now have their needs for care and their financial circumstances assessed by SSDs. However, as we have pointed out, state support, whether by central or local government, was rigorously means-tested before this change.

Another factor which may have influenced the population's perception that care provision has changed is the gradual withdrawal of long-term care in health settings. Since 1976 the number of long-term care beds for older people in the health service (which were, therefore, free at the point of use) in England has fallen from 55,600 to 37,500. At the same time, the numbers of people aged 75 and over increased from 2.4 million to 3.3 million. However, the number of beds overall for long-term care for elderly people has grown in the same period, and at a faster rate than the population of older people who might need them (all figures taken from Health Committee, 1996). This increase has taken place exclusively in the independent sector – and has to be paid for at the point of use by the resident or by the state on his or her behalf.

This latter point is related to a further misperception. Some believe that the money released by the sale of housing when people enter residential care goes to the state. For example, one of our respondents in the second stage, when asked for views on the current situation where people with above £10,000 in assets pay something towards the cost of care and those with more than £16,000 pay all the costs, said:

> Assets should not be used to pay for nursing homes – ie handed over to the state. That person will have saved all their lives just to give it back to the state.

In fact, the 'state' receives none of the money used by elderly people to finance care, unless they choose to enter the rapidly shrinking pool of homes in the local authority sector. All of it goes rather to independent sector care home proprietors and owners. In some sense, perhaps, the state saves money by not having to pay for these people, but, as described above, the state has never paid for those who had more than very modest means of their own.

Beliefs about the role of national insurance and taxation
The second set of reasons for respondents' apparently contradictory views about paying for care relates to the role of taxation and national insurance. Many believe that past and present payments made through national insurance and tax are both intended and

sufficient to guarantee state support of care for elderly people. One respondent's words, when asked about his views on taking out long-term care insurance, sum up what most others who were negative about the idea also felt:

> I've already paid considerably more than that [LTC insurance premium] each month, so has my wife, to the state. We believe that this kind of thing would be covered, that this was insurance. Why should we have to pay twice?

Again, we are dealing here with the inaccurate historical view that national insurance and tax have been paying for long-term care in the past and therefore should continue to do so. However, such views are strongly held; more than one respondent in the second stage interviews referred to what they believed to be the 'contract' between individuals and the state in relation to care. Talking about who might provide help with shopping or cooking if he needed it in old age, one person said:

> This should be the responsibility of the state. Because I will have paid NI contributions and income tax, with no breaks, and I consider I'm in credit and if I need it the debt should be honoured.

Beliefs about the state's ability to pay for care
The third factor which influences people's willingness to consider dipping into their own pockets to pay for care relates to scepticism about the state's professed inability to meet that need. In the first stage we tested opinions about several areas of state expenditure. We used the questions from the British Social Attitudes Surveys about whether people wanted to see more or less spending on a number of state services or benefits, and added one about 'special care for older people'. Enthusiasm for 'much more' state spending was greatest for health (chosen by 31 per cent), followed by education (24 per cent), old age pensions (21 per cent) and our category of special care for older people (20 per cent). By contrast, 38 percent wanted to see 'less' or 'much less' spending on military and defence provision and 20 per cent on unemployment benefits. This suggests that people might be happy to see increases in some aspects of state expenditure off-set by decreases in others, without necessarily having to increase the budget overall. This belief that there might already be sufficient resources in the system to care for older people was also evident in responses to a series of attitude

statements. Only a third (34 per cent) of respondents said that they agreed with the statement 'The state cannot afford to provide adequate care for all elderly people' while over half (55 per cent) disagreed.

The role of capital held as housing
The fourth factor which contributes to people's reluctance to pay for care is the very specific nature of capital holding in the UK. As we see in chapter 6, the majority of households in Britain are now owner occupiers. Their home is, for home owners, the largest capital resource they are ever likely to hold. In a country where the state has paid for residential care for only the least wealthy, a large capital holding is the obvious place to look for financial resources when the need for care arises. However, the fact that this is held as housing is a major stumbling block to making it 'work' for care.

Thaler (1990) has pointed out that in the theoretical economic 'life-cycle' model of savings all forms of income and wealth holding are seen as equivalent and, therefore, equally likely to be used to fund consumption, when needed. The model thus predicts that rational individuals will follow the rule:

> in any year compute the present value of your wealth, including current income, net assets, and future income; figure out the level annuity you could purchase with that money; then consume the amount you would receive if you in fact owned such an annuity (pp. 193–4).

However, he argues, empirical evidence suggests that people behave otherwise. Consumption is actually sensitive to income and various sources of wealth do not appear to be as close substitutes for each other as the theory would suggest. 'In particular, households appear to have very low marginal propensities to consume either pension wealth or home equity, compared to other assets' (Thaler, 1990, p. 194). The theory assumes that home equity is 'fungible' and therefore perceived as a good substitute for other forms of wealth but, again, empirical evidence challenges this, especially for the elderly 'who do not dis-save fast enough' (p. 201).

Our evidence suggests that there is, indeed, a great deal of resistance to the idea of using housing capital to finance care but also that people are beginning to feel that they might use this form of wealth in this way because they will have no option.

Respondents in the first stage were unlikely (19 per cent) to feel that elderly people needing residential or nursing home care should have to sell their home if they wished to bequeath it to family members. We explored these issues in more detail by asking owner occupiers what their feelings were about ownership. Between a quarter and a third (24 per cent in the first stage and 31 per cent in the second stage) said that the most important reason for owning their own home was as an investment for the future. Only 12 per cent and 13 per cent in the two stages chose the more specific reason of providing security for old age.

However, those in the oldest sub-group (55 to 70 years) in the first stage were significantly more likely than the younger sub-groups to mention security in old age as a reason for owning their own home. Moreover, age seemed to be much more strongly associated with this view than were beliefs about the role of the state and the individual.

In the second stage we also asked owner occupiers whether they felt that people of their generation still bought their homes expecting to be able to pass them on to their children or other close family. Over half (52 out of 91) said that they did but only 34 that they had personally bought their home with that expectation. Of these 28 said that they still felt that way. There were differences between the sub-groups we identified for the second stage sample. Those in the 'mixed economy' sub-group were least likely to say that they thought people of their generation still expected to pass on their homes. Those who were 'pro-individual' were most likely to say that they had personally bought their home expecting to be able to pass it on and that they still felt that way. This suggests that people's views about the role of housing in 'cascading wealth down the generations' – to coin John Major's phrase (Dolan, 1995) – may be changing. Those who are older and those whose views remain in favour of personal responsibility may retain the more traditional view.

The proportion of owner occupiers in each sub-group was about the same. However, we found in the second stage that the 'pro-individual' sub-group were most likely to be in favour of the current capital test for state support for residential or nursing home care. Overall 38 per cent of the whole sample said that the current system was a 'good idea' but over half (57 per cent) of the 'pro-individual' sub-group. This was the reverse of the pattern in all the other sub-groups, where the majority said that they thought it was a 'bad idea'.

The open-ended question which explored why people felt the way that they did about this issue revealed that many of those who were broadly in agreement with the capital test felt that the threshold should be higher and also recognised the difficulty, in the current situation, of liquidating housing capital. For example, one respondent said:

> Well, residential care is expensive and you should be left something to pass on to your children, but I'm not sure that £10,000 is enough to pass on. I think, though, that it would cause a lot of headache to give up your home and there should be an element of state help.

A question about how respondents would expect care to be provided or paid for if they themselves needed to enter a residential or nursing home by the time they reached the age of 85 identified a substantial minority of sixteen out of the 102 who felt that they would have to sell their homes or other assets. We also asked whether respondents would expect the state to pay for their care when needed if they had a house to pass on. Just under two-thirds of the whole sample said that they would, but the 'pro-individual' sub-group were significantly more likely than the others to say that they would not expect the state to provide for their care if they had a house that they wished to pass on. This suggests that this sub-group, at least, remains consistent, but their responses raise some interesting policy dilemmas. It also, of course, begs the question of whether these respondents would actually behave the way their responses suggest, if it came to it.

DECISION MAKING IN UNCERTAINTY

A key issue in individuals' decision making about whether or not to take out insurance, and in insurers' decisions about whether to let individuals do so, is that of risk. In relation to long-term care in the UK, however, both insurers and the potentially insured are operating in conditions of great uncertainty. Despite the Institute of Actuaries' and others' heroic efforts to provide some guide to the risk of need for long-term care (Nuttal *et al.*, 1993; Richards, 1996), it remains the case that there are no longitudinal studies in the UK which can sensibly guide either the industry or the individual (Bone, 1996).

The most recent census indicated that around 25 per cent of

people over the age of 85 in 1991 lived in some form of 'communal establishment'. This figure has provoked much anxiety, with the assumption that similar proportions of the growing numbers of people who will survive to 85 in the future will also need such care. However, there are several reasons why this figure does not help in judging risk for the future. First, the census does not distinguish between people who entered 'communal establishments' in old age and those who entered when much younger. Secondly, women aged 85 and over in 1991 (and who constituted the bulk of the 'communal establishment' population) were a unique historical cohort. Their chances of marriage, and all that that entails of family networks and access to financial resources, were curtailed by the effects of the First World War. Marital status is important in determining whether or not disabled elderly people enter long-term care and elderly women who have never married are particularly at risk (Bernard and Parker, 1995). This cohort cannot therefore be used as a safe guide to likely risk in the future. Thirdly, even if we knew the proportion of those over the age of 85 who would need long-term care in the future, this would tell us little about overall risk for the population as a whole or for individuals. At the least we need to know what proportion of any cohort is likely to reach the age of 85, taking into account behavioural, environmental and genetic factors which might influence length of life and our physical and mental state at the end of it, but about which science currently knows little.

This lack of knowledge about risk is in clear contrast to most other situations where we might be making insurance decisions as 'we all die sooner or later, we generally have some idea of how risky our neighbourhoods are in terms of car theft or household burglary, and if we take up hang-gliding we at least suspect that we might suffer more broken limbs than the average' (Parker and Clarke, 1996, p. 8).

Further, even if people could be given accurate assessments of their risk, there is some doubt that all would respond to this knowledge. Experience in the USA suggests that even elderly people are reluctant to buy insurance 'because they either view such future benefits as theoretical or simply deny the aging process and the possibility of needing such care' (Merrill, 1992, p. 179). How much more will this be the case with younger people?

We explored perceived risk, and respondents' reactions to it in a number of ways.

In the first stage we examined planning for the future generally by asking about savings and investment intentions. First we used vignettes to explore what people thought should be priorities for saving or investment at different life stages. We presented scenarios about a married couple in their forties who were able to save some of their income each month, a married couple close to retirement and who had adult children, and a retired couple who had sold their home and moved to a smaller house, giving them £20,000 to invest. We then asked people to chose the most and second most important reasons for saving or investment, giving the options of leaving money to children/grandchildren, for their own old age, or to pay for care for their own parents, if needed. In this forced choice situation, saving for their own old age was chosen by 82, 79 and 76 per cent as the most important reason at the three life-stages respectively. Saving in order to leave money to their children or grandchildren followed, chosen by 13, 16 and 19 per cent respectively. Paying for care for their own parents came a very poor third, chosen by 4, 3 and 2 per cent respectively.

On the face of it, then, it seems that people do perceive the need to save for their old age – or, at least they say so when being interviewed about long-term care! However, as with so much that has emerged from this research, we found that respondents were not always consistent when it came to their own behaviour. So, for example, when we asked them what they would do with extra money if their outgoings were much lower, only 16 per cent said that they would be 'very likely' to put the money in a pension or some sort of savings plan. Spending more on themselves or the family, buying new things for the house, or home improvements were far more likely to be mentioned as 'very likely'. (It is possible that the way in which the question was phrased – referring to reduced outgoings rather than increased income may have influenced the responses we obtained here. Increased income may be seen as being more 'permanent' than reduced outgoings and therefore a safer basis on which to take out pensions or regular savings plans.)

Further, there were some interesting differences between the age groups in their views about what should be the priorities of people in their 40s. Here, the youngest group of respondents (25–39) was significantly more likely to prioritise leaving money to children than they were saving for their own old age. By contrast, the oldest age group (55–70) were more likely to think that the couple in their forties should be saving for their own old age. This pattern was not repeated in answers about the other life-stages. A cynical interpretation of the youngest group's response about people in their forties might be that it is influenced by their own hopes about inheriting from their parents. It may also reflect that younger people have difficulty in ever imagining that they will grow old and that, for those who already have young children, their more immediate preoccupation is with the next generation. By contrast, the responses of those nearer to old age may reflect a degree of regret that they had not themselves saved enough for old age while they were in their forties.

In the second stage we explored how people saw both overall and personal risk. First, we asked them how many 85 year old people out of a hundred they thought would need help with cleaning and shopping, help with washing, dressing and getting in and out of bed, and admission to residential care. They were then asked how likely they thought it that they personally would need these forms of care by the time they were 85.

On the basis of what we know about people who are currently 85 or over, our sample seemed consistently to overestimate both the population and personal risk of needing care. The degree of overestimation varied with the type of care. National figures indicate that around 68 per cent of current 85 year olds need help with a single activity of daily living such as cooking or cleaning (Bone, 1996). The average risk figure given by respondents for help with cooking and cleaning was 75 out of 100, and 77 per cent felt that they were 'very' or 'fairly' likely to need such help themselves at that age. Our sample's estimates were somewhat on the high side, but not excessively so. By contrast, risk estimates for help with personal care and for admission to residential or nursing home care were very exaggerated. National figures suggest that only 21 per cent of those still living in the community need help with personal care (ibid). Our respondents felt that, on average, 59 out of 100 85 year olds would need help with personal care, and 59 per cent felt that it was fairly or very likely that they would themselves at that age. While only 25 per cent of 85 year olds are in residential or nursing home care (but see above for provisos about this figure), our sample felt that 50 out of a 100 85 year olds would need residential or nursing home care and 40 per cent that it was fairly or very likely that they would themselves by that age.

Respondents also over-estimated the average length of stay in residential or nursing home care. Research carried out in 1992 suggests that 63 per cent of completed long-term stays in residential care homes are for three years or less and that the comparable figure in nursing homes is 78 per cent (Darton, 1992 cited in Joseph Rowntree Foundation, 1996). Only 18 per cent of our second stage sample thought that people stayed in care for three years or less, 33 per cent between three and five years, and 36 per cent over five years.

Given that knowledge about risk is so limited, does giving respondents information about risk levels alter their views? After we had asked people whether they would currently take out long-term care insurance (to which only 6 per cent said they would, see above) we presented them with a series of potential risk figures for admission to residential and nursing home care at the age of 85 to see if having such information would alter their answer. The rider 'if you could afford it' was added to get over the perceived problem of cost. We started with the current figure of one in four (25 per cent risk) and, for those who still said that they would not take out insurance, proceeded to one in two (50 per cent risk) and three out of four (75 per cent risk). At the one in four figure some 47 per cent of the second stage sample said that, knowing these risk figures, they would take out long-term care insurance, if they could afford it. However, those who said that they would not remained largely steadfast; another 5 per cent changed their mind at a risk of one in two, but there was no further change at the risk of three in four. The 'pro-state' sub-group were significantly less likely and the 'pro-individual' sub-group more likely to say that they would take out insurance at the first risk level. However, at the higher risk levels there was no obvious differences between the sub-groups. This suggests that just over half of the people we interviewed are resistant to insurance at current risk levels, and just under a half are resistant even at substantially inflated levels of risk.

An open-ended follow-up question highlighted the difference between those who are risk averse and those who are not and also underlined the difficulty government or the insurance industry would have in persuading the latter to insure. As well as those ideologically opposed to private insurance for care, there were those who did not feel that at current risk levels it was a good enough 'bet'. For example, several mentioned the issue of surviving to 85 in the first place:

I'm not sure that I'm going to make it to 85. It's quite good odds that I wouldn't need it anyway. If I did it would only be for a few years and I'd have paid out more than my care would cost.

There was also a reluctance to accept that the risk applied to all, particularly if there was some evidence to support this view:

Because I think what my parents are like at that age at the moment and they wouldn't need that sort of care.

However, the more risk averse saw the current odds as convincing:

Well, the statistics are quite high and I'd rather go in a home than be a burden on my family.

Another area of uncertainty for people planning for their old age is, of course, government policy. Few policy analysts – still less the 'average' person – could have predicted in 1976 how radically the face of care provision in the UK would have changed by 1996. Planning for care in old age requires very long lead times – even decisions made around pensionable age are unlikely to come into play for fifteen or more years. It is not surprising, then, that people are wary of making major investment or insurance decisions in this area where they have little real knowledge and where policy appears highly labile.

The second stage interviews threw an interesting light onto what people believed would happen in reality with the provision of care in the future. We asked respondents who would provide or pay for the three different types of care (domestic, personal and residential) if they themselves needed it by the time they reached 85 years of age. In all three examples, between a quarter and a third thought that the state would provide help, and similar proportions that they or their family would pay. Among the third who expected to have to pay themselves for residential or nursing home care almost half spontaneously mentioned having to sell property or liquidate assets to meet costs. Around a tenth also expressed the view that they expected to have to fund domiciliary care themselves because they believed that the state would 'no longer' do so.

These responses contrast starkly with the more general beliefs people held about who 'should' pay for or provide care, suggesting that many have got the message about having to fund care themselves, although they do not like it.

CONCLUSIONS

We have explored our material here using two key themes – notions of justice and fairness, and decision making in uncertainty. Our research shows that the population at large is not ready for policies which require them to take on overt individual responsibility for paying for care in old age.

The majority of people believe that it is right for the state to retain a level of responsibility for this area, whether exclusively or in partnership with individuals. However, this belief is founded on the related belief that the state is currently largely responsible for care or, at least, was in the past responsible to a greater degree than it is at present. As we have shown, this is not the case, but such strongly held beliefs pose substantial problems for politicians committed to home ownership as a way of 'cascading wealth down the generations'. It is precisely because people in the UK have been encouraged to have their major capital holdings in the form of housing that we find ourselves in this impasse. Even if there is no increase in the proportion of older people needing long-term care, the increasing level of home ownership will of itself mean that more will face the need to liquidate their housing capital to pay for care.

People in our surveys who were 'pro-state' opposed increased individual responsibility for care largely on principle. However, even this group were unhappy at the prospect of using housing capital to pay for care. Yet it is difficult to imagine that the 'pro-state' group would feel that it was right for someone who held thousands of pounds in shares or savings not to contribute from that towards the cost of care. Home ownership is a form of forced saving – how many of us would accumulate similar amounts through other forms of saving or investment? Moreover, it is subsidised by the state through mortgage interest relief. Further, as economists would point out, we have already derived substantial value from our investment through living in the accommodation which it ensures. On a purely rational basis, then, we should not be so resistant to liquidating this asset when needed.

However, economic rationality, as the whole programme has shown, does not always guide financial decision making. Homes have an emotional meaning which makes it difficult to think of selling up in order to pay for care. Further, the use of housing capital has become negatively associated in people's minds with admission to residential or nursing home care. It is difficult to liquidate housing capital partially, to fund care while still living at home. If this were easier to do people's attitudes towards the fungibility of their housing capital might well change (and we might find fewer people needing to go into residential or nursing home care). Finally, there is the strong sense of 'broken promises' which makes people resistant to using capital. Many were encouraged into home ownership as a way of increasing wealth, without full knowledge that, come the time, they would have to use that wealth for their care needs.

Broken promises also come into play in respondents' feelings about the future. They are resistant to the idea of making insurance provision because they thought national insurance and taxes paid for welfare services. The fact that future policy is uncertain makes them perhaps more realistic about what is likely to happen to them, but they are unhappy because it appears to break another promise.

Political thinking about the appropriate role of the state in guaranteeing personal welfare has changed dramatically in the past twenty years, and not just among right-of-centre politicians. However, our research suggests that the bulk of the population has not changed its thinking in line with this radical change, and even less its behaviour. A national debate about the levels of state support we wish to see devoted to long-term care and the contributions we are prepared to make, whether individually or through taxation, is long overdue.

3 Entrepreneurial Activity in the Public Sector: Evidence from UK Primary Care

Christine Ennew, Teresa Feighan and David Whynes

INTRODUCTION

The late 1980s and early 1990s witnessed some of the most fundamental changes in the provision of health care in the UK since the
introduction of the National Health Service (NHS) itself over fifty
years ago. The basic thrust of these reforms was to reproduce the
characteristics of a market within a public sector activity, in order
to enhance efficiency and improve quality. The central feature of
this process was the institution of a purchaser-provider split to create
a quasi-market in health care. Thus, while the state continues to fund
the provision of health care, it ceases to be the sole provider. Instead the state or its agents purchase health services on behalf of
consumers from a range of different providers. Two mechanisms drove
the process of reform in the primary care sector; first, the institution
of a new General Practitioner contract in 1990 which changed the
terms and conditions under which GPs were required to provide
care and second, the introduction of fundholding which devolved
budgetary responsibility for the provision of primary care and the
purchase of certain forms of secondary care to individual GP practices.
   Entrepreneurial activity is often seen as a key element in driving
the effective operation of private sector markets (Baumol, 1968).
If private sector markets rely on entrepreneurship then it seems
likely that quasi-markets in the public sector may also require some
form of entrepreneurial activity in order to function effectively. To
the extent that the reforms to primary care provide GPs with greater
flexibility and discretion with regard to the provision of health care,
they create an opportunity for change which could lead to efficiency

gains and improvements in quality. The realisation of efficiency gains and quality improvements will depend upon the willingness of individual GPs to innovate in the way in which they deliver health care to their patients. This process of exploiting enhanced levels of flexibility and discretion can be thought of as the public sector equivalent of the entrepreneurial activity observed in the private sector. With respect to primary care, the main source of discretion arises with respect to fundholding. Fundholding presents general practitioners (GPs) with a budget which is controlled and allocated by them for the provision of primary care and the purchase of secondary care. In principle, the scheme gives GPs responsibility for determining the allocation of resources in relation to the type, quantity and quality of care provided. Accordingly, it can be argued that the fundholding reforms create the opportunity for and even require entrepreneurial activity on the part of those GPs involved. However, the changes in the GP contract also provide an element of flexibility for those GPs not involved in fundholding. Thus, from a conceptual perspective, there is no reason to assume that entrepreneurship should be restricted to fundholding GPs although it might be reasonable to expect it to be more prevalent among this group.

The extent and nature of entrepreneurship among fundholding and non-fundholding GPs remains essentially an empirical question. Accordingly, this chapter provides an empirical investigation of the meaning and nature of entrepreneurial activity in the context of primary care. The discussion proceeds first by examining briefly the changes to primary health care provision in the UK. Thereafter, we explore the links between markets, quasi markets and entrepreneurial activity in order to develop an understanding of the concept of the public sector entrepreneur. The following sections outline the data collection process and present the results of the analysis. The chapter concludes with a with a discussion of the implications of the results.

QUASI-MARKETS AND THE REFORM OF PRIMARY HEALTH CARE

As with the reform of the public sector in general, structural changes in the NHS have been instituted with the intention of creating an operating environment which, although not a true market, embodies the principal characteristics of such a market (Le Grand, 1991). For a quasi-market to operate in health care, the purchaser and provider roles within the NHS had to be separated. Whilst this was largely to be achieved through a respecification of the role of local health authorities and the creation of autonomous hospital trusts, an additional element was added to the purchasing side by the introduction of the Practice Budget Scheme, or 'fundholding' (DoH, 1989). Fundholding allowed GPs to hold their own budgets for the provision of primary care and the purchase of secondary care, services. It is evident that the intention of fundholding was to confer enhanced market power on the individual practice, whilst at the same time requiring that practice to subject itself to the financial discipline of a pre-determined budget. Although membership of the fundholding scheme was, and has remained, optional, new terms of service were simultaneously imposed, covering all GPs contracting services to the NHS. The 1990 Contract radically revised the structure of GP remuneration, by diminishing the importance of fixed allowances and by increasing the proportion of gross income generated by the performance of specific activities and the assumption of responsibilities for patients (Whynes, 1993). These changes in the operating environment were expected directly to affect agents within the NHS, encouraging the types of behaviour consistent with an unregulated market (Ferlie, 1992). More specifically, the introduction of private sector models into the public sector should encourage the replacement of existing administrative and professional cultures with entrepreneurial cultures (Stewart and Walsh, 1992).

Recruitment into fundholding has proceeded in a series of annual 'waves', commencing in 1991; the take-up of fundholding was initially limited by practice size such that only practices with a list size in excess of 9,000 were eligible for the first wave, but over time, the scope of the scheme has increased. The minimum list size necessary for eligibility was progressively reduced and, by 1993, smaller practices were being permitted to form consortia in order to meet the minimum list size requirement. In 1995, two new fundholding options were introduced. 'Community fundholding', with a low list size requirement, was similar to 'standard fundholding', although the range of purchasable services was more restricted. At the other extreme, large practices and consortia were able to opt for 'total purchasing', which implied a fund covering, in principle, the purchase of virtually all patient services. By 1995, more than 10,000 of the UK's 35,000 GPs were operating within fundholding practices (Office of Health Economics, 1995) and, it is estimated that over half of the population was being served by fundholders (Audit Commission, 1996). Although the future of fundholding remains politically uncertain, most proposals for reform seek to involve GPs in some form of commissioning activity, as implied by the proposal in the 1997 Labour party manifesto for 'GPs in an area to bring their combined strength to bear on individual hospitals to secure higher standards of provision' (Labour Party, 1997, p. 21). Despite the strong commitment to fundholding in some quarters and substantial support for GP commissioning (from all political parties), the evidence for the effectiveness of fundholding is still partial.

Anecdotal evidence of both the costs and benefits of fundholding is provided by Bain (1993) and McAvoy (1993) who both note that patients of fundholding practices have experienced improvements in service quality but equally, both recognise that this has imposed costs on patients in non-fundholding practices. Chambers and Belcher (1993) comment on the increased workload imposed on GPs as a consequence of the NHS reforms more generally including the changes to the GP contract. More recently, the Audit Commission Report (Audit Commission, 1996) noted that the administrative costs of fundholding have exceeded the reported costs savings by some £26 million. Whilst this has been accompanied by improvements in the quality of service provided by fundholders, there is evidence that quality improvements have not been as extensive as might have been expected. As Newton *et al.* (1993) observe, it will inevitably be some time before the long-term impact of the scheme can be fully assessed. Much of the existing research, conducted in the early stages of fundholding, provides valuable preliminary evidence but typically lacks a clear theoretical framework. We believe that the concept of the entrepreneur and entrepreneurial behaviour provides a theoretical and conceptual basis which can be used to shed further light on the impact of fundholding and contribute to theoretical and empirical developments relating to entrepreneurship in the public sector.

ENTREPRENEURSHIP IN THE PUBLIC SECTOR

The introduction of fundholding arguably puts the GP in a position which is akin to that of an entrepreneur. The term *entrepreneur* has been used to describe not only the fundholding GP (Bain, 1993), but also headmasters in schools as a consequence of educational reform (Boyett and Finlay, 1992) and business managers in hospital trusts (Boyett and Finlay, 1995). More generally, the climate created by the recent public sector reforms has been described as *entrepreneurial* (Stewart and Walsh, 1992). However, the concept of the *entrepreneur* in the private sector continues to be imprecise and the subject of considerable debate (Chell *et al.*, 1991); the concept of *entrepreneurship* in relation to the public sector, even more so. Nevertheless there appears to be a widespread agreement that entrepreneurship is relevant outside the private sector (Gartner, 1990; Schultz, 1975, 1980) and it can be argued that when the public sector is characterised by quasi-markets, the concept of entrepreneurship is likely to be particularly relevant. Arguably, if markets need entrepreneurs in order to function effectively (Baumol, 1968) then quasi-markets will also require individuals who fulfil this type of role. However, this begs an obvious question about the nature of entrepreneurship in the public sector given the absence of the profit motive, lack of ownership and other private sector characteristics which condition entrepreneurial activity.

There are many different concepts of the entrepreneur. Schumpeter (1934), for example, sees the entrepreneur as having a decision-making role and his/her main function is to innovate (i.e. introduce new goods; introduce new methods of production; open new markets; acquire new sources of supply; create new types of industrial organisation). Indeed the Schumpeterian view essentially emphasises the idea of the entrepreneur as a source of disequilibrium. By contrast, the Austrian School (e.g. Kirzner, Hayek) focus on the idea of the entrepreneur as arbitrageur who exploits opportunities which arise from differences between markets (the simplest example being that of buying at a low price in one market and selling at a higher price in another). This approach emphasises the role of the entrepreneur in moving a system back toward some sort of equilibrium. While apparently diametrically opposed, these two concepts are by no means inconsistent and may simply recognise the fact that the role and activities of the entrepreneur may be context specific (Cheah, 1990). A third approach is concerned with the idea of the entrepreneur as someone who achieves success by avoiding the inefficiencies (whether in terms of management or production) to which other people or organisations are prone (Leibenstien, 1968); this activity is often referred to as the reduction of x-inefficiency.

Casson (1982) attempts to identify a shared element that runs through these theories by introducing the concept of entrepreneurial judgement. The attempt to identify a shared element suggests that Casson's theory has generality, and may be applied to all kinds of entrepreneurship. Casson (1982, p. 23) specifically defines an entrepreneur as *someone who specialises in taking judgmental decisions about the co-ordination of scarce resources*. In Casson's view the concept of entrepreneurial judgement is of paramount importance; judgement is not based on the simple application of marginalist rules regarding resource allocation but rather is based on individuals, their perceptions and the information that they have available (or choose to acquire). Central to this concept is the recognition that different individuals will make different decisions which will produce different outcomes because information is necessarily imperfect and costly to acquire.

Private sector entrepreneurship has typically been studied in terms of attitudes, behaviour or some mixture of the two and there is an extensive body of literature dealing with typologies and characteristics of entrepreneurs (Woo, Cooper and Dunkleberg, 1991; Ennew, Robbie, Wright and Thompson, 1993). Although there is no generally accepted definition of the entrepreneur it is widely recognised that there are a number of attributes or styles of behaviour which will be in some way typical (Chell *et al.*, 1991). These include opportunism, innovative behaviour, the ability to think strategically, being imaginative and being proactive. Bull and Willard (1993) attempt to formalise these ideas into a theoretical framework for entrepreneurship in which they suggest that the emergence and development of entrepreneruial activity requires certain personal characteristics including task related motivation, perception of gain and expertise combined with an appropriate and supportive environment.

Typically entrepreneurs are identified as being profit motivated although this may simply reflect the predominance of private sector work in this area. Indeed, broadening the concept of profit to be more akin to the concept of utility provides a more general source of motivation for entrepreneurial behaviour. Similarly there is considerable uncertainty as to whether there is some basic pool (or fixed supply) of entrepreneurs or whether anyone can become entrepreneurial given the right environment (Schultz, 1980).

In principle, the GP managing a practice budget and making decisions relating to the purchase and provision of health care can

be classified as an entrepreneur in terms of Casson's broad definition. Given an allocated budget, the fundholding GP must make
judgmental decisions regarding the provision of services and although these decisions are not necessarily profit motivated, they
may be viewed as being utility motivated in the sense that the GP
can improve his or her utility (sense of well being) by delivering
an improved quality of service and greater patient satisfaction.
Certainly, as indicated above there is anecdotal evidence of innovative behaviour in relation to service delivery which would be
consistent with aspects of the Schumpeterian view of the entrepreneur. Equally, if GPs are behaving in a manner which is consistent
with the expectations of the reformers then we might expect to see
efficiency gains and resource savings consistent with Leibenstein's
view of the entrepreneur. Finally, given the ability of GPs to choose
providers we might anticipate that behaviour consistent with the
Austrian view would be observed as GPs seek to exploit price differentials between providers. Furthermore, given the increased flexibility associated with the new GP contract, it is at least possible
that the opportunity to engage in entrepreneurial behaviour of the
sort described above may not be restricted to fundholders.

Indeed, if the types of behaviour described above do not materi-
alise, then the extent to which NHS reform in general and primary
care reform in particular will realise their stated objectives will be
significantly constrained. The extent to which GPs do engage in
entrepreneurial behaviour will depend on the supply of individuals
capable of so doing. If the pool of innovative/entrepreneurial individuals is in some sense fixed and less than the existing number of
GP practices then the extension of fundholding may not be effective in generating more extensive improvements in service delivery
because only a limited number of GPs will be able to innovate.
Alternatively, if we accept the view of Schultz (1980), that changing economic conditions will encourage an increased supply of entrepreneurs, then the extension of fundholding has the potential to
generate future improvements in quality. While measuring the supply
of actual and potential entrepreneurs is difficult, if not impossible,
an empirical examination of the activities of fundholding and non-
fundholding GPs may at least help to shed some light on these
issues.

AN EMPIRICAL ANALYSIS OF ENTREPRENEURIAL BEHAVIOUR AMONG GPs

The relative novelty of the idea of the public sector entrepreneur and the uncertainty surrounding the concept more generally suggest that any attempt to research this area must initially be exploratory in nature. Past research examining the nature and characteristics of entrepreneurship has focused on a range of issues including motivation (Lafuente and Salas, 1989), goals (Dunkleberg and Cooper, 1982) and social orientation, managerial style and competitive environments (Davidsson, 1988). These characteristics have then been employed to develop typologies of entrepreneurs in order to improve understanding of the complex concept of entrepreneurship. The problems associated with this type of approach have been well documented (Woo, Cooper and Dunkleberg, 1991, Chell, Haworth and Brearley, 1991). If there are problems in establishing typologies of entrepreneurs in relation to private sector activities, those problems are likely to be even more acute in relation to the public sector.

Consequently, the analysis contained in this section of the chapter is essentially exploratory and seeks to identify broad general patterns of attitude and behaviour among GPs using both qualitative and quantitative approaches. The qualitative analysis is based on a series of 58 interviews with fundholding (29) and non-fundholding (29) GPs in Nottinghamshire and Derbyshire conducted during 1995 and 1996. The interviews lasted between 30 and 90 minutes and sought to explore motivation, beliefs and behaviour with respect to the provision of health care in the reformed NHS. The quantitative data was collected by means of a postal questionnaire distributed to a sample of over 2,000 GPs (fundholders and non-fundholders) from a range of different health authorities throughout the country. The questionnaire was sent out in the summer of 1996 and around 800 responses were received, making the survey one of the largest of its kind. The questionnaire collected basic practice data, illustrative examples of the range of practice activities and data on GP attitudes. For both data sets, the analysis was concerned with identifying patterns or forms of entrepreneurial behaviour (innovating, resource saving, and arbitrage) and the extent to which these patterns were linked to specific characteristics of the respondent including motivations and attitudes and specific characteristics of the practice such as fundholding status and the stage at which it was adopted.

Analysis of Interviews

The analysis of interview data aimed to explore in detail various aspects and forms of entrepreneurial behaviour. Particular attention was devoted to the identification of entrepreneurial behaviour through the reduction of x-inefficiency, arbitrage within and between markets and genuine innovation. Although it was anticipated that the opportunities for various forms of entrepreneurial behaviour would be greater for fundholders it was not assumed that entrepreneurship was necessarily absent among non-fundholders.

- *X-Inefficiency (organisational slack)*
  Arguably, the opportunities for reducing organisational slack are greatest for fundholders who have direct control of their budget and their referral patterns. As a broad indication of the extent to which savings which have been made, some 15 fundholders reported that they had been able to make budget savings which were then ploughed back into the practice in the form of waiting list reductions, building refurbishments and IT improvements. However, 12 fundholders (primarily in the third, fourth and fifth waves) reported no cost savings. This finding must be interpreted with care as it may reflect the greater experience of the early wave fundholders or the tighter budgets allocated in later waves. Staffing decisions, increases in generic prescribing and the increased use of IT were all identified as sources of cost saving.

  The process of contracting with hospitals for the provision of secondary care is an important mechanism for enhancing efficiency (for example by specifying when patients are seen, by whom and how frequently). However, the extent to which fundholders are actually able to reduce x-inefficiencies depends on how contract provisions translate into actual behaviour. Some practice were quite specific about the type of care required and attempted to monitor the extent to which providers conformed to contract specifications. However, the majority had not developed formal monitoring systems (at least in part because of the costs of so doing) and consequently were less able to ensure that providers were delivering up to the required standard. In a small number of cases GPs were unaware of monitoring processes, having devolved these to their fund or practice managers. An examination of invoicing and payment arrangements also highlights some missed opportunities to reduce organisational slack. Fundholders are entitled not to pay invoices which are not presented within a specified period, thus placing pressure on providers to improve their own internal systems. In practice, around half of the fundholders indicated that they were reluctant to ignore invoices however late they may be. However, among those who did a number noted that provider systems did improve. Furthermore, many of those who did restrict payment of late invoices also checked those invoices carefully resulting in additional savings. For example;

> Another thing is that the hospitals have tried a few things on us. We do obstetric scans for miscarriages and thats an area where they are trying it on, but our astute manger picks them up. (Fundholder, first wave)

Evidence of efficiency gains among non-fundholders is much more difficult to identify because they do not have direct control over their spending. Certainly, one non-fundholder commented on the potential for efficiency gains through a different allocation of staff (the use of nurse practitioners) and a small number of others commented on the beneficial effects of IT. Interestingly, the majority of non-fundholders commented adversely on the increased administrative workload which had resulted from the new contract which appeared to have limited their potential for cost savings.

- *Market Arbitrage*
  The Austrian view of the entrepreneur is as an arbitrageur, exploiting gaps that exist between and within markets. In principle, both fundholders and non-fundholders have the potential to perform such roles in that the purchase of secondary care by the former gives them the opportunity to select the best price-quality configuration from a range of providers, and patterns of referral among the latter provide an opportunity to exploit apparent gaps in service provision. In many instances, the scope for arbitrage may be restricted by geographic considerations and a substantial number of GPs observed that there had been little change in their pattern of referrals simply because of the dominant position of the main hospitals, one in each of the main conurbations (Nottingham and Derby).

  The interviews revealed that in practice, most fundholders have purchased services similar to their referral pattern prior to fundholding. Less than 25 per cent of fundholders indicated a substantial change in referrals with the remainder reporting moderate to marginal changes. Six of the non-fundholders (21 per cent) indicated a minor or moderate change in referral patterns but none indicated substantive change. Generally, this change in referral patterns was facilitated by the activities of a non-fundholding consortium in Nottinghamshire to which all but one of the non-fundholders belonged. Like fundholders a small number of non-fundholders attempted to exploit differences in waiting times. For example;

> We would refer to [hospital] for ENT because they don't have to wait as long as they do in [hospital]. Basically we refer to different hospitals because of waiting times. (Non fundholder)

Among those fundholders who were willing to make significant changes in their purchasing pattern, some made long term shifts in response to an improved price-quality configuration, others used the ability to switch provider as a mechanism to force a preferred supplier to provide the desired service. For example

> One of the big problems we had was with pathology. We were approached by [hospital] who said they would collect specimens everyday and fax us back the results everyday. So we went to our local hospital and said to them – what are you going to do? So what they developed (this isn't just for fundholders) was a van service which now collects the specimens at lunchtime ... and the following day the results are delivered back to the practice. If its urgent, they phone us, so that's much better. I think it was just a bit of a threat. (Fundholder, first wave)

Longer term changes in contracting include six practices which have moved a number of different specialisms away from their traditional, local provider on the grounds of quality of service grounds and waiting times. In general though, ad hoc diversifications in referral patterns were probably more common than major long term shifts which is consistent with a greater reliance on cost-per-case contracts rather than block contracts.

- *Innovation*

  The strong association between entrepreneurship and innovation suggests that it is appropriate to examine the extent and nature of innovation by GPs. While it seems plausible that innovation would be greatest among fundholders, there is no a priori reason why it should be restricted to this group. By far the most significant form of innovation has related to service delivery. Almost all of the fundholders interviewed had introduced new services and around half had established 'satellite' clinics at their own surgeries. Such clinics have two particular advantages from the patient's point of view: they bring the consultant to the patient rather than sending the patient to the consultant and they reduce waiting times (as well as costs in some instances). The staffing of these clinics varies. In some instances, the provider sends its own staff as part of its service to the fundholder; in instances in which the provider is unwilling to offer such a service, the clinic will be staffed by consultants working on a private basis.

Although less extensive, there was evidence of innovation in service delivery among non-fundholders. Around half of the non-fundholders interviewed reported extensions in the range of services offered, typically in the form of counselling and physiotherapy. Interestingly, those GPs who were offering such services believed that they had been able to do so despite being non-fundholders whereas those who had not been able to do so typically felt that this was because they were non-fundholders. One non-fundholding practice had even been able to arrange consultant-led clinics at their surgery:

> We arranged some special sessions which we call teach and treat where we get a consultant along to do a teaching session on our patients so ... all the partners and practice nurses are there and we present our own patient to the consultant and he/she then teaches us on that patient so we all learn from the referral. It works extremely well ... the patient likes it. We have done it with orthopaedics, dermatology and ear nose and throat and we are going to have a go with eyes. (Non-fundholder)

One of the major problems with respect to service delivery has been waiting times. Problems with long waiting lists have been tackled by one-off contracts with other providers (if necessary, at a higher price). In instances where GPs have an ideological objection to going private, these contracts have been with other NHS providers – sometimes at a moderate distance from the patients home. However, the majority of GPs had no ideological objections to private medicine and have used that sector to reduce waiting times. Thus, as one interviewee commented:

Physiotherapy – we went private with that ... we could offer physiotherapy in a day or two where it was taking weeks, months sometimes to get to the orthopaedic department. (Fundholder – first wave)

Behaviour of this sort may be regarded as innovative in that it breaks with the long standing tradition of retaining patient management within the NHS and in many cases also displays an element of traditional Austrian style arbitrage.

In exploratory research of this nature care must be taken in introducing the notion of types of entrepreneur as developed in private sector research. In many senses, all those GPs who have opted for fundholding may be regarded as being in some sense entrepreneurial and many of those who elected to remain as non-fundholders will still have undertaken innovations. However, it is clear from the interviews that there is considerable variation in the motivation for adopting fundholding, subsequent behaviour and the extent to which the GP and the practice have been able to exploit opportunities for the benefit of patients. From discussions with interviewees, the motives for adopting fundholding appear to fall into two broad (and occasionally overlapping) categories: the positive motives which emphasised the opportunities offered by fundholding and the negative motives which are typical of the reluctant participant. The two broad categories are outlined below in table 3.1.

A similar categorisation of motives can be identified when considering non-fundholders as table 3.2 shows. In this case the interesting distinction is between those who identified essentially pragmatic reasons for retaining non-fundholding status and those who were politically or ideologically opposed to system. Interestingly, a small number of GPs indicated that they had initially been interested in fundholding, were too small to enter and subsequently became committed to non-fundholding. This particular perspective may well reflect the significant role played by the Nottingham Non-Fundholders Consortium which covers the majority of non-fundholding practices in the area and has a negotiating role on behalf of its members. As such it provides a context within which non-fundholders can see themselves have a voice and having a system to which they can display commitment.

The interviews suggested some pattern linking attitudes, motives and behaviour. While no attempt was made to formally categorise

Table 3.1 **Reasons for Fundholding (figures in brackets indicate the number of citations)**

Positive	Negative
Better treatment for patients (11)	Pressure because other practices fundholding (3)
Control of budget (3)	Pressure from FHSA (3)
Manipulate system in favour of patients (1)	Improved resources (computers, cost-rent etc) (2)
Exploit new opportunities (2)	Consequences of 1992 election (1)
Reducing waiting time (3)	Waited till dealt with other issues (2)
Efficiency gains	
In favour but initially too small (7)	Personally opposed but felt it best for patients (2)

Table 3.2 **Reasons for Non-Fundholding (figures in brackets indicate the number of citations)**

Reasons for Non-Fundholding	
Pragmatic	Ideological
Not the right time	Affects doctor–patient relationship (4)
Too much work/weight of bureaucracy (7)	Political stunt (2)
Lack of agreement among partners (2)	Morally wrong (5)
Too busy initially (2)	No benefit to patients (3)
Initially too small – became committed to non-fundholding (3)	Disapprove of competition
	Not GP's role to ration care (2)

each interviewee, there was evidence to suggest the presence of different types of GPs, with the highly innovative GPs at one extreme and the rather disenchanted at the other. The GPs (largely but not entirely fundholders) who display the more positive motivations are typically much more likely to innovate in service delivery, much more likely to shop around (considering both price and quality issues), display a greater awareness of the market in which they operate and make a greater effort to improve efficiency. By contrast, the more disenchanted GPs (often non-fundholders) tend to display negative motivations, limited, even minimal service innovation, limited changes in referral patterns and limited efficiency gains. Many of the more disenchanted remain strongly committed to their profession but are clearly highly disillusioned with the way in which the new system operates. Indeed, this type of GP is rather more likely to consider retiring early. Between these two extremes is a group of GPs (both fundholders and non-fundholders) who display a mixture of both positive and negative motivations and correspondingly moderate degrees of innovation, shopping around and cost savings. Similar patterns of attitudes and behaviour have been identified among fundholders in other areas (see for example Ennew *et al.*, 1994) which might suggest some generality for this framework.

Survey Analysis

The analysis of survey data sought to identify broad general trends in the relationship between the beliefs and attitudes of GPs and their behaviour as manifested in the range of activities undertaken within practices. The basic characteristics of the respondents to the survey were as follows;

- 42 per cent of respondents were fundholders and 58 per cent were non-fundholders
- two thirds of respondents were senior partners
- the majority of respondents came from the third, fourth, fifth and sixth waves
- 78 per cent of respondents were male
- the average age of respondent was 47
- 20 per cent came from families in which either parents or grandparents were medical doctors.

A major part of the questionnaire was concerned with the collection of data relating to attitudes. Each respondent was confronted with 21 statements, on a scale from 'strongly agree' (coded 1), through 'unsure' (3) to 'strongly disagree' (5). These statements were designed to reflect various characteristics of entrepreneurship (motivation, skill, personal gain and perceived environmental support) based on the framework suggested by Bull and Willard (1993). In all cases the statements were presented in a specific NHS context. For example, and taken in isolation, strong agreement with the statement 'I enjoy playing my part in managing the activities of the practice' was used as an indicator of the extent to which the respondent was motivated by the process of actually managing their practice.

Factor analysis enabled the twenty-one statements to be aggregated into five underlying dimensions which broadly corresponded to the Bull and Willard framework (see Ennew, Feighan and Whynes, 1997, for more detail). These were then used as input to a cluster analysis and three broad types of GP were identified.

- *True Entrepreneurs*
  The first group of GP's were most positive about the opportunities for innovation and change which have been created within the NHS. They recognise few constraints on their activity, they enjoy their work and they have few doubts about their expertise. However, they do perceive that the nature of their role has changed. This group was described as the *true entrepreneurs*.

- *The Disenchanted*
  The second group of GPs had a distinctly negative perspective of the reforms and felt that their activities were significantly constrained; they did not appear to enjoy their job and were concerned about their ability to manage. The also perceived a substantial change in the nature of their work. This group was described as the *disenchanted*.

- *The Traditionalists*
  The third group were relatively positive about the opportunities within the NHS and did not perceive any substantial constraint on their activities. They enjoyed their job and were not unduly concerned about their abilities to manage. Most noticeably, they did not perceive a substantive change in their role. This group was described as the traditionalists and following further analysis was subdivided into small and large sub-groups.

The distribution of fundholders and non fundholders across and within the different categories is shown in Table 3.3 below. The first set of figures show the way in which fundholders and non-fundholders were divided across different categories. The second set of figures describes the way in which each category is split between fundholders and non-fundholders. Thus, we can see that

Table 3.3   **Distribution of Respondents Across Categories (per cent)**

	True Entrepreneurs	Disenchanted	Large Traditionalists	Small Traditionalists
Distribution of practice types across categories				
Fundholders	34	22	25	19
Non-fundholders	10	30	29	31
Distribution of practice types within categories				
Fundholders	72	36	39	32
Non-fundholders	28	64	61	68

fundholders dominate the group of true entrepreneurs while non-fundholders are more prevalent among the disenchanted and the traditionalists. However, it is significant that some 10 per cent of non-fundholders were classed as true entrepreneurs, notwithstanding the more limited opportunities for entrepreneurial behaviour which confront this group.

The different groups of GP were then examined across a series of behaviours which were thought to be indicative of enterprise and innovation. These behaviours were chosen to correspond with different types of entrepreneurial activity (innovation, arbitrage and reduction of x-inefficiency). Indicators of innovation were primarily in the form of the introduction of new services such as physiotherapy and complementary medicine; arbitrage was rather more difficult to measure but potential indicators included applications under the cost-rent scheme, the adoption of health promotion incentives (measured as the proportion in band 3) as well as efforts to become customer aware via patient satisfaction surveys. Reductions in x-inefficiency were measured in the form of cost saving activities such as computerisation, the use of nurse practitioners and the use of a prescribing 'formulary' – the restriction of prescription to an agreed list of medicines to control prescribing costs.

Evidence on the extent of innovative activity by the different groups is provided in the following tables which indicate the percentages of each practice undertaking each type of activity. Table 3.4 considers a range of different managerial activities which may be undertaken. Table 3.5 considers computerisation and Table 3.6 concentrates specifically on new services.

The true entrepreneurs were clearly the most enterprising of the

Table 3.4 Practice Activities by Type of GP

Activities undertaken	True Entrepreneurs	Disenchanted	Large Traditionalists	Small Traditionalists
Training Practice	44	16	37	27
Prescribing formulary*	58	38	40	42
Patient satisfaction survey*	56	38	49	46
Employ nurse practitioner	48	54	48	49
Health Promotion	93	91	94	93
Owns premises	78	70	76	71
Cost Rent*	73	60	64	62

*Significant at p ≤ 0.05.

Table 3.5 Computerisation Across Practices

Computers used for	True Entrepreneurs	Disenchanted	Large Traditionalists	Small Traditionalists
Medical records*	92	79	82	82
Repeat prescribing	93	90	94	89
Patient appointments*	45	30	43	35
Financial management*	75	36	58	50
Hospital Referrals*	72	53	58	55
Medical audit*	88	66	83	79

* Significant at p ≤ 0.05.

Table 3.6 New Services Offered by Practices

Practices offering	True Entrepreneurs	Disenchanted	Large Traditionalists	Small Traditionalists
Speech therapy	59	50	56	55
Counselling*	78	67	76	67
Dietetic advice	82	78	77	77
Chiropody	69	63	65	64
Physiotherapy*	83	68	75	68
Consultant-led clinics*	38	27	30	24
Minor surgery*	95	87	97	90
Complementary medicine	23	19	21	23

* Significant at p ≤ 0.05.

groupings; they had typically introduced a much larger range of new services (innovation), they made more extensive use of computers and restricted prescription lists (reduction of x-inefficiency); they were more likely to have applied under the cost-rent scheme and were more likely to undertake patient satisfaction surveys (possible indicators of arbitrage activity). By contrast, the disenchanted GPs (including a number of fundholders) appear to have been the least likely to introduce new services and the least likely to adopt major cost saving changes such as computerisation. Interestingly, health promotion clinics which attract a direct financial payment for the introduction of new services have been almost universally, adopted suggesting that at least in some areas financial incentives can have a strong impact.

Although a large proportion of the true entrepreneurs were fundholders, nearly 30 per cent were non-fundholders. This strongly suggests that innovative and entrepreneurial activity, although more prevalent among fundholders is not restricted to that group. Similarly, although the disenchanted group is dominated by non-fundholders, a surprisingly large proportion (35 per cent) of the group is fundholders.

What is clear from the figures above is that there are behavioural differences across the three groups; however, some of the similarities are perhaps as interesting as the differences. For example there is little variation in the use of nurse practitioners across the groups, little variation in the extent of minor surgery and little variation in the use of computers for repeat prescribing. Furthermore, where differences are evident they are not as substantial as they could be, suggesting that what appears to be a marked difference in attitudes is only partially translated into a difference in behaviour.

CONCLUSIONS AND IMPLICATIONS

The concept of entrepreneurship in the public sector and the ways in which entrepreneurial activity are manifested is still poorly understood. The concept of the entrepreneur as a resource allocator and a co-ordinator appears relevant in the public sector on the basis of this analysis of primary care. However, the results suggest that, irrespective of status, not all GPs would wish to or are able to adopt an entrepreneurial role. Simply creating the opportunity for entrepreneurship and innovation to occur does not ensure that it will. The point is of particular relevance in the public sector where there is the potential for considerable ideological resistance to the principle of entrepreneurship. Creating a quasi market in the public sector may create an environment in which individuals can behave entrepreneurially but it does not necessarily guarantee that they will. Specifically, while there is evidence of an association between fundholding and increased levels of innovative activity, it is important to note that not all fundholders are innovators and not all innovators are fundholders.

In addition to findings in relation to the specifics of entrepreneurship and general practice, the research has broader relevance. It provides insights into the impact of quasi-markets and economic incentives on the behaviour of agents in the public sector. The analysis of the interviews and particularly of the survey findings highlights the imperfect nature of the relationship between motives, incentives, beliefs and behaviour. The introduction of fundholding represented a fundamental change in the structure of primary care provision and introduced a new and different system of incentives. However, these structural changes do not automatically produce changes in behaviour (introducing a market does not make everyone behave in a market oriented way) and their impact on beliefs appears even weaker. Pure economic or financial incentives may be effective in inducing behavioural change on a small scale in an area where the is clear agreement among professional opinion (for example in the case of health promotion) but the extent to which they can stimulate large scale behavioural changes in a direction decided by government appears to be more questionable.

4 British Asian Entrepreneurs: Culture and Opportunity Structures

Tariq Modood, Hilary Metcalf and Satnam Virdee

INTRODUCTION

Asian Britons have rapidly assumed a major role in small business. However, this prominence conceals substantial diversity in the pattern of entrepreneurship and the nature of business across the three main South Asian groups. Indians, Pakistanis and African Asians differ markedly in their approach to business and in their success. They also differ in terms of the economic resources they bring to self-employment and in the cultural values which surround their economic activities. This diversity allowed a study of South Asian entrepreneurs to examine the complex interaction between culture and economic rationality in economic behaviour.

This chapter uses material from a recent study of British Asian entrepreneurs to analyse the role of this group in the expansion of the small business sector in the UK and also to improve our understanding of the part played by cultural factors in influencing economic decisions in the context of entrepreneurial activity (for a fuller analysis see Metcalf, Modood and Virdee, 1996).

DIFFERING EXPERIENCES OF SELF-EMPLOYMENT

In 1974 self employment accounted for 12 per cent of the white as against only eight per cent of South Asian working men (Smith 1977: 92). By 1982 the comparable statistics were 14 and 18 per cent. Self-employment amongst Asians has continued to expand into the 1990s. However, participation in self employment has been uneven across groups whose origins lie in the Indian sub-continent. The most recent survey, in 1994, shows that one in four Indians and

African Asian men were self employed compared with one in five Pakistanis and one in ten Bangladeshis (Modood *et al.*, 1997:122). Ethnic minority groups also diverge in their socio-economic position and in their cultural backgrounds. African Asians and Chinese people have a much more advantaged educational and economic profile than groups such as the Pakistanis, Bangladeshis and African-Caribbeans (Jones, 1993; Peach, 1996; Modood *et al.*, 1997). To what extent these differences are due to economic, cultural or other factors is a matter of current debate. Self-employment is a focus of these debates. On the one hand, it is clearly related to structural factors: Asian self-employment took off at a time of high unemployment. On the other, it is clearly related to ethnicity, since it is to be found more amongst some groups than others.

Explanations of the Move Towards Self-Employment among British Asians: Adverse Circumstances versus Enabling Culture

Different approaches to British Asian self-employment rest on practical issues to do with the circumstances in which the communities find themselves and on their cultural backgrounds, and offer different perspectives on their situation. The 'blocked upward mobility' approach suggests that Asians enter into small business in order to escape racial discrimination which confines them to low-status low-waged sectors of the labour market (Aldrich *et al.*, 1981: 175; Jones *et al.*, 1994; and Ram, 1992). Since entrepreneurship is the result of the push of discrimination rather than a more positive appraisal of market opportunities and access to capital, skills and other relevant resources, it is seen as unlikely to be highly successful. Studies of the experience of Asian entrepreneurs from this perspective concluded that they 'are entering not an upward ladder leading to material enrichment, but a dead-end on the fringe of the modern economy' and could be characterised as a sort of 'lumpen bourgeoisie' (McEvoy *et al.*, 1982: 10).

An alternative approach emphasises the 'cultural resources' of Asian entrepreneurs. In a study of Pakistani entrepreneurship, Werbner argues that the critical factor in the success of Pakistani businessmen is their cultural heritage, which stresses thrift, deferred gratification, industriousness and self-reliance (1990a and 1990b). Such attributes no less than the wider environment are central to the development of Asian business. Werbner emphasises the importance of kinship and friendship networks which provide support in getting work and other economic opportunities such as partnership, credit, customers and market information and reinforce the ties of mutual trust, interdependence and reciprocity. This approach offers a more positive view of Asian entrepreneurship than the view that it is to be understood in terms of a racism that denies Asians opportunities for upward mobility. Srinivasan also points to the advantages of flexible working hours without the necessity of 'clocking in and out', the possibility of dual occupations, a varied social life within the work environment, the utilisation of female labour within cultural constraints, and for the ethnic shopkeeper, a position of power vis-a-vis white customers (Srinivasan 1992: 68).

Waldinger and colleagues (1990) have suggested an approach which combines the economic constraint perspective with that which lays stress on the contribution of an enabling ethnic culture. Their interactive approach is built on two dimensions: opportunity structures and characteristics of the ethnic group. While this is a theoretical advance, it does not take the idea of 'interaction' far enough. It still assumes that 'opportunity structures' can be culturally-neutral and can be defined independently of ethnic group norms and attitudes. Our study shows that what counts as an opportunity is conditioned by cultural factors. Values associated with religious background, cultural assumptions about the social status of a business owner and future aspirations for children are relevant to understanding the experiences of British Asians in self-employment, the routes followed by different British Asian minorities into self-employment and the routes that, in many cases, they then plan for their children away from self-employment.

Asian groups differ substantially in their success in self-employment. The most recent national survey of ethnic minorities showed that the mean weekly earnings of Pakistanis in self-employment was substantially less than that of whites; for African Asians it was more; and for Indians substantially more (Modood *et al.*, 1997:127). African Asians, however, have the largest proportion of high earners: a quarter of all African Asian male employees and a fifth of self-employed, compared to a tenth and a quarter of Indians respectively, and a seventh of white men, earnt more than £500 per week in 1994 (Modood *et al.*, 1997:127). Differences by religion are even starker, especially at the top. Twelve Asians feature in the top 500 of *The Sunday Times Rich List 1997* (Beresford with Boyd, 1997) and, according to *Eastern Eye* calculations, about 50 Asians are amongst the richest 1,000 in Britain (Beresford and Merchant,

1997) – well beyond the three per cent that Asians comprise of the population. Hindus probably make up not much more than a quarter of British Asians (Modood *et al.*, 1997: 16). Judging by their names, we estimate that more than half of Britain's 100 richest Asians are Hindus, including at least 10 in the top 15 with a personal wealth of more than £50 millions (Beresford and Merchant, 1997).

The different success of different ethnic minorities in self-employment suggests that culture as well as the racism that blocks opportunities is important in this area. In this chapter we will consider the interaction between economic circumstances and cultural factors in influencing the decisions by different South Asian groups to enter into self-employment and also their varying success once they enter that sector. The research will also give an indication of the likely future development of South Asian entrepreneurship.

The research was based on a sample of 129 self-employed British Asians derived from the Fourth National Survey of Ethnic Minorities. The interviews took place in 1995 and were carried out in appropriate languages by British Asian interviewers. The sample of self employed people reflected the national composition of Asian self employment in terms of ethnic and gender composition. However, it should not be seen as a representative sample, as it was confined to areas of high concentrations of Asian self-employment for convenience in interviewing. It consisted mainly of prime age married males with children. Nearly all were migrants to Britain, mainly emigrating as a child or young adult and arriving in Britain before 1980.

THE INFLUENCE OF CULTURAL AND ECONOMIC FACTORS ON SELF-EMPLOYMENT

There are strong differences between the three main ethnic groups (Indians, African Asians and Pakistanis) in the operation of cultural and economic factors: in entry into self-employment, development of the business and satisfaction with self-employment. There are also differences between sub-groups within them.

Entry into Business

Self-employed Indians and Pakistanis formed two fairly homogeneous groups with similarities within each group of experience in business. However, African Asians were more varied. Part of the explanation seemed to lie in the greater educational homogeneity of Indians and of Pakistanis compared with African Asians, who tended to be either unqualified or highly qualified. The more mixed characteristics of African Asian businesses may also have been related to this group's greater religious diversity, compared with Indians, nearly all of whom were Hindus or Sikhs, groups who are similar to each other in terms of cultural adaptation (Modood, Beishon and Virdee, 1994; Modood *et al.*, 1997), and Pakistanis, all of whom were Muslims.

Both economic and cultural factors played an important role in the decision to pursue a small business career. As in other studies we found the movement into self-employment was not usually from unemployment. Pakistanis, however, appeared to suffer more from poor employment prospects and racism at work and the majority of them referred to these factors as reasons for going into business. For example, 40 per cent of Pakistanis set up in business to escape racial harassment compared with eight per cent of Indians; 63 per cent did so due to poor job opportunities compared with eight per cent of Indians. A substantial minority of African Asians (33 per cent) suffered the same problems, although satisfaction with pay prospects and skill development prior to self-employment was high in this group. These 'push' factors interacted with rather different 'pull' factors for each group. Pakistanis (53 per cent) and African Asians (44 per cent) tended to see running a business as conferring status within their family (and, to a lesser degree, in the community), indicating either that status in general was more important to these two groups or that self-employment was identified with status for these groups. Equally, the weaker employment and income situation of Pakistanis prior to self-employment may have led them to associate self-employment with a gain in status. Indians, in contrast, seemed to attach more importance to the possibility of increasing their income (52 per cent) and the degree of self-determination that being their own boss conferred (47 per cent). Thus while all groups exhibited both push and pull factors Indians, to the greatest extent, appeared to be making positive choices to enter business whereas Pakistanis and, to a lesser extent, African Asians were using self-employment as an escape from racism and poor employment prospects.

Complementing their tendency to enter self-employment for positive reasons, Indians seemed to have better access to start-up capital. Only one in ten reported experiencing problems in this area, as against a quarter of African Asians and a fifth of Pakistanis. More Indians than other groups used institutional loans as well as savings to finance their business – 53 per cent as against 31 per cent for African Asians and 30 per cent for Pakistanis. Given the need for entrepreneurs to draw up business plans and often to offer security for bank loans, this suggested Indians had greater initial wealth combined with a more developed business orientation. Over one third of Indians entered self-employment by taking over an existing business, a less risky approach than starting from scratch, and this may contribute to their greater success in gaining loans. Most (58 per cent) Indians ran retail or catering businesses, particularly small groceries or off licences and newsagents, although one fifth were engaged in manufacturing or construction and a further fifth in non-retail services. Indian businesses were least likely to be single-person concerns and generally had more employees.

African Asians were least likely to require loans but also seemed to have the weakest access to finance, with over one third reporting problems in this area. As a result, they tended to rely on savings rather than bank loans. This group was more oriented towards developing business around pre-existing skills, which was reflected in the line of business, with one fifth in business as craft workers and a further fifth in manufacturing or construction. Retail and catering were less important than in the case of Indians, although these areas accounted for 41 per cent of businesses.

Nearly all Pakistanis established their business from scratch and tended to rely on a single source of finance, most frequently their own savings. This may be partly explained by Muslim conceptions of economic justice and disapproval of at least some kinds of interest-based loans (Kuran, 1995, p. 157), and also by the finding that bank managers and others may have negative stereotypes of Muslim entrepreneurs in comparison with Sikhs or Hindus (Deakins, Hussain and Ram, 1995). Half went into retail and catering, with a further quarter running taxi-cab businesses. Few went into manufacturing or construction. Religion may have influenced the choice of business for some, as religion influenced the goods and services provided for two thirds of Pakistanis and one quarter of African Asians. It may also have constrained business development for some Pakistanis. Once a line of business had been entered into, the handling of alcohol did not figure as a constraint for Indians and African Asians. However, a quarter of all Pakistanis in business in areas where the sale of alcohol was a possible sideline did not handle it for religious reasons.

Community and family support were important in many ways, through encouraging self-employment, helping with finance and providing assistance in the business (paid or unpaid). More than half the respondents did in fact have a family history of self-employment, though few had worked in a family business. About one fifth may have benefited from access to knowledge specific to the business they themselves would eventually own through having relatives in the same line of business. The fact that a high proportion had relatives who were in business may well have encouraged or assisted a move to self employment. The family was clearly important to the respondents. Between two-thirds and three-quarters in each group said that what was best for their family took precedence over their own personal well-being.

We found no evidence of the moral individualism that some commentators associate with self-employed people (Bechhofer *et al.*, 1974; though see Hakim, 1988). Indeed, the data was suggestive of the benefits of the intangible social capital formed by family ties of mutual obligation and trust, and of its spill-over into more tangible contributions by family members (Sanders and Nee, 1996). Family members provided a source of labour for many businesses, with one-third using family workers only in the business initially. Community and family financial support was more important for Indians and African Asians than for Pakistanis. Indians, too, tended to enter self-employment as a joint enterprise with one or more partners and were more likely to have members of the family working in the business (58 per cent as against 44 per cent for African Asians and 38 per cent for Pakistanis). This was partly because Indian women were more likely to be self-employed than other women, and most Indian men found it acceptable for married women to work outside the home (in the family business or elsewhere). Pakistani men were divided on whether married women should be permitted to work outside the home, and this may lead to higher start-up costs and act as a constraint to development in the case of some Pakistani businesses. While very few respondents said they did not trust British people, the highest levels of trust were expressed for family members, followed by people from one's own religious (rather than ethnic) group. At the same time, the desire to increase one's status within the family was linked with running a business particularly for Pakistanis and African Asians, and this will have reinforced the intention to enter business.

The differences in the type of business and finance are likely to reflect differences in orientation towards self-employment and in family support as well as differences in educational levels and in financial resources between the groups. Indians, who had a concentration of medium-level qualifications and better access to capital, seemed to exhibit a strong business orientation. African Asians combined business orientation with experience in the relevant lines of business and appropriate technical skills. Pakistanis, however, seemed to suffer from both financial and skill constraints, and demonstrated little business orientation. This is perhaps unsurprising, since members of this group often entered self-employment in order to escape from inferior conditions of employment and as a route to higher status within the family. Even though Pakistanis and Indians were concentrated in fewer lines of business than African Asians, the latter seem to have been better prepared for the particular line of business they entered. Despite these differences just over one half of each group aimed to expand their business on becoming self-employed, in most cases to increase income although a quarter regarded expansion as primarily a means of raising their status.

DEVELOPMENT OF THE BUSINESS

Other cultural differences emerged between the three groups which were likely to influence their approach to entrepreneurship, in addition to the stronger association between business and family status for Pakistanis and African Asians. Indians appeared to be more risk averse, cautious and conservative, like the Edinburgh shopkeepers studied by Bechhofer (Bechhofer *et al.*, 1974). African Asians, while generally risk averse, were more likely to welcome new ideas, and Pakistanis were most welcoming of new ideas and also least risk averse. For example, about three-quarters of Indians interviewed agreed with the statement 'It is better to be cautious about making major changes in life' as against two-thirds of African Asians and two-fifths of Pakistanis. Religious beliefs may have played a part in these attitudes. Nearly all Pakistanis said religion was very important to how they led their lives, compared to less than a third of Indians and African Asians, a finding supported by the large samples studied in the Fourth Survey (Modood *et al.*, 1997:301). Moreover, nearly all Pakistanis said that the success of a business was largely dependent upon the will of God compared to two-thirds of Indians and two-fifths of African Asians. It may be that individuals who believe that their success or failure is dependent upon divine providence have less reason to be cautious.

These groups differ in their attitudes to risk-taking and innovation despite the fact that Indians and African Asians display less conservative views than Pakistanis on gender roles (for more discussion of the cultural conservatism of Pakistanis see Modood, Beishon and Virdee, 1994 and Modood *et al.*, 1997). Contemporary society has been characterised by risk and uncertainty (Beck, Giddens and Lash, 1994; Giddens, 1994). If they are to flourish, it is said, individuals need to embrace uncertainty. Risk-taking among Pakistanis in this study, however, seems to arise from a mixture of economic insecurity and religious faith, with the latter providing a sense of security from which risk could be faced. These Muslims and perhaps some of the other Asians can be compared to Weber's Protestants who developed an entrepreneurial ethic based upon the ideas of predestination and the belief that God will look after those who are God-fearing but economically aspiring. However, the Calvinists who measured their faith by their works were able to flourish in business for they had superior access to capital. For the Muslim group, religious security may encourage entrepreneurship, but also encourage exposure to excessive risk and lead to a low rate of success.

The approach to business entry and the circumstances surrounding it are likely to exert a strong influence on later business development. Those with a more business-like orientation, better initial funding and more developed business plans are likely to achieve greater success. To some extent this was apparent, with fewer Pakistani businesses being successful in terms of growth in turnover – 41 per cent had increased turnover, compared with 50 per cent of the Indian-owned businesses and 62 per cent of those owned by African Asians. Only eight per cent of Indian businesses declined, and although Indian businesses did not have the highest proportion growing, this pattern should perhaps be expected from the cautious and conservative approach described earlier. African Asian businesses were most likely to grow but, as in the case of Pakistani businesses, a substantial proportion had undergone contraction (21 per cent and 34 per cent). It was unclear if this pattern was due to the heterogeneity of this group or because they had a greater propensity to enter businesses chosen on the basis of their existing skills rather than as a result of business considerations so that fluctuations in the success of the enterprise due to chance were more likely. Indians further display their more rational business orientation through their development as entrepreneurs: just as they were more likely to buy existing businesses in order to enter into self-employment, so they were more likely to sell their original business and buy another. Only six per cent of the sample had ceased being self-employed in the previous year, and none had ever gone bankrupt.

Self-employment has been seen as an avenue to the expansion of employment at a time when the capacity of traditional industries to provide jobs is in decline. We investigated the extent to which South Asian businesses were developing new sources of employment and the extent to which such businesses relied on or sought to provide family employment.

As businesses developed, they increasingly became a vehicle for providing work for people, whether as employees or as unpaid family workers. From initially employing (paid or unpaid) 362 people, employment had grown by nearly 60 per cent to 576 by the time of the survey (or, including the respondents themselves, from 491 to 699, by 42 per cent). This was mainly accounted for by expansion in businesses employing more than one person. There was no change in the proportion of single person businesses, at about 50 per cent. Taking into consideration the long period of operation of many of the businesses and that our methodology did not allow us to identify businesses that had failed before the Fourth Survey, self employment cannot be seen as a source of employment sufficient for a majority of an ethnic group. Most Asian self-employment is not capable of creating much employment other than for the owner. There was some evidence however that the largest ten per cent of the businesses have generated a considerable number of jobs. Six per cent of the sample had come to own two businesses, with two per cent owning three.

Indian business were more likely to employ a larger number of people, family members and others, both at the outset and as the business developed. They are also more likely to be jointly run and thus can be characterised as family concerns. The employment potential of African Asian businesses was lowest: businesses were often sole ventures and rarely employed non-family members. Pakistani businesses started in a similar manner to businesses run by African Asians, with many owners working alone. Pakistanis who employed others were rather more likely to offer employment outside the family. They also showed most developmental change, increasing employment provision, particularly in providing work for family members.

While business growth was the main driving factor behind employment growth, there was also evidence that the business was used to provide employment for the family. Avoiding unemployment was a factor in employing family workers, although all groups were equally influenced by the lack of decent employment opportunities. Businesses were also used explicitly as a vehicle for family cohesion, especially amongst Indians and African Asians. Economic factors also entered the picture. Family members were often employed as a result of problems in affording the wage-costs of others. Some entrepreneurs, mainly Indians and African Asians, also preferred to employ family members since they had greater confidence in the quality of their work. Overall, the number of family workers increased from 92 to 145, with a slightly smaller increase in Indian-owned business. The proportion employing family members, however, was unchanged for Indians and African Asians, but increased from 39 per cent to 55 per cent for Pakistanis. The contrast between Indian businesses – jointly run and employing family members – and Pakistani businesses, which were less likely to employ family members, may be partly due to the differences in attitudes to working women held by these groups.

SELF-EMPLOYMENT AND UPWARD MOBILITY: SUCCESS AND SATISFACTION

Measures of upward mobility are culturally based and depend on what it is that different cultures value. Srinivasan, for example, has argued that Asian shop-keepers are motivated by the desire for status, but that the status in question is defined by specific criteria and rankings and is not identical with that recognised by the white British (Srinivasan, 1995). We examined upward mobility primarily in terms of individuals' views of their success in business and of measures of satisfaction rather than in terms of income and occupation change. We were also aware of the difficulty found in the Fourth Survey in eliciting information on income. The study examined success and benefits along a number of dimensions, including self-worth, independence and satisfaction as well as finance. Because it was difficult to get precise information on level of income respondents were asked to rate their income on a scale from very high to very low. This approach was likely to be a good guide to satisfaction with income.

Overall, most South Asian self-employed people felt they had been successful in business. Pakistanis, who had the worst performance in terms of turnover, were least likely to feel they had been successful. The same pattern was reflected in views about income. Over two-thirds felt that their income was at a medium level. Few Indians and African Asians but nearly half of the Pakistanis interviewed considered their income to be low. This tallies with the reports of earnings given in the Fourth Survey. Information on incomes indicates that even when interpreted in purely financial terms, the economic dead-end thesis is too pessimistic in relation to the African Asians and Indians although it may accurately describe the experience of a substantial number of Pakistani small businesspeople.

Not surprisingly, a large minority (36 per cent) of Pakistanis reported financial problems and frequent money worries, whereas 22 per cent of African Asians and only nine per cent of Indians did. However, Indians and Pakistanis were equally likely to save regularly, whereas African Asians were not. These differences cannot be explained in terms of the importance attached to money between ethnic groups, since there was little variation in this. If one accepts that individuals' views on the level of their income bears a relationship to the income they find acceptable, it is tempting to attribute the difference to cultural factors. Both African Asians and Indians tend to see their incomes as medium or high. Indians tend to be more cautious, while African Asians are more willing to accept risk. These factors may explain the higher levels of saving and fewer money worries among the former compared with the latter. The degree of individual responsibility may also play a part, with a higher proportion of African Asians taking greater personal responsibility for their success than other groups (20 per cent of African Asians said God's will had nothing to do with success, compared with virtually no Indians and Pakistanis). This approach suggests that fewer Pakistanis, almost all of whom attributed business success to God's will, would have money worries. Nonetheless, this group is more likely to see their income as low and this may explain their financial concerns.

Business brought benefits in terms of self-esteem: nearly all derived feelings of self-worth from their business and more than four-fifths felt the business gave them standing with their family. Business was also seen as conferring higher status in the wider community and in British society by two-thirds of the sample. Differences between ethnic groups in the satisfactions sought from business and their achievement suggest that Indians (who were less concerned about achieving status through their business) and African Asians (who reported a gain in status) were successful in gaining the benefits they sought, but that Pakistanis were not.

Business also conferred feelings of independence, an important benefit since many gave the desire for independence as a reason for seeking self-employment. Feelings of independence were high across all groups and ranged from about 70 per cent for Pakistanis and African Asians to about 50 per cent for Indians. However, only about half of Indians had sought independence through self-employment, while 70 per cent of African Asians and 80 per cent of Pakistanis had done so.

Indians were more likely to work with their family and so be less independent than other groups, while the desire for independence amongst Pakistanis may have been promoted by the poor labour market conditions from which self-employment offered an avenue of escape. Nevertheless, given their position in relation to measures of business success (fewer businesses experiencing a growth in turnover, lower average profits, less personal satisfaction from the business and a desire to work longer hours) the high proportion of Pakistanis who did derive feelings of independence from their business was surprising and may well have been influenced by their comparatively inferior position prior to self-employment.

Issues of control and satisfaction were also examined through the hours worked. Most respondents worked between 40 and 59 hours per week with only ten per cent working fewer hours and little variation across ethnic groups. Although most people wanted to work fewer hours, dissatisfaction with the number of hours was greatest amongst Indians. This is partly explained by the longer hours that Indians work, but cultural and economic factors also appear to operate. Indians place a higher value on leisure than other groups and most appear to be reasonably satisfied with the level of income gained for the hours worked.

EXPLANATIONS OF DIFFERENCES IN SOUTH ASIANS' PROFILE IN SELF-EMPLOYMENT

The research shows that the experience of British Asians can only be understood if the interaction between cultural and economic factors is taken into account, and that this interaction is complex and differs between the three groups, resulting in variation in business growth and success.

Pakistanis

Many Pakistanis entered business as an escape from poor employment prospects and racism in the labour market rather than as a positive choice. The resources they brought in terms of finance and skills were poor. The decision to enter self-employment in these circumstances may have been reinforced by cultural factors which include an optimism about the results of economic activity ultimately based in religion. In addition, the Pakistanis placed value on self-employment as a means of improving standing with the family. Against this background it is not surprising that Pakistani businesses tended to be less successful in objective terms although religious outlook may reduce the associated stress. Self-employment brought both satisfaction and problems.

Indians

Indians appeared to have a greater business-orientation. Self-employment was more often entered for positive reasons and entry and development seemed to take greater account of business opportunities. Indians were typically better educated and able to call on resources such as savings, commercial and family loans. In relation to cultural factors, perceptions of status were less likely to encourage entry into self-employment, family cohesion was a support, with Indians more often entering businesses with family partners. Their greater risk aversion may have influenced both the initial decision to move into business and its subsequent development. The sounder initial background probably explains the greater stability of Indian businesses. Fewer declined and fewer expanded rapidly.

African Asians

African Asians were a more heterogeneous group in terms of qualifications and seemed to exhibit a mix of the circumstances and attitudes of both Pakistanis and Indians. A large minority escaped into self-employment from labour market discrimination. Cultural values concerned with self-employment and family standing also pushed some into self-employment. They shared the business orientation of Indians, but were more likely to develop business around their skills and less likely to buy existing businesses, perhaps because they did not have good access to capital. The heterogeneity of the African Asian group was reflected in the development of their businesses: these were among those most likely to grow and also among those most likely to decline.

While various 'push' and 'pull' factors were present for each of the three South Asian groups in different degrees and combinations, there does not appear to be a strong predisposition to self-employment as such among any of them. Each group was well-represented with a family history of self-employment, self-employment was seen as a vehicle to increase standing with the family for African Asians and Pakistanis, and family resources and capital were forthcoming for Indian entrepreneurs. While this certainly makes self-employment viable and attractive for some Asians, the strength of these factors also depends upon the alternatives and how they are perceived.

Self-employment has been appealing to Asians in Britain as a result of their marginality and exclusion from more mainstream opportunities. Poor labour market prospects and racism had played a major role in the decision of Pakistanis to enter business and a lesser role for African Asians. Available evidence indicates that these 'push' factors are less important than in the past (Iganski and Payne, 1996; Modood *et al.*, 1997). Existing South Asian self-employment has been a result of particular kinds of interactions between opportunity structures and cultures. The character and scale of South Asian self-employment will be affected by changes in either of these elements.

THE FUTURE OF SELF-EMPLOYMENT: THE BRITISH-BORN GENERATION

A major issue is whether the high incidence of self-employment amongst South Asian immigrants will continue amongst the British-born. The study had hoped to look at differences in attitudes between first and second generation immigrants but the low proportion of British born in the sample (and therefore in business) precluded firm conclusions.

The wishes of current entrepreneurs about who should inherit the business reinforce the idea that the very high levels of self-employment among British Asians may be a passing phase. The migrant generation's employment expectations for themselves differ markedly from their aspirations for their children. They may have been willing to put family before self and to prioritise work over leisure, but few entrepreneurs felt that the business provided what they would wish for a son in his first job. Only one fifth wanted their children to take over their business. Indians, in particular, were uncertain. Pakistanis had more definite views, with one third wanting a child to take over the business and about a third not wanting this. Parental wishes may or may not be fulfilled, but it cannot be assumed that the current high levels of self-employment combined with a youthful age-structure mean a continuing trend in high rates of self-employment.

A study of white shopkeepers has shown that their children are disproportionately likely to succeed in joining prestigious professions (Bland, Elliot and Bechhofer, 1978) and it seems this is what the South Asian migrants desire for at least some of their children. The qualification levels of the children (for those over 18, 45 per cent of Pakistanis, 65 per cent of African Asians and 83 per cent of Indians had attained A-levels or a degree) lend support to the thesis that self-employment acts as an intergenerational 'springboard' into the professions. The 'economic dead-end' thesis that self-employment does not contribute to upward socio-economic mobility may be misleading, but at the same time it may also be true that many Asian entrepreneurs do not believe that their children's future lies in self-employment. If an environment of racial discrimination elsewhere in the labour market contributed to high levels of entry into self-employment among British Asians in the past, the experience of long hours of work coupled with cultural values about the status of professions may fuel an aspiration for children to pursue educationally based mobility. This argument is reinforced by suggestive evidence that migrants tend to come disproportionately from the better educated and the professional classes from South Asia and East Africa (Daniel, 1968: 60–1; Smith, 1977; Heath and Ridge, 1984). Some Asians are reversing the initial downward mobility produced by migration and racial discrimination in the early years of settlement. Self-employment has played a role in this process.

CONCLUSION

Although self-employment was often entered for negative reasons, it frequently provided entrepreneurs with status and satisfaction. However, the success of the business and benefits to the individual were related to the circumstances of entry into self-employment. Substantial differences emerged between ethnic groups. This has implications both for policies designed to promote entrepreneurship and for the theoretical discussion of economic behaviour in this area.

The evidence on business success suggests that in order to create a thriving small business sector it is desirable to ameliorate the labour market conditions that push South Asians into self-employment (racism and poor labour market prospects), so that entry is based on positive reasons, and businesses are more likely to be successful and stable. Access to finance also needs to be improved, especially for Pakistanis, perhaps through schemes whereby financial institutions can take a stake in the business as an alternative to interest-based loans. There is a need for greater education and advice to encourage a more business oriented approach: for example focusing on market opportunities as well as skills and developing business plans to improve access to commercial loans and other institutional funding. It is important that advice and support should not assume that South Asians are a homogeneous group, so that assistance can be targeted to the particular needs of different groups.

At a theoretical level the study shows that the economic decisions involved in entrepreneurship cannot be understood simply as a result of 'rational' choices or of culturally determined behaviour but the interaction between the two, and that this varies between different cultural groups. Cultural values determine the objectives that feed into goal-oriented behaviour, for example the values attached to owning a small business, irrespective of its success, or to providing employment for family members. Similarly, cultural values influence constraints on economic behaviour, for example, different religious beliefs appear to be associated with differences in risk aversion between Muslim and Hindu communities. Historical studies have demonstrated that the rise of market capitalism was driven by ideological values as well as by awareness of economic opportunities (Weber, 1930; Tawney, 1926). The same point applies to the growth of the contemporary British Asian small business sector.

5 What Drives Support for Higher Public Spending?[1]

Lindsay Brook, Ian Preston and John Hall

INTRODUCTION

Year after year, evidence from the Social and Community Planning Research's annual British Social Attitudes (BSA) survey and elsewhere consistently shows both high levels of public support for increased spending on such front line public services as education and the National Health Service alongside a marked reluctance for individuals to countenance increases in their own tax bills. Using evidence from the 1995 BSA survey, we examine the popularity of seven major spending programmes (health, education, the police, defence, the environment, culture and the arts and public transport), linking any advocated changes in spending explicitly to the resultant changes in tax payments for the respondent's household.

We examine the effect of respondents' circumstances and opinions on each spending programme, taking account of many other influences on support for higher spending. In Brook, Hall and Preston (1996), we pointed out that some groups in the population, such as the elderly or those with children, are more likely than others to support increases in certain types of spending. However, not only might individuals whom we group together as 'the elderly' face widely varying household characteristics, these other characteristics may not be typical of the population as a whole. The elderly, for example, include rich and poor households but are on average less well-off than younger groups. Some elderly people have private health insurance but fewer than amongst other age groups. To separate out the effect of age on support for spending from the influences of these other factors requires the sort of analysis we conduct here, controlling for all other socio-economic, demographic and behavioural influences which are likely to affect attitudes towards public spending. We report also the results of a similar analysis to examine the individual characteristics associated with support for increased provision of social security benefits.

79

In the next section, we describe the British Social Attitudes Survey data set and our approach to question design in the 1995 survey. The third section describes our methodology. The fourth section presents our findings on which individual characteristics are associated with support for higher spending on a range of seven government programmes and on five types of social security benefits.

DATA AND QUESTION DESIGN

British Social Attitudes is an annual survey of around 3500 respondents aiming to yield a representative sample of British adults. Since the first survey in 1983, the series has included questions about attitudes to a variety of public spending programmes, some questions designed to establish priorities for extra spending and others designed to establish willingness to pay for increases, or accept decreases, in spending. Questions of the latter type have focused on six items of publicly supported service provision (health, education, police, defence, culture and the arts, and the environment) and two items of publicly funded cash transfers (state pensions and unemployment benefit).

Our aim in revising these questions for the 1995 survey was both to put the tax implications of extra (or reduced) state spending into much sharper focus and to investigate some additional areas of interest such as support for spending on public transport and social security benefits for single parents, the disabled and working parents on low incomes.

Self-interest versus National Interest

In previous years, BSA surveys have asked respondents what they would 'like to see' happen to each of a range of government spending programmes. This did not spell out clearly the considerations to be taken into account when responding. Both individuals' private interests and their perceptions of the national interest are likely to influence what they might 'like to see' happen. Since individuals may weigh the importance of the two considerations differently, and these may differ in interesting ways, we have separated out these two influences on attitudes towards public spending.

There are several reasons for our interest in examining support for changes in public spending out of self-interest separately from support resulting from perceptions of the common good. For instance, assessing the distribution of actual benefits from public spending requires knowledge of how individual interests (narrowly interpreted) vary. For predictions of voting and other sorts of political behaviour, on the other hand, answers based on wider considerations may be pertinent. The extent to which electoral support is based on self-interest is itself an important question since it may well determine the political sustainability of public spending programmes in a changing environment. We therefore asked all respondents two sets of questions: first, would higher or lower spending on each programme be 'best for the country as a whole' and second, which would be 'best for you and your household.'

For most spending programmes, a broadly similar proportion of respondents thought higher spending was both in their own interest and in the interest of the country as a whole. However, in respect of both education and health, a larger proportion of respondents thought higher spending would be good for the country than thought it would be good for themselves and their households.[2]

Making the Size and Incidence of Tax Changes Explicit

We sought to clarify the tax implications to respondents of choosing higher or lower spending on each programme. Questions asked in previous years had hinted that choosing 'much higher spending' might lead to tax rises – but it was not clear what the size of these tax changes would be, or who would be asked to pay for them. Moreover, those who chose lower spending were not reminded that this might lead to lower taxes.

Unsurprisingly perhaps, there is some evidence to suggest that some respondents were allowing themselves to imagine that adverse tax consequences might be borne by others. Thus, in 1994, for example, 87 per cent of respondents supported increases in health spending, and 73 per cent supported higher spending on education, even if taxes might have to rise. However, in the same year, only six per cent of those who said they were middle income and three per cent of those who claimed to be on low incomes felt that their own taxes were too low. This suggests that many respondents were hoping that any higher spending that they endorsed would be paid for through somebody else's taxes.

We explicitly linked increases or reductions in public spending to specified changes in household tax bills in the form of either a

Figure 5.1   **Impact of Specifying the Size and Incidence of Tax Changes on Percentage of Respondents Supporting Higher Spending**

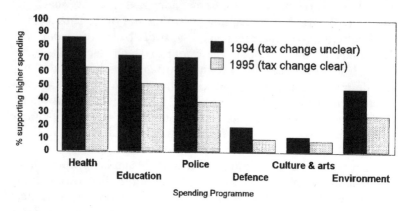

Source: Brook, Hall and Preston (1996).

change in the basic rate of income tax by a penny in the pound up or down, or a flat rate £35 charge or rebate per adult living in the household. The impact on the numbers supporting higher spending for the six spending programmes which were asked about in both years is illustrated in Figure 5.1. Support for higher spending fell in every single one of the six spending programmes which were asked about in both 1994 and 1995, in one case (police) by almost a half. However, a majority of respondents still supported higher spending on the core services of the Welfare State, health and education, even if their own tax bills would rise as a result.

Does the Tax Instrument Make a Difference?

We can think of at least two reasons why support for higher public spending may vary according to household income. First, richer individuals may expect to receive a different share of the benefits of additional spending than poorer individuals. They may, for instance, use different types of public services from those used by the poor. Second, if respondents believe that spending changes are to be financed through changes to income related taxes, then richer individuals may expect the highest burden of any tax changes to fall on their tax bills. Thus, any variation in the support for higher spending between different income groups may be attributed to some combination of two effects – an 'income effect' (the impact of higher incomes on support for spending due to either the expected pattern of benefits or simply because higher incomes make a given tax rise more affordable) and a 'price effect' (the impact of shouldering a larger share of the additional tax burden on support for spending). Separating out these effects may be important but is difficult without making explicit which tax instrument is to be used and doing so in a way which allows the tax price to vary in a way not perfectly correlated with income.[3]

Whenever politicians worry about losing the support of the well-off for a spending change if they use progressive taxes to finance the additional public spending, they are worrying specifically about the strength of tax price effects. Separating out the income and tax price effects is also essential if we are to understand how increasing affluence may affect support for higher public spending. To investigate this, the respondents to the 1995 BSA were divided randomly into two equally sized groups. We asked one group about their attitudes to spending changes financed by raising or lowering the basic rate of income tax by one penny in the pound and the other half about their attitudes to spending changes financed by a flat £35 per head increase or decrease in the tax payments of all adults. This meant that two individuals with similar household incomes but who faced different tax instruments would face different increases in household tax bills as a result of choosing higher public spending. This variation in tax prices independent of variations in income should allow the separate identification, in principle, of income and tax price effects.[4] In other words, if tax price effects are strong, we might expect richer households to be noticeably less inclined to see higher spending as in their own interest if offered spending increases financed through a more progressive tax instrument.

METHODOLOGY

Individuals will support increases in public spending only if their willingness to pay for higher spending exceeds the tax cost that they would face. Willingness to pay is likely to depend on the household's income, since this influences its ability to pay, and on any household characteristics which affect the benefits which the respondent might expect to receive from higher spending on each spending programme. The cost, in terms of a higher household tax bill, depends on whether the respondent was faced with a flat rate tax change or with a change in the basic rate of income tax. For individuals asked to consider a tax change of £35 per adult in the household, this is proportional to the number of adults in the household; for individuals asked to consider a change to the basic rate of income tax the tax cost will, of course, be an increasing function of gross household income.

We estimated a separate ordered probit equation for each of the seven spending programmes using maximum likelihood techniques.[5] We investigated the influence which a range of individual and household characteristics might have on support for changes to public spending.[6] The variables used are listed in the appendix to the chapter. Variations in support for changes in a particular public spending programme between individuals were explained in terms of variations in the household income, level of education, economic activity and other characteristics of the respondents. The BSA surveys measure household incomes only in a banded form, so that we know only within which range each household's income lies. We chose to fit a lognormal distribution to this banded data, using the known endpoints for the bands,[7] and using the predicted values as regressors.

We also included a variable to pick out those respondents who were confronted with the income related tax instrument. We then interacted this variable with household income and the number of adults living in the household in order to pick up variations in the 'tax price' of higher spending between respondents. Economic theory suggests that individuals who would pay more under each tax regime should be less willing to support higher spending, just as a higher price for a particular good might deter an individual from purchasing the good. Individuals with high incomes, for instance, should have been less likely to support increases if faced with an income-related tax burden. Thus, we might expect that the interaction of household income with the dummy variable for those who were faced with the income tax question would enter negatively into the regression equation.

We are also interested in investigating the impact of use of private sector alternatives on support for public spending increases. To this end, we include variables reflecting purchase of private medical insurance, private schooling for children or car ownership as additional regressors in the analysis. Other behavioural and 'value driven' variables include newspaper readership and support for particular political parties.

We report results with and without the inclusion of these additional variables separately for a number of reasons. Firstly, support for particular political parties, for instance, might be regarded as primarily playing a role in mediating the influence of socioeconomic characteristics on support for public spending rather than having an independent effect. If this is so then it may be of interest to see the total effect from socio-economic characteristics including those operating through political affiliation in this way.

Secondly, the use of private alternatives to state services or identification with particular political parties may be associated with support for particular spending programmes primarily through the influence of common attitudinal factors, such as general antipathy to the public sector. This could mean that the coefficient estimates in equations which include these individual characteristics as explanatory variables could give a misleading impression if taken as evidence of the causal impact that these factors might have on support for higher spending. Thus, for example, any association between having private medical insurance and a reduced level of support for higher health spending may not represent any causal effect, but simply the fact that those who have purchased private insurance were less inclined to support higher state spending on health in the first place.

On the other hand, leaving these variables out of the equation would render estimates of included effects inconsistent if there *were* a causal impact and the causal influences we were omitting were correlated with included variables. We therefore present results excluding and including these variables, with the caveat that either approach will yield consistent estimates of the effects of interest only under strong assumptions, for instance, about the influences which affect choices over the use of private health insurance or educating one's children in the private sector. Reassuringly, conclusions about effects of other variables are not very sensitive to the inclusion of these variables.

We applied similar models to examine two further sets of issues:

- Which characteristics appear to influence the likelihood that an individual will support higher spending on a particular spending programme as being in the interest of the 'country as a whole'?
- Which individual characteristics are associated with support for changes in spending on five classes of social security benefits?

In the latter case, we include a set of explanatory variables which reflect the likelihood that the respondent would qualify for each of the social security benefits that we asked about. These include whether the individual is retired or disabled.

RESULTS

Household Interests

Table 5.1 presents the results of seven ordered probit estimates,[8] each of which attempts to explain variations in support for changes in spending on one of the seven public spending programmes which respondents perceived as being in their own interest. We organise the discussion of the results according to four groups of individual and household characteristics which we use to explain variations in attitudes to changes in public spending. These are household composition, socio-economic variables, use of private sector alternatives, and other possible influences such as newspaper readership.

Household Composition Influences

The age of the respondent appears to be positively associated with support for higher spending on all seven programmes, but significantly so only for police, defence and public transport. Higher support for spending on the police seems to fit with other evidence from the BSA survey revealing greater concern about crime in older age groups. Higher support for improvements to public transport may reflect the greater reliance of older individuals on the public transport network. Support for higher spending differs little between male and female respondents. The only programme towards which the attitudes of women seem significantly different to those of men is defence. Perhaps surprisingly, it is women who express greater support for spending on defence. Unsurprisingly, the number of children in the household was associated with a substantially greater enthusiasm for increased education spending. The explanation for increased support for spending on the police amongst those respondents whose households contained a larger number of adults is less obvious. Other than this, there is little evidence that household size has much impact on support for higher public spending.

Table 5.1 **Household Interests: Ordered Probit Estimates**[17]

	Health	Education	Police	Defence	Culture & arts	Envir-onment	Public transport
Age	0.017	0.009	0.056	0.019	0.006	0.010	0.022
.	(1.658)	(0.894)	(5.633)	(4.757)	(1.660)	(1.178)	(2.567)
Female	0.027	0.050	-0.002	0.040	0.021	0.006	0.000
.	(0.842)	(1.493)	(-0.077)	(3.084)	(1.743)	(0.245)	(0.006)
Adults	0.043	0.077	0.126	-0.008	-0.027	0.081	0.010
.	(0.792)	(1.297)	(2.082)	(-0.337)	(-1.213)	(1.526)	(0.193)
Children	0.111	0.537	0.094	0.030	-0.003	-0.015	-0.002
.	(1.563)	(7.613)	(1.413)	(1.045)	(-0.108)	(-0.265)	(-0.029)
Household income	-0.033	-0.009	-0.047	-0.008	0.007	-0.018	-0.035
.	(-1.109)	(-0.280)	(-1.479)	(-0.624)	(0.540)	(-0.669)	(-1.341)
Manual worker	0.014	0.042	0.002	0.015	-0.026	0.019	0.006
.	(0.427)	(1.233)	(0.063)	(1.082)	(-2.022)	(0.681)	(0.210)
Self-employed	0.063	-0.048	0.089	0.027	0.008	0.089	-0.069
.	(0.985)	(-0.735)	(1.423)	(0.950)	(0.304)	(1.490)	(-1.527)
A Level education	0.074	0.136	0.074	0.004	0.072	0.190	0.147
.	(1.465)	(2.615)	(1.483)	(0.167)	(2.998)	(4.257)	(3.206)
Higher Education	0.037	0.071	0.032	-0.023	0.090	0.125	0.149
.	(0.958)	(1.732)	(0.803)	(-1.478)	(4.996)	(3.617)	(4.404)
Owner Occupier	0.056	-0.019	0.005	-0.039	-0.021	0.022	0.016
.	(1.606)	(-0.514)	(0.159)	(-2.590)	(-1.482)	(0.718)	(0.537)
Car owner	-0.022	-0.026	-0.019	0.017	-0.017	-0.066	-0.123
.	(-0.568)	(-0.647)	(-0.501)	(1.095)	(-1.111)	(-1.957)	(-3.467)
Lives in South	-0.003	-0.070	-0.039	-0.007	0.038	0.014	0.058
.	(-0.106)	(-2.111)	(-1.236)	(-0.561)	(2.969)	(0.531)	(2.152)
Scotland/Wales	0.014	-0.021	-0.099	-0.028	0.001	-0.054	-0.015
.	(0.325)	(-0.473)	(-2.399)	(-1.719)	(0.065)	(-1.561)	(-0.425)
Asked income tax question (δ_i) .	-0.248	-0.249	-0.450	0.049	0.184	-0.067	-0.123
	(-0.778)	(-0.757)	(-1.481)	(0.345)	(1.397)	(-0.242)	(-0.452)
$\delta_i \times$ Income	0.034	0.026	0.065	-0.008	-0.019	0.012	0.012
.	(0.934)	(0.694)	(1.778)	(-0.475)	(-1.380)	(0.385)	(0.406)
$\delta_i \times$ Adults	-0.022	-0.004	-0.162	0.053	0.003	-0.073	0.036
.	(-0.286)	(-0.044)	(-2.076)	(1.655)	(0.102)	(-1.046)	(0.543)

Log likelihoods

	-793.58	-946.63	-937.66	-911.12	-884.55	-1011.73	-1049.59

Tests for exclusion of all tax instrument effects

χ^2_3	4.46	0.69	7.88	2.78	2.36	1.36	1.04
P value	0.22	0.88	0.05	0.43	0.50	0.72	0.79

Ordered probit estimates: Asymptotic t-values in italics

Socio-Economic Influences at Household Level

The impact of household income on support for higher spending is insignificant for all seven of the spending programmes.[9] We have included variables intended to capture income-related variation in tax prices so it seems unlikely that this is arising simply because the 'income effect' and 'price effect' on support for higher spending are cancelling each other out. However, there is little evidence of any effect from these variables either.[10] The tax instrument dummy and associated interactions are neither individually nor jointly significant in any of the seven spending regressions, except in the police spending equation. Moreover, the signs of the interaction effects in the police spending equation are in conflict with any interpretation in terms of tax price effects.

We could interpret this as evidence that economic influences on support for public spending increases are indeed slight. If so, this would have profound implications – above all, public support for spending increases would be insensitive to the distribution of the implied tax burden. Support for spending changes among the better-off would not be jeopardised by finance through progressive tax instruments. However, other factors may be at play here. Respondents are answering questions about hypothetical situations without prior deliberation and as part of a lengthy questionnaire. They may have decided opinions about which aspects of public spending deserve more funds but little idea about the size of extra finance needed to secure the sort of improvements they want. Our interpretation is based on an underlying assumption that each individual would be prepared to countenance some maximum increase in their tax burden in order to receive the benefits from higher spending and that they would reject tax rises greater than this. However, any figure suggested in the wording of the question could plausibly have established itself in the respondent's mind as a reasonable benchmark for what it might cost to make a significant difference to the level of provision offered, severely attenuating the impact of the sort of economic influences we are trying to uncover. These sorts of 'anchoring' effects are discussed, for instance, by Tversky and Kahneman (1974) and Green, Jacowitz, Kahneman and McFadden (1995).

Current household income can clearly only be an imperfect indicator of the household's expected long term living standards, especially for those with highly unstable incomes like the self-employed. Moreover, individuals who have only recently entered the job market or who are undergoing a period of training or study, might reasonably expect to have higher incomes in the future. We therefore take account of various characteristics of individuals, such as the level of formal education they have received, and characteristics of their jobs, such as whether or not they work in a manual occupation.

Any impact of the level of an individual's formal education on support for public spending can be interpreted in a number of ways.

Increased formal education may be associated with changes in underlying values or it could reflect the likelihood of higher lifetime earnings. It is interesting to note that education, whether beyond age 16 or beyond age 18, is associated with increased support for higher spending on all spending programmes other than defence. Experience of post-compulsory education is associated with an increased interest in spending on the 'quality of life' items – culture and the arts, the environment and public transport. Those who have undertaken post-compulsory education themselves are also more likely to see an interest in expanded public education spending.

One might expect that support for higher public spending will vary between different regions of the country, even allowing for variations in incomes and other household characteristics. This could be because of regional variation in tastes or attitudes or it could be because of regional variation in either existing levels of spending or in the anticipated location of any additional spending. To examine this, we include two regional effects – a dummy variable for respondents living in London and the South of England and another for those who live in Scotland or Wales. Living in the South is associated significantly with support for spending on culture and public transport. This is presumably because of the concentration of both cultural institutions and commuters in the South, especially in London. The Scots and Welsh respondents differ mainly in being less supportive of extra spending on the police.

Household Use of Private Sector Alternatives

One might expect that individuals who purchase private alternatives to public services might express different levels of support for increased spending on these services within the state sector. Such individuals might still make use of the state sector – individuals with private health insurance still rely on the NHS for accident and emergency provision, for example – so support need not be completely undermined. However, one might nonetheless expect lower support for spending increases unless the individual were a reluctant and marginal user of private alternatives who might be tempted back into the public sector by the increase. Some individuals might prefer to relinquish their use of private services if the quality of provision within the state sector was sufficiently improved.

Table 5.2 shows the difference which purchase of private medical insurance, private schooling for one's children or ownership of a car makes to support for higher public spending on each of the seven programmes. It is clear that having private health insurance is associated with a significantly lower probability of supporting increases in public health spending. It has previously been noted that this is true of the group covered by private medical insurance, without taking account of their economic and demographic characteristics (see Besley, Hall and Preston 1996 or Calnan, Cant and Gabe 1993). Our results establish that this remains true even when we make allowance for other characteristics of those with and without private insurance such as the privately insured typically being richer and more prone to support the Conservative party than most. We should be careful, however, to recognise that purchasing such insurance could be influenced by attitudes toward the public sector. An alternative explanation for the correlation we are noting could be that the sorts of people who tend to buy private health insurance could be the sorts of people who are ill-disposed to the public sector, whether they buy private insurance or not.

We did not find any strong evidence of a link between the use of private schooling and support for higher public spending on education. We have noted elsewhere (Brook, Hall and Preston 1996), that, taken as a group, those with children in private education actually seem *more* interested in increased state spending than others, but this is clearly not statistically significant once we control for other characteristics.

Ownership of a private car can be seen as another way of opting out of the public sector. A privately owned car and public transport can be considered as alternative ways of making journeys. Taking all other characteristics into account, we observe that individuals who own a car are rather less inclined to support increased spending on the public transport system or the environment than those who do not.

Other Influences at Household Level

Even taking in to account the differing socio-economic and demographic characteristic associated with the supporters of particular political parties, it seems that political affiliation is linked with pronounced differences in support for changes to public spending. Conservative supporters are distinguished from others predominantly in being considerably less inclined to support extra spending on the NHS whereas Labour supporters, on the other hand, express

Table 5.2   **Household Interests: Private Services – Ordered Probit Estimates**

	Health	Education	Police	Defence	Culture & arts	Environment	Public transport
Age	0.015	0.003	0.053	0.017	0.004	0.005	0.016
.	(1.434)	(0.256)	(5.055)	(3.849)	(1.012)	(0.580)	(1.816)
Female	0.038	0.068	0.001	0.035	0.018	0.011	0.004
.	(1.187)	(1.976)	(0.043)	(2.653)	(1.529)	(0.425)	(0.166)
Adults	0.030	0.092	0.118	−0.008	−0.029	0.086	0.012
.	(0.539)	(1.493)	(1.902)	(−0.353)	(−1.346)	(1.602)	(0.238)
Children	0.060	0.512	0.074	0.017	−0.004	−0.024	−0.009
.	(0.833)	(7.030)	(1.082)	(0.579)	(−0.168)	(−0.415)	(−0.164)
Household income	−0.011	−0.010	−0.037	−0.012	0.002	−0.024	−0.034
.	(−0.353)	(−0.278)	(−1.136)	(−0.874)	(0.156)	(−0.857)	(−1.300)
Manual worker	−0.012	0.039	0.004	0.012	−0.020	0.025	0.013
.	(−0.351)	(1.089)	(0.133)	(0.893)	(−1.538)	(0.892)	(0.455)
Self-employed	0.083	−0.013	0.107	0.027	0.003	0.091	−0.078
.	(1.290)	(−0.185)	(1.642)	(0.961)	(0.103)	(1.450)	(−1.636)
A Level education	0.083	0.124	0.070	0.005	0.067	0.169	0.133
.	(1.594)	(2.305)	(1.393)	(0.221)	(2.798)	(3.704)	(2.871)
Higher Education	0.010	0.037	0.024	−0.025	0.075	0.105	0.121
.	(0.232)	(0.858)	(0.575)	(−1.547)	(4.140)	(2.944)	(3.480)
Owner Occupier	0.073	−0.020	0.014	−0.036	−0.022	0.021	0.014
.	(2.067)	(−0.502)	(0.397)	(−2.352)	(−1.542)	(0.697)	(0.452)
Car owner	−0.000	−0.019	−0.028	0.015	−0.019	−0.073	−0.129
.	(−0.008)	(−0.461)	(−0.719)	(0.925)	(−1.176)	(−2.085)	(−3.518)
Private health	−0.116	−0.039	−0.044	−0.003	0.005	0.016	−0.048
.	(−2.422)	(−0.823)	(−1.027)	(−0.176)	(0.269)	(0.412)	(−1.376)
Private school	0.108	0.048	0.064	0.026	0.022	0.099	0.094
.	(1.658)	(0.776)	(0.946)	(0.992)	(0.858)	(1.634)	(1.894)
Reads Tabloid	0.034	−0.088	0.007	0.007	−0.042	−0.066	−0.089
.	(0.996)	(−2.446)	(0.214)	(0.521)	(−3.361)	(−2.433)	(−3.144)
Conservative	−0.147	−0.032	−0.015	0.026	−0.007	−0.051	−0.051
.	(−3.127)	(−0.693)	(−0.317)	(1.318)	(−0.388)	(−1.278)	(−1.448)
Labour	0.056	0.158	0.011	−0.012	0.035	0.065	0.063
.	(1.592)	(4.380)	(0.314)	(−0.802)	(2.354)	(2.086)	(2.044)
Lives in South	0.004	−0.068	−0.039	−0.011	0.040	0.022	0.068
.	(0.116)	(−1.979)	(−1.191)	(−0.824)	(3.134)	(0.783)	(2.446)
Scotland/Wales	0.005	−0.011	−0.104	−0.029	0.008	−0.042	−0.003
.	(0.124)	(−0.245)	(−2.485)	(−1.734)	(0.466)	(−1.202)	(−0.083)
Asked income tax question (δ_i) .	−0.239	−0.322	−0.456	0.075	0.144	−0.134	−0.178
	(−0.721)	(−0.949)	(−1.447)	(0.529)	(1.097)	(−0.473)	(−0.637)
$\delta_i \times$ Income	0.034	0.035	0.065	−0.011	−0.016	0.018	0.017
.	(0.912)	(0.898)	(1.728)	(−0.667)	(−1.124)	(0.567)	(0.539)
$\delta_i \times$ Adults	−0.061	−0.033	−0.166	0.051	0.010	−0.063	0.052
.	(−0.757)	(−0.387)	(−2.071)	(1.599)	(0.348)	(−0.895)	(0.756)
Log likelihoods	−747.61	−901.75	−903.88	−876.36	−844.67	−970.31	−1004.09
Tests for exclusion of all tax instrument effects							
χ^2_3	3.66	1.11	7.25	2.45	1.48	0.91	1.65
P value	0.3	0.77	0.06	0.48	0.69	0.82	0.65

Ordered probit estimates: asymptotic t-values in italics.

high level of support for additional spending on education, culture, the environment and public transport.

We show in Table 5.2 that the readers of tabloid newspapers are less well-disposed than others (whether or not they read other newspapers) to spending on the 'quality of life' items – education, culture, environment and public transport. This could arise from readership influencing attitudes or because choice of paper is influenced by pertinent attitudinal and cultural factors. Our estimates of the impact of other individual characteristics on support for public spending appear fairly robust to whether or not we include these attitudinal variables in our analysis.

Many of the characteristics which appeared to be associated with support for particular public spending programmes in the simple crosstabulations presented in Brook, Hall and Preston (1996) remain important once we have taken account of other influences on spending using the more sophisticated techniques used here. We now go on to apply these techniques to examine perceptions of national interest in public spending changes and support for higher spending on five types of social security benefit.

National Interest

As well as asking respondents whether they thought increases or reductions in public spending on each of the seven spending programmes would be in the interests of their own household, we also asked them which reforms would be for the good of the country as a whole. Figure 5.2 illustrates how the proportion who would support increases in spending on each of the seven programmes as being in the interests of their own household compares to the proportion who thought that higher spending would be in the interest of the country as whole. As can be seen, the levels of support were broadly similar, although rather larger proportions of the public thought that higher spending on health and education would be in the national interest than thought it would be in the interest of their own household. There is, of course, no inconsistency in this – it all depends on how individuals interpret the interests of 'the country as a whole'.[11]

Whilst proportions of the public supporting higher spending as being in their own interest and as being in the national interest are similar for most programmes, it does not necessarily follow that it is the same respondents who hold these views. We therefore

Figure 5.2 **Proportions Who Thought Higher Spending Would Be in the Interest of Their Household and in the Interests of the Country as a Whole**

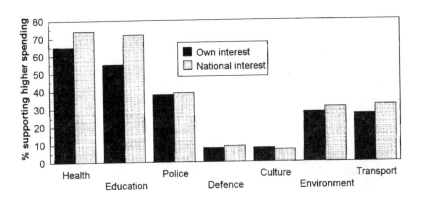

Source: Brook, Hall and Preston (1996).

attempt to explain support for higher spending on each programme as being in the national interest in terms of the same types of individual characteristics and attitudinal variables as we used to explain patterns of support for higher spending in the household's interest in Table 5.2. The results for support for higher spending in the national interest are reported in Table 5.3.

These results suggest that the factors associated with an individual supporting higher spending as being in the national interest are remarkably similar to those associated with higher spending being perceived as in the interest of the respondent's own household. It is difficult, having looked at these tables, not to believe that individuals own interests exert a considerable pull on what they also think to be good for the nation.

Nonetheless there are some noteworthy differences. In particular, the presence of children in the household has far less impact on support for increased education spending when respondents are asked to consider whether or not increased spending is in the national interest. When respondents were asked to consider the national interest rather than the interests of their own household, car ownership was less associated with reduced support for spending on the environment and public transport, and private health insurance was

Table 5.3   **National Interest: Ordered Probit Estimates.**

	Health	Education	Police	Defence	Culture & arts	Envir- onment	Public transport
Age	−0.022	−0.012	0.043	0.021	0.002	−0.009	0.010
.	(−2.081)	(−1.187)	(3.790)	(5.127)	(0.545)	(−0.977)	(1.054)
Female	0.066	0.015	0.048	0.036	0.016	−0.002	−0.065
.	(2.062)	(0.460)	(1.464)	(2.857)	(1.649)	(−0.065)	(−2.293)
Adults	−0.072	−0.058	0.065	0.006	−0.027	0.025	−0.059
.	(−1.359)	(−0.997)	(1.005)	(0.247)	(−1.539)	(0.451)	(−1.088)
Children	−0.187	0.071	−0.031	0.047	0.019	−0.026	−0.078
.	(−2.647)	(0.953)	(−0.430)	(1.701)	(0.855)	(−0.438)	(−1.184)
Household income	0.076	0.073	−0.030	−0.011	−0.007	0.002	0.043
.	(2.560)	(2.384)	(−0.933)	(−0.836)	(−0.642)	(0.081)	(1.465)
Manual worker	0.015	−0.034	0.018	0.026	0.001	−0.002	−0.033
.	(0.492)	(−1.108)	(0.538)	(1.936)	(0.134)	(−0.079)	(−1.039)
Self-employed	−0.003	−0.056	0.096	0.018	−0.012	0.013	−0.094
.	(−0.047)	(−0.833)	(1.469)	(0.633)	(−0.604)	(0.214)	(−1.710)
A Level education	0.077	0.039	0.091	0.015	0.054	0.146	0.164
.	(1.634)	(0.804)	(1.650)	(0.684)	(2.747)	(3.143)	(3.337)
Higher Education	0.039	0.064	−0.028	−0.020	0.053	0.071	0.127
.	(0.982)	(1.613)	(−0.663)	(−1.271)	(3.457)	(1.873)	(3.283)
Owner Occupier	0.021	0.023	0.018	−0.018	−0.001	0.017	0.009
.	(0.630)	(0.644)	(0.513)	(−1.235)	(−0.070)	(0.514)	(0.275)
Car owner	0.012	−0.034	−0.012	0.028	−0.011	0.015	−0.035
.	(0.328)	(−0.895)	(−0.303)	(1.875)	(−0.859)	(0.441)	(−0.963)
Private health	−0.060	0.030	0.003	0.004	0.009	0.050	−0.001
.	(−1.390)	(0.639)	(0.071)	(0.193)	(0.553)	(1.193)	(−0.022)
Private school	−0.015	0.083	−0.026	0.020	0.001	0.030	0.017
.	(−0.239)	(1.370)	(−0.399)	(0.781)	(0.067)	(0.474)	(0.314)
Tabloid reader	0.048	−0.014	0.029	−0.011	−0.045	−0.108	−0.129
.	(1.489)	(−0.440)	(0.831)	(−0.804)	(−4.282)	(−3.894)	(−4.209)
Conservative	−0.134	−0.086	−0.038	0.009	−0.010	−0.086	−0.121
.	(−2.927)	(−1.923)	(−0.819)	(0.464)	(−0.721)	(−2.129)	(−3.008)
Labour	0.019	0.109	−0.019	−0.014	0.031	0.093	0.154
.	(0.567)	(3.201)	(−0.515)	(−0.984)	(2.453)	(2.702)	(4.601)
Lives in South	0.015	0.017	−0.059	−0.021	0.032	0.037	0.141
.	(0.494)	(0.545)	(−1.759)	(−1.687)	(2.907)	(1.310)	(4.578)
Scotland/Wales	0.063	0.030	−0.108	−0.017	0.013	0.001	0.063
.	(1.534)	(0.723)	(−2.536)	(−1.046)	(0.846)	(0.035)	(1.443)
Asked income tax question (δ_i) .	0.139	0.094	−0.581	0.034	0.023	0.584	0.262
	(0.446)	(0.288)	(−1.920)	(0.247)	(0.215)	(2.176)	(0.866)
$\delta_i \times$ Income	−0.010	−0.013	0.079	−0.007	−0.004	−0.070	−0.029
	(−0.271)	(−0.347)	(2.093)	(−0.417)	(−0.336)	(−2.061)	(−0.826)
$\delta_i \times$ Adults	0.118	0.139	−0.120	0.034	0.003	0.066	0.051
.	(1.519)	(1.791)	(−1.448)	(1.056)	(0.118)	(0.880)	(0.685)
Log likelihoods							
	−631.31	−666.56	−838.36	−889.69	−842.15	−898.06	−880.92
Tests for exclusion of all tax instrument effects							
χ^2_3	17.75	5.76	6.05	1.86	2.22	5.27	1.56
P value	0.00	0.12	0.11	0.60	0.53	0.15	0.67

Ordered probit estimates: asymptotic t-values in italics.

Figure 5.3 Support for Increases in Social Security Benefits[16]

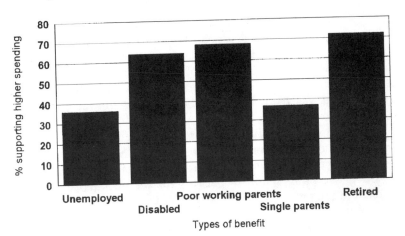

less associated with reduced support for public spending on health. Indeed in all these cases the effects cease to be statistically significant. Whilst these differences are all readily explicable, some other differences are less easy to explain. Income, for instance, seems more important to perceptions of what is in the national interest and owner occupation less so.

ATTITUDES TO WELFARE SPENDING

The 1995 BSA survey asked individuals whether they would support higher or lower spending on five types of social security benefit – benefits for unemployed people, disabled people unable to work, working parents on low incomes, single parents and retired people. Whilst the exact size and incidence of any resulting tax changes was not made explicit, respondents were reminded that choosing higher or lower spending was likely to mean they would have to pay higher or lower taxes. Figure 5.3 shows the large variations in the extent of support for higher spending across the different types of benefits with 72 per cent of respondents supporting higher spending on pensions whilst only 37 per cent supported higher spending on benefits for single parents.

We estimate the impact of a range of individual and household characteristics on support for spending on each of these social security benefits, using ordered probit equations as before. In addition to the individual characteristics which were useful in explaining variations in support for higher spending on the seven major spending programmes, we added some characteristics of individuals which are associated with the likelihood of the respondent qualifying for each of the benefits. These are whether the respondents are themselves retired, disabled, a single parent or unemployed.[12] The results are shown in Table 5.4.[13]

Unsurprisingly, our results suggest a clear tendency for individuals to be more sympathetic to spending on the sorts of benefits which they might receive themselves. The keenness of the unemployed to see more spent on benefits for the unemployed, of the disabled to see more spent on benefits for the disabled and of single parents to see more spent on benefits for single parents are pronounced and strongly significant. Furthermore, these do not typically translate into greater keenness to see more spent on benefits for *other* vulnerable or low income groups.[14] This pattern could simply reflect self-interest or it could be that respondents can empathise better with the straitened circumstances of those in similar positions to themselves than with vulnerable groups with different characteristics.

The retired do not seem any more inclined than anyone else to favour state help for retired households but what is clear is that age does have a strong positive impact. Other effects worth noting in this regard are the antipathy of higher income households to higher spending on benefits for the unemployed and the enthusiasm shown by households with children for benefits for working parents on low incomes and single parents. Those respondents living in Scotland and Wales appear more supportive of higher spending on benefits for unemployed people than those who live in England.

The effects of political allegiance are strong. Those identifying with the Conservative Party are less inclined than others to favour increases in spending on any form of social security outlay. Labour identifiers, on the other hand, are more supportive of extra spending on all five benefits, and significantly so in the case of all but the retired.

Table **5.4   Attitudes to Welfare Spending: Ordered Probit Estimates**

Benefits for:	Unemployed people	Disabled people	Parents working on low incomes	Single parents	Retired people
Age	0.022	0.017	−0.013	−0.022	0.046
.	(1.443)	(1.109)	(−0.837)	(−1.476)	(3.492)
Female	0.009	0.010	0.016	−0.020	0.017
.	(0.277)	(0.296)	(0.528)	(−0.593)	(0.576)
Adults	0.074	0.037	0.005	0.053	0.018
.	(1.570)	(0.833)	(0.124)	(1.137)	(0.457)
Children	0.006	−0.031	0.110	0.141	−0.021
.	(0.075)	(−0.378)	(1.364)	(1.756)	(−0.297)
Household income	−0.066	−0.047	−0.023	−0.040	−0.036
.	(−2.448)	(−1.735)	(−0.804)	(−1.460)	(−1.515)
Manual worker	0.020	0.090	−0.009	0.006	0.063
.	(0.585)	(2.663)	(−0.277)	(0.174)	(1.969)
Self-employed	−0.063	−0.137	−0.031	−0.069	0.001
.	(−1.100)	(−1.797)	(−0.445)	(−1.076)	(0.018)
A Level education	−0.011	−0.019	−0.037	−0.015	0.001
.	(−0.226)	(−0.383)	(−0.771)	(−0.265)	(0.025)
Higher Education	0.059	0.028	−0.016	0.056	−0.011
.	(1.410)	(0.657)	(−0.388)	(1.367)	(−0.285)
Owner Occupier	0.008	−0.040	−0.064	−0.059	−0.009
.	(0.222)	(−1.103)	(−1.855)	(−1.658)	(−0.290)
Car owner	−0.040	0.064	0.058	−0.011	0.011
.	(−0.914)	(1.530)	(1.463)	(−0.274)	(0.302)
Private health	−0.097	−0.029	−0.063	−0.101	−0.005
.	(−2.212)	(−0.603)	(−1.298)	(−2.351)	(−0.129)
Private school	−0.049	0.087	0.111	−0.022	−0.015
.	(−0.692)	(1.384)	(2.077)	(−0.315)	(−0.253)
Tabloid reader	−0.030	0.054	0.024	−0.045	0.077
.	(−0.866)	(1.565)	(0.690)	(−1.249)	(2.469)
Conservative	−0.163	−0.088	−0.147	−0.108	−0.183
.	(−3.940)	(−1.807)	(−3.313)	(−2.552)	(−4.126)
Labour	0.164	0.076	0.101	0.093	0.056
.	(4.280)	(2.059)	(2.894)	(2.486)	(1.691)
Lives in South	0.020	0.090	0.001	0.067	0.039
.	(0.596)	(2.644)	(0.018)	(1.951)	(1.344)
Scotland / Wales	0.142	0.054	0.036	0.073	0.052
.	(3.106)	(1.245)	(0.869)	(1.640)	(1.387)
Retired	−0.085	−0.035	−0.000	−0.105	−0.051
.	(−1.391)	(−0.572)	(−0.006)	(−1.703)	(−0.921)
Single parent	0.239	0.045	0.012	0.315	0.006
.	(2.862)	(0.613)	(0.154)	(3.824)	(0.079)
Unemployed	0.318	0.071	0.045	0.056	0.009
.	(4.347)	(1.121)	(0.636)	(0.784)	(0.154)
Disabled	0.086	0.182	0.106	0.060	−0.029
.	(1.531)	(3.716)	(2.061)	(1.074)	(−0.613)
Log likelihoods	−947.14	−797.69	−799.13	−971.47	−816.05

Ordered probit estimates: asymptotic t-values in italics.

CONCLUSIONS

We have examined the role of individual and household character-istics in explaining patterns of support for higher public spending on seven of the most important public spending programmes in-cluding health, education, the police and defence. We found that some groups in the population, such as the elderly, those who are highly educated, and those who support particular political parties, tend to support distinctive types of spending, even when we con-trol for a range of other factors which might affect their attitudes. We also found some evidence that use of private alternatives to public services reduced support for higher state spending in the fields of health care and transport, although we could not find any evidence that this was true for education.

We found a fair degree of consonance between the factors affecting support for higher spending which individuals perceive as being in their own interest and that which they support as being in the interests of the country as a whole. Those differences that were found ap-pear readily explicable. The association between having children in the household and supporting higher spending on education, for instance, was far stronger in the case of private interests than for the country as a whole. Personal use of private sector alternatives also appeared to have less impact on perceptions of the national interest in expanded public provision than on perceptions of self interest.

We found some evidence that individuals tend to express a greater degree of support for those benefits which they might or do qualify for themselves. We also observe that some groups, such as better-off households and Conservative supporters, are more hostile than others to spending on social security spending generally.[15]

Appendix: Definition of Variables

Age	Age of respondent in years (divided by 10)
Female	1 if respondent is female; 0 if male
Adults	Logarithm of number of adults in the household
Children	Proportion of household members under the age of 18
Household income	Predicted logarithm of gross household income
Manual worker	1 if manual worker; 0 otherwise
Self-employed	1 if self-employed; 0 otherwise

A Level education	1 if possesses A-level qualification; 0 otherwise
Higher Education	1 if possesses a degree or other higher qualification; 0 otherwise
Owner Occupier	1 if owner occupier; 0 otherwise
Car owner	1 if owner of car; 0 otherwise
Private health insurance	1 if covered by private health insurance; 0 otherwise
Privately educated	1 if any child educated at private school; 0 otherwise
Reads Tabloid	1 if regular reader of Sun, Daily Mirror or Star; 0 otherwise
Conservative	1 if supporter of Conservative Party; 0 otherwise
Labour	1 if supporter of Labour Party; 0 otherwise
Lives in South	1 if resident in South of England; 0 otherwise
Scotland/Wales	1 if resident in Scotland or Wales; 0 otherwise
Asked income tax question (δ_i)	1 if asked to consider spending financed by extra penny in the pound on or off income tax; 0 if asked to consider spending financed by raising or lowering taxes for every adult by £35 per annum.
Retired	1 if retired; 0 otherwise
Single parent	1 if single adult with children aged under 18; 0 otherwise
Unemployed	1 if unemployed; 0 otherwise
Disabled	1 if disabled; 0 otherwise

Notes

1. We are grateful for comments from Timothy Besley, Carl Emmerson, Paul Johnson and Michael Ridge.
2. We also ask a series of questions on support for changing the level of public spending on five social security programmes, using the original BSA form of questioning. We did not make a similar distinction between household and national interest for questions on welfare spending.
3. Previous questions in the BSA series have asked respondents which tax instrument they would prefer to be used to pay for higher public spending, but most respondents typically choose the one (an increase in the higher rate of income tax) through which they would not pay themselves.
4. Of course, this works only if respondents understand the implied incidence of tax changes specified. We prefaced the spending questions by a question exploring understanding of the cost to the household of changing the basic rate of income tax by one penny in the pound. Brook, Hall and Preston (1996) present evidence that the implications of the different tax instruments were understood reasonably well.
5. In an ordered probit specification the probability of supporting more or of not supporting less spending are each regarded as a function of

the same linear combination of the explanatory variables. To be specific, for an ordered probit equation this function is the cumulative distribution function of a normal distribution.

6. A fairly simple economic model of responses to the BSA questions on public spending justifying the econometric techniques adopted is presented in Brook, Hall and Preston (1997).

7. The ranges of incomes covered by the bands are unequal. Strictly speaking the generated nature of the income regressor necessitates a correction to the standard errors on the probit coefficients – however, Preston and Ridge (1995) find that the correction makes little difference in a similar context and we follow them in ignoring it.

8. Under an ordered probit specification the conditional probability of supporting more spending, or of not supporting less, is a function of the same linear combination of the explanatory variables. For continuous variables the reported coefficients are expressed as marginal effects on the probability of supporting an increase in spending at the mean values of the explanatory variables. For these variables, the marginal effects on the probability of not supporting a reduction in spending are proportional to those reported. For dichotomous discrete explanatory variables the coefficients are expressed as the effect of changing from a value of zero to a value of unity for mean values of all other variables.

9. This perhaps helps understand the lack of any clear impact from household size, which might have been expected to matter through its effect on household living standards (more people sharing the same household income) if through nothing else.

10. Brook, Hall and Preston (1996) present a simple cross tabulation suggesting that there are no strong effects from *perceived* tax cost either.

11. If, for instance, respondents took the phrase to indicate the interests of the median respondent then it would be quite consistent for only just over half of the population to see an increase as in their own interest but for everyone to correctly acknowledge it to be in the national interest.

12. We did investigate whether these variables might also influence attitudes to other spending programmes but could find no strong evidence to suggest that they should be included in the equations of earlier sections.

13. In this case respondents were given a wider range of options, including supporting 'more' or 'much more' spending.

14. There is some evidence to suggest that single parents want more help for the unemployed and the disabled want more help for poor working families.

15. One extension of our approach would be to analyse correlations between the unexplained variation in support for spending on the different programmes. Results of such an analysis are presented in Brook, Hall and Preston (1997).

16. Since the question format is different from that used for the seven major spending programmes above, these figures are not comparable with those of Figure 5.1.

17. We have chosen to report coefficients expressed as marginal effects on the probability of supporting any increase in spending at the mean value of the explanatory variables. In the case of discrete variables, we report the impact on the probability of supporting increased spending which would result from moving from the zero state to the one state. (e.g. moving from not being an owner occupier to becoming an owner occupier).

6 Choices in Owner-Occupation

Moira Munro, Ruth Madigan and Clodagh Memery

INTRODUCTION

> Two, a priori different, kinds of questions can be asked of any decision situation under uncertainty. The normative question is what constitutes rational behaviour in such a situation, while the positive question is what constitutes human behaviour in such a situation (Muthoo, 1996, p. 1357).

This chapter is concerned with the process of making choices in the uncertain housing market. It is more centrally concerned with the positive rather than the normative question as distinguished by Muthoo as this emphasis is, arguably, more appropriate for contributing to debates about housing policy. If people, whether because of inadequate reasoning power or because of limitations in the time and effort devoted to the decision-making process, systematically deviate from making truly rational decisions, it is more relevant in policy terms to develop understandings of the actual rather than the ideal determinants of behaviour. The chapter touches on many of the themes that recur in the book. It is centrally concerned with how people make an essentially complex decision, exploring the ways in which the economic and social context impact upon choices made. Housing as a policy arena is mainly in the private sector. It is particularly useful to consider whether measurable economic experience, perceptions and expectations impinge on choices in the ways that would have been predicted from economic theory.

The potential complexity of housing decisions arises from the fact that housing is itself a complex commodity. In economic terms its most salient characteristic is its durability (Fallis, 1986; Maclennan, 1982). This has practical as well as theoretical impacts. As an asset it has gained in real value over the long-term (Munro and Tu, 1996).

Therefore when buying a house, consideration of consumption value; whether it is judged to meet a household's demand for space, privacy, housing and neighbourhood quality and so on, are also overlaid with the longer term considerations of the expected investment value of the asset that is being bought. Future expectations are also potentially important for the consumption aspects of housing, for as housing is traded relatively infrequently (it is costly both to buy and sell), choices are made with a view to remaining in the house for some period of time. During the period of expected stay it would also be expected that interest rates, inflation (in both housing and other prices), incomes and family demands may change. It is hardly surprising that rational economic choice is hard both to model and to carry out in this context.

A further layer of complexity exists. The house as 'home' embodies familial meanings and decisions and may therefore be subject to ideologies and social norms as well as to economic rationality (Darke, 1996; Benjamin, 1995; Allen and Crow, 1989). It has been argued that owner-occupation as a tenure also has attendant meanings, such as providing greater social status, independence and ontological security that increase its inherent desirability (Saunders, 1990). The home, as the locus of family life, may thus be overlaid with norms about the perceived appropriateness of particular choices at given points in the family life-cycle that cross-cut economic considerations. The social and the economic context are both important in the shaping of public policy. This chapter also explores the influence of social norms on choices and on beliefs about the role the state should play in housing policy and provision. First we discuss recent trends in the housing market.

THE HOUSING MARKET CONTEXT

The great majority of households are now owner-occupiers – 67 per cent in Britain by 1994 (Wilcox, 1996). Marked changes have occurred in the housing system since the early 1980s. The promotion of owner-occupation was a significant part of the broad agenda of privatisation and an important aspect of policy to create a 'property owning democracy' as espoused by Thatcher's Governments (Hamnett *et al.*, 1991; Boleat, 1997). Policy measures supported this emphasis both implicitly and explicitly. The 'right to buy' policy, introduced in the Housing Act of 1980, had the greatest impact in increasing the proportion of owner-occupiers (Forrest and Murie, 1988). The Act allows tenants of local authority houses to buy at a discount which varies depending on the length of tenancy. The policy was a popular success and resulted in over one million tenants becoming owners.

Other policy measures indirectly promoted owner-occupation. Support for development of new social rented housing or refurbishment of the old was reduced, so that local authority tenancy became less desirable and less easy to access (Coles and Furbey, 1994). The deregulation of the financial services industry in the early 1980s greatly increased the availability of mortgage finance at competitive rates, in contrast to the quantity-rationed queues for mortgage finance created by the price-fixing building society cartel which operated until the late 1970s (Miles, 1994; Stephens, 1993).

Owner-occupation is regarded as the preferable tenure by many people in Britain. Traditionally owner-occupiers were drawn from more affluent sectors of society and the tenure was therefore associated with the best quality housing and neighbourhoods. Even if it was not possible to gain immediate access to these benefits, owner-occupation was widely presented and perceived as a 'ladder' of opportunity, up which it was possible to advance by taking advantage of real house price appreciation. Inflation further increases the apparent benefits of owner-occupation as it erodes the real value of the mortgage debt and increases the (nominal) value of the house, so that owner-occupiers can quickly find themselves paying relatively low amounts (based on historic values) for an asset which has greatly increased in value. In this context, even if house price rises are not stable, owner-occupation will be more financially attractive than becoming a tenant, as rents remain broadly pegged to changing price levels. As Pahl argued in the early 1970s (after a period of rapid house price inflation) 'a family may gain more from the housing market in a few years than would be possible in savings from a lifetime of earning' (1975, p. 291).

The mid-1980s witnessed a major boom in house price inflation. As figure 6.1 shows, average house prices in the UK more than doubled between 1983 and 1989, an increase far greater than general price inflation. While on the one hand rising prices can bring windfall gains to existing owners, there is a parallel decline in affordability for those wishing to become owners for the first time. Of particular relevance for the present study is the fact that house prices began to fall, first in real and then in nominal terms after the boom of the late 1980s.

Figure 6.1   Regional Trends in House Prices

Index (1983 = 100)

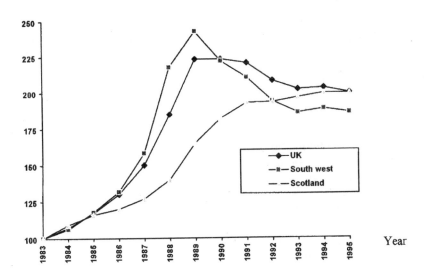

Source: Nationwide Building Society Price Bulletins, various issues.

This was an unexpected shock to the housing system. The downturn was exacerbated by an over-exposure to mortgage debt, the rapid increase in interest rates from 9.5 per cent in May 1988 to 15.4 per cent in 1990, the rise in unemployment and the economic recession of the early 1990s (Forrest and Murie, 1994). As these authors note: '... an overheated, over-indebted hypermobile housing market rapidly degenerated towards a gridlock of immobile households adjusting to very different expectations of home ownership' (Forrest and Murie, 1994, p. 55).

The market downturn revealed that many of the advantages associated with owner-occupation were not an inevitable adjunct of the tenure but been created by the specific market conditions of the time (Forrest *et al.*, 1990). Many people found that owner-occupation now imposed financial loss and severe limitations of choice. 'Losers' in the housing market included those whose house value fell below the amount they had borrowed for it (somewhat euphemistically described as having negative equity). If they were able to sell (and the market downturn was associated with a large reduction in the number of prospective purchasers) it would be at the cost of incurring a real debt to be repaid by some other means (Gentle, Dorling and Cornford, 1994). The labour market recession was a further source of difficulty, as rapidly increasing levels of arrears and repossessions revealed. For many owners the inability to sell without loss exacerbated repayment problems (Ford, 1994).

The recession also revealed various troubles in the deregulated financial services industry. It emerged that some of the lower cost mortgage products might not perform well enough to repay capital at the end of the mortgage term. It also became evident that few vestiges of the philanthropy traditionally associated with mutual status remained among Building Societies or in the competitive financial services industry more generally. Debates surrounding the Financial Services Act clarified, in a way that had not previously been generally evident, that financial advisors were motivated as much by profit as any other business and would therefore encourage customers to buy products more geared to increasing those profits than to their own needs. Thus while competition and apparent choice had expanded in the process of financial deregulation, it also emerged that some people had been sold quite inappropriate financial products, particularly in the areas of mortgage schemes and pensions.

The instability in the housing market was not evenly felt across the country. There have been marked regional differences in the experience both of boom and slump, often characterised as a North-South divide (Hamnett, 1989; Holmans, 1995). As Figure 6.1 illustrates, comparing the South West region and Scotland with the trend in the UK as whole, prices in Scotland were more stable, marked neither by as rapid increases in the 1980s nor by price falls from 1989 (though the trend rate of increase falls after 1991). In contrast, the South West experienced both a sharper boom and a more dramatic fall in prices than the UK average. This regional differentiation in the experience of the housing market creates an ideal context in which to investigate empirically the ways in which instability in the housing market affects owners' beliefs and behaviour as they make housing decisions.

METHODS

The original research on which this chapter is based consists of two closely related elements. Each takes advantage of the significant differences in the housing market experience across the country by focusing on Glasgow and Bristol. These cities reflect the regional contrasts revealed in Figure 6.1. Glasgow had relatively slower price rises in the 1980s and was a fairly stable housing market in the early 1990s while Bristol underwent the more dramatic rise and fall of the boom and slump in house prices experienced in the South-west.

Two complementary surveys were conducted in each area. The first was a semi-structured interview survey with a total of 45 people who had been recently or were currently active in the housing market, including both trading owner-occupiers and first time buyers. The interviews explored the factors respondents said they took into account when making the decision to move and how they made their housing choices and were transcribed and analysed as qualitative data. It is, of course, recognised that those who make the decision to buy in the context of a slow housing market may be atypical in some way.

The second study was a structured sample survey of over 800 owners divided between Glasgow and Bristol. It permitted examination of the differences between those who have decided to move rather than stay put, as well as providing larger scale evidence on attitudes and behaviour in the housing market. They were not a random sample, but instead were randomly drawn across three quotas; namely those who had bought for the first time in the previous three years, those who had bought for the second or subsequent time in the last three years and those who had not moved. While this sample design does not produce a representative cross-section of owners it was chosen because the core questions for the research required sufficient data to be gathered from those who had traded in the housing market during the downturn (who would be a smaller proportion in a randomly drawn sample) while gathering enough information from those who had either been discouraged from moving, or who simply had no desire to move, to enable reliable comparisons to be drawn. The survey work was completed in late 1995, at which time there was no sign of any upturn in house prices.

These two methods provide complementary insights, as the qualitative work allows respondents to express ideas in a more detailed manner than is possible in answer to the closed questions of a structured survey. Exploring these more complex responses enables a better understanding of the relationships identified in the analysis of the larger scale survey.

We will first examines the extent to which economic factors account for housing market expectations and influence choices, and then consider how people describe their choices and deal with risks. Finally, we consider views about the appropriate role for public policy in the housing sector.

ECONOMIC BELIEFS AND EXPECTATIONS

This section considers expectations in the housing market and for the wider economy. It might be expected that perceptions and expectations would be systematically different amongst owners in the two areas, shaped by the contrasting local experiences. Table 6.1 compares the responses in Glasgow and Bristol as to expectations of the future and shows a considerably more pessimistic view in the latter than in the former city. Under half of all respondents in Bristol expected house prices to increase in the next two years, and nearly 20 per cent of those surveyed believed that house prices would continue to fall. In Glasgow a clear majority expected house price increases over the next two years, although there was a minority view that prices would decrease, despite the fact this had not been generally experienced in the city. It is also clear that Glasgow respondents perceive greater stability in the housing market in terms of the riskiness of buying a house.

Table 6.1 also reports expectations with respect to two major economic variables of relevance to housing market decisions: interest rates and tax relief on mortgages. The general pessimism in relation to the future of interest rates and tax relief on mortgages was clearly evident. Only a small minority in both cities expected the economic conditions to change in a way favourable to owner-occupiers. Glasgow respondents were more pessimistic overall than those in Bristol: a greater majority expected interest rates to increase and more expected tax relief to fall.

The survey showed that the relationship between housing market and more general economic expectations was relatively weak. For example, there was no significant association between expectations about future house prices and expectations about interest rate

Table 6.1 **Expected Future Changes in the Housing Market, by Area**

Housing market change	Glasgow	Bristol
House prices will[1]:		
Increase	63.4	45.3
Stay the same	22.6	36.6
Decrease	14.0	18.2
Total (= 100%)	372	358
Buying a house is now (cf. 3 years ago)[1]:		
More risky	40.5	43.2
Same	46.5	32.2
Less risky	13.1	24.6
Total (= 100%)	383	382
Change in economic policy variables:		
Interest rates will[1]:		
Rise	62.6	50.4
Stay the same	22.4	35.0
Fall	15.0	14.5
Total (= 100%)	366	351
Tax relief on mortgages will[3]:		
Rise	18.8	18.4
Stay the same	31.3	39.1
Fall	49.9	42.6
Total (= 100%)	351	343

Source: Household Survey, 1995.

Note: Chi square significant at: [1] 1 per cent [2] 5 per cent [3] 10 per cent.

or tax rate changes, and this pattern persisted even when the data were controlled for area and type of buyer. This may explain why these variables did not prove to be strongly significant in explaining outcomes in the housing market.

There was, however, evidence of significant associations between some socio-economic characteristics and expectations in housing market. This would be consistent with the view that people's own circumstances are more salient to their assessment of the relative riskiness of house purchase than are general market conditions and political trends. There was a strong association between respondents' assessment of how their own financial position had changed over the last three years and their beliefs about the riskiness of house purchase. Those who believed that they were now better off were relatively more likely than other groups to believe that house purchase had become less risky, while those who believed that they had become worse off were more likely than others to state that house purchase had become more risky. However, multivariate analysis revealed that the most important and consistently significant explanatory factor in relation to the anticipation of house price rises was area. Those in Bristol were only about 40 per cent as likely to expect price rises, holding other factors constant as those in Glasgow. This relationship remained, even when controlling for a range of personal variables (including recent experience of unemployment, perceived labour market security and change in personal financial circumstances) and also taking into account the range of other attitudinal variables. Analysis consistently showed that recent local housing market experience was the most significant factor shaping future housing expectations.

The next stage in the analysis explores how attitudes and expectations shape choices. Table 6.2 shows the relationship between the decision to move or buy a house and the degree of optimism about the state of the housing market and the future development of economic variables.

The table confirms the associations between activity in the housing market and expressed beliefs both about the housing market and the future course of economic variables. First time buyers were the most optimistic and 'stayers' the most pessimistic about the housing market overall. First time buyers were most likely to think that buying a house had become less risky, although this remained the minority view. However, there was more pessimism about the future course of economic variables among those who had bought or sold recently than among those who had not moved. First time buyers, in particular, were most likely to expect interest rates to rise in the next three years and movers were more likely than stayers to believe that mortgage interest tax relief would fall in the future. This was somewhat unexpected, since a simple link might have been anticipated between general economic optimism and the propensity to move and buy a house. Instead the data suggest a more complex picture where housing market risks are assessed and buyers enter the market with a generally pessimistic view. They take the risk of buying despite expectations that economic variables will move against them. The decision to move did not seem to reflect any 'feel good' factor. A partial explanation of this phenomenon would be provided if those who had not moved had less reason to give

Table 6.2   **Expected Future Changes in the Housing Market,
by Type of Owner**

	Stayer	*Recent mover*	*First time buyer*
Housing market change			
House prices will[3]:			
Increase	47.9	53.5	60.5
Stay the same	33.2	31.3	24.6
Decrease	18.9	15.1	14.8
Total (= 100%)	190	284	256
Buying a house is now (cf. 3 years ago)[1]:			
More risky	52.1	42.4	32.3
Same	34.7	39.5	43.1
Less risky	13.1	18.1	24.6
Total (= 100%)	213	304	248
Change in economic policy variables			
Interest rates will[2]:			
Rise	53.9	54.3	61.2
Stay the same	31.4	33.0	21.6
Fall	14.7	12.7	17.2
Total (= 100%)	191	276	250
Tax relief will[2]:			
Rise	19.8	16.2	20.3
Stay the same	43.3	33.9	30.1
Fall	36.9	49.8	49.6
Total (= 100%)	187	271	236

Source: Household Survey, 1995.

Note: Chi square significant at: [1] per cent [2]5 per cent [3]10 per cent.

serious consideration to what might happen to these factors in the future. Stayers, however, were also most likely to believe that buying a house had become more risky in the recent past, suggesting that some of this group would have entered the housing market had they believed that conditions in the market were better.

Multivariate analysis showed that locality also influenced these relationships. In Bristol pessimism was general across movers and stayers, while in Glasgow optimism about housing market variables was more clearly associated with a decision to move. However, when the distinction between 'traders' and 'stayers' was analysed in detail, it became clear that demographic and socio-economic variables exerted the strongest effects on the decision to move. Expectations either about housing market variables or economic variables did not make a significant contribution to explaining the decision to move when these more traditional factors were taken into account.

In summary, analysis of the data from the structured survey showed a complex picture. At the most aggregate level, expressed expectations about the housing market are consistently shaped by local experience and support the hypothesis that the lack of general housing market confidence caused the marked decline in the market activity. However, it was also clear that individual respondents did not make consistent connections between what they expected to happen in the housing market and other policy changes nor did these expectations strongly distinguish movers and non-movers. The qualitative analysis contributes to an improved understanding of how expectations shape decisions.

EXPLAINING HOUSING MARKET CHOICES

For the owners in the qualitative sample who were buying or selling, experience of the housing market had been of considerable instability. The high interest rates which prevailed at the end of the 1980s were clearly remembered by some. The fact that interest rates had fallen more or less constantly since that time was regarded as a bonus since it reduced housing costs more rapidly than expected, but the pessimism about the future described above was clearly evident in the interviews. It influenced the way financial choices were made, creating a reluctance to take the maximum mortgage possible. This is an important way of reducing risk in an uncertain world; where those with high costs and debts are vulnerable to financial, economic, labour market or family changes.

> Interviewer: 'How would you see interest rates going in the future?'
> Ms Graham: 'Probably up (laughs). . . . probably up, I'm not sure. . . . At the time I was told that the highest they had been for so long had been 15 per cent and I asked them to work out what my mortgage would be at 15 per cent, just to see how I could afford it. I could, I wouldn't have a life, but I could still make it. So I didn't mortgage myself to the hilt and I had no intentions of ever doing that.' (First time buyer: Glasgow)

> Mr Martin: 'I would see them (interest rates) rising, but I don't see them going . . . much beyond, much over 10 per cent. I would

not see them going up to 15 per cent. However, when we bought this property on a similar sort of ratio of income, then they were about 15 per cent so. . . . I don't think we've over-stretched ourselves against the next property.' (Trader: Bristol)

Other respondents remember the period of high interest rates as more of a struggle.

Mrs Walker: 'At one point we were paying 16 per cent in interest rates and of course it was spam we were eating, spam (laughs)! Um, yes I think our first two years were hard.' (Trader: Glasgow)

Mrs Robb: 'When I bought this house, interest rates were $15\frac{1}{2}$ per cent. The mortgage payments took over half my disposable income – you know take home pay. . . . How we ever paid it, I don't know.' (Trader: Bristol)

These comments also implicitly reveal the extent to which people were willing to risk large debts in the booming property market of the late 1980s; indeed the conventional wisdom of the time was that it was worth taking the risk of a large mortgage because of the promise of returns in the future. These attitudes had not completely disappeared; one respondent directly echoes the sentiments of that time in relation to current choices.

Mrs Orr: 'Next time, we've said, we always said we didn't stretch ourselves enough this time, we should have stretched up to the two bed (house). We should have done it, we would have had more space, it would have been easier to sell . . ., but we said oh no, we want to go out, we want to do this that and the other and we don't want to stretch ourselves . . ., we said next time we will stretch ourselves to the limit, we won't make the same mistake twice.' (Trader: Bristol)

This reflects the particular problems that impinged on the very bottom end of the market in Bristol; the relative affordability of larger and more attractive houses appeared to have left the small starter homes market stranded, with little effective demand, as the current cohort of first time buyers was able to by-pass this part of the market and buy bigger properties. It is however interesting that the direct linkage made was between their unwillingness to have taken more of a risk last time and their selling difficulties. There is, for instance, no comparative consideration of how much money might have been lost had they borrowed more. It also appears that the phrase 'stretching ourselves' which is frequently used in discussion about debts and financial management with the largely negative connotation of being in a position which is risky or hard to manage, is here used to suggest that they should have made more of an effort. Despite these sentiments, the respondent ultimately made a more cautious financial choice then implied above, selecting a house some £10–£15,000 less than they could afford at the maximum.

The interviews showed that most people were actively seeking to find ways of reducing the risks they felt to be inherent in house purchase at this time. Limiting the amount of borrowing so that repayments would remain manageable if economic factors were to change was a common strategy. Other respondents were very conscious of the merit of accumulating some equity in their house, reducing the likelihood of negative equity and easing the process of moving even when selling conditions were difficult. In order to do this, respondents either sought to put a larger deposit down or to take a repayment mortgage.

> Mr Todd: 'A friend of mine has got a negative equity situation of about £9,000, but he's paid off that much on his mortgage, through the repayment mortgage. It means he's got to take out another 25 year mortgage when he starts, but in theory he hasn't lost any on it. Well, he hasn't got to pay any hard cash for it, it's just sort of paper money... We'd probably stay in the next house for at least 10 years.... If we take out a repayment mortgage hopefully that would cover any negative equity we had.' (Trader: Bristol)

An interesting aspect of this account is that his friend's continuing monthly mortgage repayments did not seem to be counted as 'real' money.

Some respondents explicitly considered the prospective saleability of the next house bought as part of their risk minimisation strategy. This might be articulated either in terms of finding a house that others would also find attractive to buy or thinking about which houses would accumulate value faster than others, and was frequently spelt out in relation to mistakes they had made in the past.

> Mrs Orr: 'I'd never do it again. I'd never buy a new property again, never, never ever.' (Trader: Bristol)

However, most respondents did not appear to consider these factors at all. For many there was a strong expectation that the next house was to be a long term prospect and resale value was irrelevant.

> Mrs Robb: 'Oh, I'm not moving again. That's it. I don't want to move anywhere again. I want to be settled, and the house that I'm going to buy hopefully is a house that I can live in, have a family and not want to move again.' (Trader: Bristol)

In general, although it was clear that people hoped they would not find themselves in financial difficulty through their choices in the housing market, very few would admit that they consider house purchase to be a potential way of making money. They were keen to debunk the idea that trading in the market could produce real returns or that indeed they had ever expected to make money on housing. However there is still a notion of investment, as a long-term return, in the sense that people identify one of the main advantages of owner-occupation as ultimately getting something in return for the money spent. The long-term notion of investment was in this way linked with having something to leave to children.

> Interviewer: 'Do you see housing as an investment for the future?' Mr Stevens 'I see at as being put to stay (laughs) oh no, I suppose it is, it obviously is an investment, but I think I would look on it more as an investment for like, I've got two children from my previous marriage and my fiancée's three children from her previous marriage. So I think I would look on it as being helping them with their future. I don't, my personal experience has been that I've never bought property, sold it and made thousands of pounds off it that you can sort of stick in your back pocket and go 'oh that was a great bit of business there'. So primarily it's somewhere to rest my head at the end of the day. In the long-term it's the children's future'. (Trader: Glasgow)

Such an approach to buying reduces the theoretical complexity of the decision, because purchasers can allow consumption motives to dominate, without having to have great regard to future resale values.

Overall, despite the uncertainties concerning the financial aspects of home ownership, and the respondents' direct experience of housing market instability and its consequences, the commitment to owner-occupation remained very high. This emerged clearly in answer to questions about whether respondents considered renting as an alternative to buying. For the established owners renting did not merit serious consideration as a long term prospect, even though a few respondents expected to fall out of owner-occupation on a temporary basis.

> Mr Martin: '(owner-occupation) suits us better. I mean, we went through a phase of renting as students and that was fine at the time, but now this is what is right for us.' (Trader: Bristol)

> Mr McLeod: 'Well, we do not want to pay rent and find out after about 20 odd years that you've got nothing for it.' (Trader: Glasgow)

For many of the first time buyers, the choice was a more real one, they were much more likely either to have been private renters immediately before their move or to have expressly considered the choice. Interestingly, on balance, their experience of the private rented sector had been satisfactory. However, the potential asset value of owner-occupation was a decisive factor for some of these respondents, particularly as buying is actually cheaper in most cases.

> Ms McDonnel: 'I'd heard about other students buying properties and I don't get any grants, it's my parents that pay for my education so rather than spending like £4,000 a year on rent surely you can invest the money in buying something.' (First time buyer: Glasgow).

Here the theoretical complexity of the decision-making process is again reduced by making the tenure choice a prior decision. Once tenure choice has been made, the choice of the next house to live in is therefore restricted to those available to buy. Overall the qualitative work shows that buyers have developed a range of strategies to reduce the risk they believe exists and that the strongly embedded commitment to owner-occupation is not shaken by the instability of the housing market.

ATTITUDES TOWARDS PUBLIC POLICY

The housing system is now dominated by private provision and there was little evidence from our survey that people would prefer to rent either privately or from a social landlord. This was so even for those who faced severe difficulties and major financial loss in selling their house. However, this does not imply that our samples of home owners believe there to be no role for government or that the retreat of the state has been unambiguously advantageous for them. These issues were considered in both the structured, quantitative work and the semi-structured interviews. In the larger scale survey, respondents were asked to say whether they agreed or disagreed with a range of statements concerning the role of government in the housing market. In addition, two further aspects of public policy were explored with the sample interviewed in the qualitative survey – their assessment of public policy as directed towards owner-occupiers and their attitudes towards council housing and the right to buy.

There was a real tension evident when people were encouraged to talk about their attitude towards the treatment of owner-occupiers by the government. This can be explained in relation to the existence of two strong ideologies, both largely accepted by respondents, but working to some extent in a contrary direction. Part of the ideology of home ownership is that it involves independence, 'standing on one's own feet' and, by implication, not relying on the state for help. In fact there has been a long-standing subsidy to owner-occupiers, given as tax relief on mortgage interest, and there has been additional support available through the benefit system for owners eligible for unemployment benefit. Both of these benefits were seriously eroded in the late 1980s. The tax relief, which was for a long period limited to the first £30,000 of any mortgage, was further reduced by limiting the rate at which relief could be claimed first to and then below the rate of standard income tax in two successive budgets (tax relief stood at just 15 per cent at the time of the survey). Further changes in the income support system (introduced in the 1994 budget) meant that those taking on a new mortgage after October 1995 had no entitlement to benefit to cover their mortgage payments for the first nine months of any spell of unemployment. The Government believed that private insurance or rescheduled mortgage payments would enable people to manage without hardship and without need for state support. Both these policy changes attracted considerable media coverage when they were implemented and were visible to owners. The reduced amount of tax relief appears explicitly on mortgage statements.

The popularity of tax relief was very evident from the responses to the structured survey. The overwhelming majority of the owners did not wish to see it abolished (61 per cent strongly disagreed with the statement that 'The government should phase out tax relief' and a further 14 per cent disagreed). This was equally true in both cities. Those who had not moved recently were slightly less staunch supporters of mortgage tax relief than either first time buyers or recent traders, but still the very great majority wished it to remain.

Respondents to the qualitative survey were able to discuss their positions more fully: it was clear that they did not like the policy changes towards tax relief, recognised the reduction in the support available from the state and regretted its loss. There was an explicit tension in reconciling this with a belief in the independence of owner-occupiers:

> Mr Martin: 'I feel that it's been fairly, a fairly radical swing by the Government that the . . . um . . . I don't expect big handouts from government anyway but whether it's right to give us that sort of tax relief I don't know. But I quite like it.' (Trader: Bristol)

> Ms Mitchell: 'I know that it's tax relief and I think they are talking of cutting it or something, ... but, I mean, we certainly didn't feel as if anybody was helping us.' (First time buyer: Glasgow)

The policy changes towards owner-occupation took some commentators by surprise: it had been assumed that because of the association between conservatism (with both a lower and an upper case 'c') and the dominance of owner-occupation amongst middle class, middle income voters, it would be political suicide for *any* party to undermine the subsidy support given to owners even though there were strong academic arguments for suggesting that reform would make the housing system fairer (Duke of Edinburgh Inquiry, 1991). Ultimately the Conservative Government's desire to generate revenue in order to make cuts in the rate of income tax possible and to exert downward pressure on public spending led them to take an alternative view. Some of our respondents voiced the opinion that the government had directly broken promises:

> Mrs Taylor: 'I think basically they have forgotten about homeowners and all the trouble that people have been through and it just seem to pile the pressure upon pressure with VAT on things and tax on this, tax on that . . . they're basically cutting the throats of the people that voted them into office.' (Trader: Bristol).

There was a clear feeling that the Conservative party, identified as the party committed to home ownership and a 'property owning democracy', had let people down. There was a sense of betrayal from people who felt that they made the choices that were encouraged and expected by a Conservative government, even while an ambivalence as to how much of the blame they themselves should accept remains.

Similar ambivalences are evident when respondents were asked to discuss the change in benefit policy. People reconciled in different ways the belief in the independence of owners from Government help, the belief that they would not, themselves, get into difficulty and the belief that the Government had an obligation to owners.

> Ms Graham: 'I have quite a hard opinion on this in that I personally wouldn't have got into this if I wasn't 100 per cent sure that I could afford to stay in it, at least for the foreseeable future. If in a few years time interest rates shoot up then I will just have to cut my losses and go and I would be willing to do that. I wouldn't expect anyone to bail me out.' (First time buyer: Glasgow)

> Ms Mitchell: 'I would say when it comes down to it, it is the people who suffer quickest are the people who can ill afford it. . . . it's people like myself and my boyfriend who are first time buyers and have sunk everything we've got into this. . . . the Conservatives have always been the ones that have pushed 'everybody should own their own home'. You know, you can't push that kind of policy and give people this dream of having their own home, help them fulfil it and then walk away and leave them with it when it all goes wrong. I don't think you can do that, you need to help people.' (First time buyer: Glasgow)

A sense that the Government was expected to retain some responsibility for outcomes in the housing market was revealed explicitly in discussion of the potential for private insurance companies to provide cover for people who had lost their jobs and were unable to pay their mortgages. Partly this was presented as fairness, implying that a government which had encouraged owner-occupation should help those who had got into difficulties. There also appeared to be little confidence that private insurance would be adequate to cover the risks; respondents feared that loopholes and 'small print' would mean that they could never claim against the policies.

> Mr Taylor: 'There's too many catches in there . . . Too many clauses that would allow them not to pay on it.' (Trader: Bristol)

Mr Stevens: 'I think there are a lot of unscrupulous advisors out there that were promising people that this would not be a problem and selling insurance policies to cover the event of whatever might happen, which when unfortunately people did lose their jobs, they found out their insurance policies were useless.' (Trader: Glasgow)

There was widespread support for a continuing government role in housing provision. The surveys confirmed the expected link between voting Labour at the previous election and agreement with statements representing traditional left wing values (such as that income should be redistributed) and disagreement with those associated with the right (e.g. 54 per cent of previous Labour voters strongly disagreed with the statement that 'unemployment benefits are too high and should be reduced' compared to 23 per cent of Conservatives). Only 22 per cent of those interviewed were willing to admit having voted Conservative at the last election, a figure which seems improbably low in view of a national proportion of 42 per cent, higher among home owners. Stated future voting intentions, while notoriously unreliable, showed a strong swing to the Labour party (from 38 per cent to 53 per cent) and those who intended to vote for different parties were clearly distinguished in their attitudes to the role of government. In answer to more general questions in the structured survey our respondents confirmed the continued support for the welfare state identified in successive British Social Attitudes Surveys and discussed in more detail in chapter 5, but the qualitative work revealed ambivalence about policy towards housing.

When asked direct questions, respondents supported council housing and endorsed an expansion in provision. In the structured survey 60 per cent of people strongly agreed that there should be an increase in the amount of council housing available and a further 24 per cent agreed. Exploring the issues with the qualitative sample in some depth revealed that this support was generally couched in terms of the availability of social housing for others. It is not seen as a universal service that everyone expects to need at some time. There is less clear cut agreement on the right to buy policy and again the divisions of opinion do not reflect party political allegiance. Owners of all political allegiances found it difficult to condemn the policy outright, in view of the fact that it enabled people to enter the tenure which they themselves prefer, but this was offset to the extent that the policy was perceived to have had adverse effects on meeting need. The ambivalence supports Taylor-Gooby's (1995) argument that the strongest support exists for those universal welfare services that everyone expects to have to use at some point.

CONCLUSION

These surveys took place at a time of widespread uncertainty in the housing market. There was a widespread expectation that this uncertainty would continue, particularly in the South where there was more direct experience of the problems created by market instability. Owners were making choices in the market in the context of this considerable uncertainty and perceived riskiness. There were various strategies to reduce the complexity of decision-making which might best be characterised as disaggregating the decision-process: people instead tried to make the best choice they could in a series of semi-autonomous decisions (whether to own, how much to borrow, whether to sell, what to buy) which recognised and tried to ameliorate the perceived risks involved. In both cities, there was a general feeling that economic and housing policy would continue to move against the owner-occupier. It is clear that the push towards privatisation in the housing market has not unambiguously increased the extent of choice available to owners or tenants and many people have been badly affected by the down-turn in the market.

However, it is also clear that there remains strong, fundamental support for owner-occupation. Although those interviewed tended to distance themselves from the suggestion that they intended to make money from housing, there was a clear belief that it remains the better choice in the long term and no perception emerges of having been forced into private provision in any sense. The strength of the other meanings attached to owner-occupation helps to explain the absence of a very clear, simple, linkage between expressed pessimism about the housing market and actions. Moving house is strongly linked to family changes (such as starting new partnerships, or having children) and people want to respond to these changes despite what is happening in the housing market. Buyers, particularly in Bristol, are therefore willing to bear relatively high costs to make moves they consider timely or appropriate. Further, when there is no expectation that circumstances will improve, respondents can argue that there is no point in delaying decisions.

There is ambivalence about the extent to which the Government is blamed for the instability in the owner-occupied market and is expected to ameliorate its consequences, complicated by the strong belief that owner-occupation is characterised by independence from Government. Yet, despite the acceptance of, and commitment to, private housing, many people apparently felt angry at what they perceived to be the broken contract with owners whom they felt had been promised advantages which did not emerge. There was little faith that market solutions would be adequate to support owners in financial difficulties. The policy shift towards greater reliance on private insurance will find it hard to gain the acceptance of the general public.

7 Impulsive and Excessive Buying Behaviour

Helga Dittmar and Jane Beattie

Interlinked social and economic changes in Britain, particularly over the last two decades, have changed the climate in which individuals make consumer choices. Higher disposable incomes, coupled with an easier availability of consumer credit, mean wider choices for a greater number of individuals. An important theme of the 'Economic Beliefs and Behaviour' programme is to highlight in diverse domains that the process of choice is more complex than the operation of purely 'rational' (in a traditional economic sense) considerations on clear pre-existing preferences. The research reported in this chapter relates to this theme by addressing the claim that widening consumer choices mean that buying behaviour has assumed a greater personal significance in individuals' lives. Through an examination of buying behaviour and buying motivations we attempt to show that choices about consumer durables are influenced by particular non-functional aspects of goods. Specifically, consumer goods also have symbolic meanings on which people can and do draw in constructing and expressing a sense of self and identity. Buying goods in order to bolster one's self-image is probably a motivation that plays some role for all buying behaviour, but may be particularly important when people engage in unplanned 'spur of the moment' purchases.

Impulsive buying refers to the purchasing of consumer goods without careful deliberation, perhaps with insufficient information, and without prior intent. Impulsive purchases are often those that one would not, on rational reflection, wish to have made (see for example Hoch and Loewenstein, 1991; Rook, 1987). While most people experience the occasional lapse of judgement in purchasing, at its extreme excessive or 'compulsive' buying affects an estimated two to five per cent of adults in developed Western economies (Dittmar, Beattie and Friese, 1996), resulting in substantial distress and personal debt.

Some of these themes can be illustrated by this summary of an interview with Mrs N., 35 years, 'compulsive' shopper:

For Mrs N, there is only impulse buying, there is no planned buying apart from food. If she sees something in a shop she likes, she must have it. She can't stop herself. It is always clothes and jewellery, smart clothes mainly, a size 12 which she desires to be. Shopping is an excuse to go outside the house. It does lift her up for a few hours. When home, she does not try on the clothes, but puts them away in the loft for fear her husband could find out. It is all her fault, she thinks. She feels guilty. She has ridden the family into debt. She says that she cannot tell her husband, because he would walk out on her. She started over-spending after the birth of her daughter about eight years ago. Since she did not have the money of her own, she applied for credit cards. She complains that it is too easy to get them, and that credit limits are increased without consideration of whether the applicant can pay the money back. When she had about £9,000 of debt on her credit cards, she decided to go to a bank and take out a loan. She is paying back £266 a month, and now has two more years and £6,000 to go. With the interest, her repayments will total about £15,000.

Such an account does not sit easily with the still dominant rational (utility) model of economic behaviour, in which consumers dispassionately weigh costs and benefits, choosing the product bundle with the highest expected utility. Preferences are assumed to be consistent over extended periods of time, and internally coherent. Impulse and excessive buying questions this assumption because the preferences at the time of purchase appear to be different from those experienced later when the consumer reflects that the purchase may have been a mistake. The traditional consumer behaviour paradigm in consumer psychology, as in economics, assumes a rational, discerning, intelligent consumer, strategically gathering information and making goal-directed trade-offs (for example, Howard and Sheth, 1969; Foxall, 1990). Like the standard economic model, this cognitive model of rational decision-making cannot explain apparently 'irrational' purchases. Before considering different theoretical models to explain impulsive and excessive buying, this behaviour needs to be located in a broader context.

There are a number of interlinked economic and social changes in Britain which are likely to have had an impact on individuals' spending on consumer goods, presumably leading to an increase in impulsive and excessive buying over the last two decades. Between

Table 7.1 **Changes in Consumer Credit and Credit Card Use in Britain**

	1976	*1982*	*1992*
Approx. amount of outstanding consumer credit in real terms (actual amount in brackets)	£5.5 billion (£5.5 billion)	£7.5 billion (£15.9 billion)	£15.2 billion (£52.9 billion)
Approx. number of credit cards in use	6.1 million	14.7 million	27.0 million

Source: Adapted from Dittmar, 1996.

1971 and 1993, personal disposable income rose by about 75 per cent (taking inflation into account), giving consumers greater spending capacity and choice, while personal savings declined somewhat (Social Trends, 1994). The figures shown in Table 7.1 indicate that the yearly amount of outstanding consumer credit almost trebled between 1976 and 1992 in real terms, and the number of credit cards in use more than quadrupled (Rowlingson and Kempson, 1994).

Alongside these developments in 'modern' consumer spending, we have to consider important shifts in the cultural, social and personal significance of mass consumption. Shopping is changing its nature in Britain, the United States and the rest of the advanced Western economies. The focus has shifted from the purchase of provisions to satisfy the physical needs of oneself and one's family towards the use of consumer goods as a distinctively modern means of acquiring and expressing a sense of self-identity (Dittmar, 1992a), regulating emotions (Elliott, 1994) or gaining social status (McCracken, 1990). Shopping has thus changed for a substantial segment of consumers from the acquisition of necessities and become a leisure and lifestyle activity. Americans now spend more time in the shopping mall than at any other single location beside work and home (Bloch, Ridgway and Dawson, 1994). An English survey identified 25 per cent of their sample as predominantly leisure shoppers (as opposed to thrifty or routine shoppers, for example), who buy goods as rewards for self and others, buy on impulse, and are close to the stereotype of modern consumerism: 'I shop therefore I am' (Lunt and Livingstone, 1992).

Social psychological research on the meanings and functions of material possessions converges with this literature in asserting that material goods can and do function as symbols of self. Belk (1988) demonstrates that people perceive a whole range of material objects as an actual part of their self, and concludes that material objects can be viewed as 'self-extensions'. Dittmar presents reviews and her own empirical studies which show that material possessions are intimately involved in the expression of one's own self-identity, as well as in perceptions and judgements about other people's self-identity (1991, 1992a,b, 1994, 1996). This work is concerned with material possessions already owned, but if concerns with self and identity do play an important role with respect to material goods, the argument can be made that they may also be an important influence when people make decisions about buying consumer durables, both in terms of the actual goods purchased and the reasons for buying. This suggests that impulsive and excessive buying need to be examined with respect to consumers' self-concept, where the motivation to express or enhance one's self-image may play an important role. Moreover, different facets of buying behaviour – impulsive, planned, excessive – may not be radically discrete, but may lie on a continuum, where concerns with identity expression are an underlying social psychological motivation that plays a role for all buying behaviour, if to a different extent.

EXPLANATORY MODELS OF IMPULSE AND EXCESSIVE BUYING

The term 'impulse buying' has had different meanings to different theoretical perspectives. It is important to disentangle these before attempting to examine behaviours which may have quite different underlying motivations (Stern, 1962). For example, presumably there is a considerable difference between 'reminder impulse buying' (in which a shopper remembers the need for an essential item on seeing it in the shop), and 'pure impulse buying' (a novelty or escape purchase which breaks the normal buying pattern). Consumer behaviourists have tended to regard any unplanned purchase as impulse buying, while economists and psychologists have generally studied the (possibly) 'irrational' aspects of pure impulse buying. We define impulse buying as a 'spur of the moment' decision in the shop, similar to Stern's pure impulse buying, and contrast it with planned purchasing, in which the buyer intended to make the purchase of a particular good before reaching the shop.

Economic Models

The backbone of standard microeconomic theory is the assumption that economic agents have well-articulated, internally coherent and consistent preferences. Pure impulse buying presents problems for this rational choice model because such purchases may be associated with a high degree of post-purchase regret. A recent study found that 80 per cent of impulse buyers reported negative consequences from their purchases (Rook, 1987). Even if some impulse purchases do not lead to regret (for example, Rook and Fisher, 1995), it is clear that after a shopping episode excessive buyers would prefer not to have carried out many of their purchases. This suggests that the preference at the point of purchase (to buy the object) is inconsistent with the later preference (regret at having bought it). This leaves open the possibility of the buyer being exploited by more sophisticated agents through money pumps (in which the individual is taken through a cycle of preferences, paying money to move to each successive stage, yet ending with exactly what he or she started with, less the payments).

Various modifications of economic theory have been proposed to account for impulsive buying (and other time-inconsistent behaviours), all of which remain within the utility framework. The standard explanation of impulse buying has been the discounting model (see Strotz, 1956), which assumes that impulse buyers discount the future at too rapid a rate. Thus, the benefits of the desired object at the point of imminent purchase outweigh the (future) problem of paying the bill. However, these preferences switch later, when the buyer comes to pay the bill and regrets the purchase. A similar model is Winston's (1980) stochastic preference model, in which people are assumed to randomly switch between two sets of different preferences: a myopic set which pushes the shopper towards the purchase, and a far-sighted set which remembers that the bill must be paid. The main problem with these models is that they do not provide an explanation for the 'mistake' itself, i.e., why discounting rates should be disproportionately high, or why and how people shift between short term and long term preferences. Finally, Hoch and Loewenstein's (1991) model of time-inconsistent preferences is a reference point model with losses looming larger than gains. Consumers are assumed to partially adapt (imaginatively) to owning the good before they actually purchase it: hence foregoing the purchase would be experienced as a loss (forcing the consumer toward the purchase). They propose a number of factors assumed to increase the probability of a reference shift (and hence impulse buying), which apply regardless of the type of consumer good in question. This application of economic theory to consumer research partially addresses the limitations of the earlier models by high-lighting the importance of consumers' *perceptions* and *evaluations* of goods as crucial to understanding impulsive buying. While all of these economic models explain some aspects of impulsive buy-ing, they fail to account for one of the most striking aspects of the behaviour: why it is the case that certain goods are bought impulsively and excessively (such as fashionable clothes) while oth-ers (such as basic kitchen equipment) are rarely subject to impulse buying.

Consumer Behaviour and Marketing

Perhaps surprisingly, the consumer behaviour and marketing litera-tures have also neglected this aspect of impulse buying. The main-stream approach has been concerned with identifying general factors (such as exposure to in-store stimuli, such as shelf location) which increase unplanned purchasing (for example, Abratt and Goodey, 1990) or with developing atheoretical lists of those goods that are likely to be bought impulsively (for example, Bellenger, Robertson and Hirschman, 1978). This information may be useful for choos-ing goods for sales promotions (for example, end-of-shelf displays), and is also unusual in recognising that certain goods have a greater potential to be bought on impulse than others. However, it does not explain why, nor predict beyond the particular goods studied. Moreover, these studies tend to use purely behavioural definitions of impulse buying, such as regarding a purchase as impulsive if it was not on the buyer's original shopping list (for example, Kollat and Willet, 1967).

Psychological Approaches

These have fallen into two types: cognitive and clinical. The cogni-tive approach places impulsive shopping within the framework of impulse control in general (Mischel, 1961). This work has shown that impulse control improves with developmental stage, and can be used as an individual difference parameter to predict perform-ance on certain cognitive tasks (for example, Baron, Badgio and

Gaskins, 1986). Like the economic and consumer behaviour approaches, the cognitive literature assumes a rational decision maker. In contrast, the clinical psychological literature has been concerned with the excessive buying of compulsive shoppers. The main perspective to date on this excessive 'urge to buy' has been a psychiatric or clinical psychology model. Although it is not listed, as yet, in the current *Diagnostic Statistical Manual* as a psychiatric disorder in its own right, this approach treats compulsive shopping as similar to other types of impulsive, mood or addictive disorders (for example, McElroy, Keck, Harrison, Pope, Smith and Strakowski, 1994; Schlosser, Black, Repertinger and Freet, 1994). A recent American clinical study reports that 95.8 per cent of sufferers described buying that resembled an impulse control disorder (Christenson, Faber, de Zwaan and Raymond, 1994). In more phenomenologically-oriented research, compulsive shopping is described as an 'inability to control an overpowering impulse to buy' (O'Guinn and Faber, 1989) or as 'excessive impulsive consumption' (Faber, O'Guinn and Krych, 1987). This approach regards excessive impulsive buying as a deviant activity, qualitatively distinct from ordinary consumer behaviour. However, our approach suggests that there may be underlying social psychological mechanisms centred on consumers' self-concept which play a role in both ordinary and excessive impulse buying. In common with economic and consumer behaviour perspective, the clinical perspective cannot explain why only certain goods tend to be bought impulsively and excessively, and it does not provide an explanation of possible underlying motivations for this behaviour.

A Social Psychological Model of Impulsive and Excessive Buying

We suggest that a consideration of the cultural context of shopping and the social psychological functions consumer goods fulfil for people can help in developing a new perspective, in which goods are linked to consumers' self-concept because they function as important material symbols of personal and social identity. The core of our theory is that impulse buys are especially likely to be those goods that project a person's self-image. Symbolic self-completion theory (Wicklund and Gollwitzer, 1982) proposes that perceived shortcomings in certain dimensions of one's self-concept produce a motivation to compensate. Amongst diverse strategies, this can involve acquiring and using material symbols which are relevant to those aspects of self felt to be lacking (for example, Braun and

Wicklund, 1989). For instance, by displaying a recognised masculine symbol, such as wearing a black leather motorbike suit, a young man can compensate for not feeling masculine enough, through using the object to tell both himself and others that he is indeed masculine. Symbolic self-completion theory may provide a general perspective on obtaining consumer goods as a possible compensatory mechanism, but a model which can explain when and why an individual engages in impulsive or compulsive buying needs to address two further issues.

Firstly, such a model needs a way of determining whether an individual uses consumption as a symbolic self-completion strategy, rather than sports or artistic achievements, for instance. Richins and Dawson (1992) conceptualise materialism as an individual value orientation, where the acquisition of material goods is a central life goal, prime indicator of success, and key to happiness and self-definition. Their materialism scale thus seems a good proxy measure for the degree to which a person uses symbolic consumption as a self-completion strategy.

Secondly, self-completion theory merely infers self-concept deficits and does not offer a conceptualisation advanced enough to make self-discrepancies amenable for empirical research. For this, we draw on Higgins' (1987) conceptualisation of self-discrepancies, which details mood-related consequences of perceived gaps between different areas of self. Discrepancies between a person's representations of how they are now – actual self – and how they would ideally like to be – ideal self – do not only lead to negative emotional states, they have also been linked to diverse physical and mental health conditions (for example, Heidrich, Forsthoff and Ward, 1994; Scott and O'Hara, 1993). Our research is the first application of self-discrepancies to the area of shopping addiction, and we designed our own measure for studies described below. Suggestive illustrations come from exploratory qualitative research with compulsive shoppers, in which it was noted that 'references to . . . lacking a clear identity' were common (O'Guinn and Faber, 1989, p. 153) and that they 'attempt to restore a depleted self' (Krueger, 1988, p. 581).

A corollary of our theory is that consumers will differ in the goods that they impulsively buy along the lines of the social categories to which they belong (for example, class, race, gender) because such categories are powerful determinants of a person's sense of self (Tajfel, 1984). Thus, for example, a young female student would be expected to use quite different objects to project a sense of herself than would an elderly male factory worker. Within social psychology, gender has been highlighted as a particularly pervasive social category, and gender differences in goods bought on impulse would link with already established gender differences both in the meanings of personal possessions (Dittmar, 1989, 1991) and the construction of object categories in decision-making (Beattie and Barlas, 1993). Moreover, Hanley and Wilhelm (1992) found that women are more likely to be compulsive buyers than men, and in O'Guinn and Faber's (1989) study, a full 92 per cent of their compulsive shopper sample were women. In our own research, we examine gender as an example of the influence of a social category on object selection for impulse buying. Other fruitful categories for future research might be social class, education level or age.

Our model is presented schematically in Figure 7.1, where arrows represent causal links. In other words, if an individual is high in self-discrepancies and is prone to use material goods as compensation, they should buy a lot on impulse, be motivated by mood and self-image buying considerations and should have high compulsive shopping tendencies. It is important to emphasise at this point that we do not propose that self-discrepancies are the *only* reason for impulsive and compulsive buying, rather they are multi-determined. We do propose that a conjunction of high self-discrepancies and materialism will lead to such buying behaviour. Indirect support for this model which views excessive buying as a form of compensatory consumption comes from studies which show that addictive shoppers have low self-esteem, want to spend money in a way that reflects status and power, buy to bolster their self-image and social image, and engage in mood repair (Elliott, 1994; Hanley and Wilhelm, 1992). Our model is also in line with recent proposals for a new 'socio-economic' approach, which views individuals as influenced by value commitments and by their membership of social groups (for example, Etzioni, 1988).

Based on this model, three general expectations can be derived for empirical study:

• If impulse purchases are those 'most likely to project a person's self-image', we should find that some goods make more likely impulse buys than others and that buying motivations related to self-image are relatively more important for goods frequently bought on impulse than for goods hardly bought on impulse.

Figure 7.1   **A Social Psychological Model of Impulse Buying**

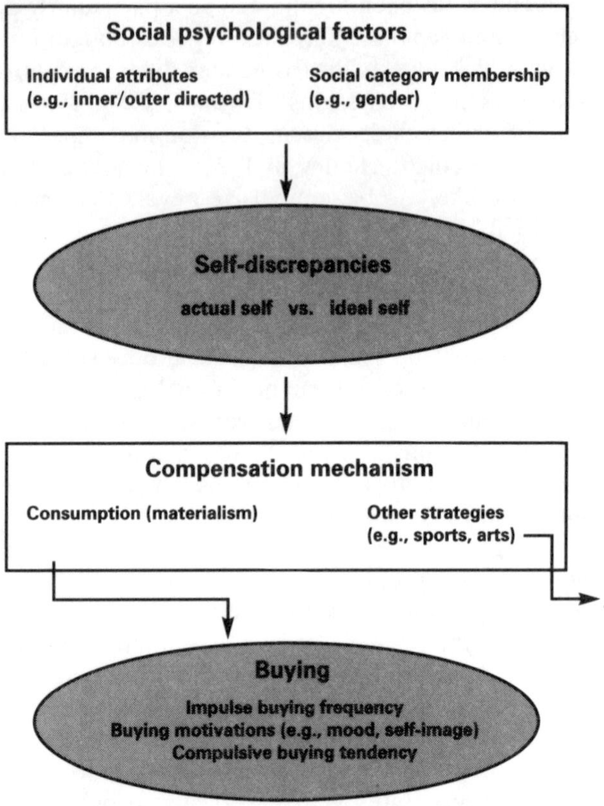

Source: Originally published in Dittmar, Beattie and Friese, 1996.

- If goods are bought impulsively to reflect and project self-identity, then we would expect that gender (as a major social category) should influence both the products bought impulsively and buying motivations.

- If excessive buying (or 'shopping addiction') is linked to consumers' self-concept and consumption values, we should find that ordinary and compulsive shoppers differ systematically (in extent of self-discrepancies and using purchases of goods as a compensation mechanism). At the same time, it should also be the case that magnitude of self-discrepancies together with the belief that consumption is an important self-completion strategy predicts individuals' compulsive shopping tendencies. This last hypotheses provides the most stringent test of our social psychological model.

Our project employed diverse methods, including computer-run experiments on discount rates and qualitative data collection through shopping diaries and interviews, but the findings described in this chapter focus on the questionnaire survey.

MAIN SURVEY FINDINGS

Our strategy of contacting respondents was aimed explicitly at producing a sample for the purpose of testing our theoretical model, rather than a sample which could be considered representative. The sample consisted mainly of two groups: respondents who had been in contact with a shopping addiction self-help organisation and a larger group of respondents whose addresses were selected so that they residentially matched (by town and street) those of the self-help group. Further addresses were obtained through 'snowballing'. The overall response rate for this postal questionnaire was 56 per cent, which compares favourably with standard rates of around 30 to 40 per cent.

The questionnaire measures consisted of six main parts:

- *Compulsive shopping scale* (d'Astous, Maltais and Roberge, 1990). This is a validated scale, which can be used as a measure of an individual's tendency towards compulsive shopping, as well as a 'screener' to divide the sample into compulsive and ordinary (noncompulsive) shoppers.
- *Frequency of buying 9 types of durable consumer goods as planned purchases.*
  Consumer goods included, for example, clothes, kitchen items or sports equipment.
- *Buying motivations for planned purchases.*
  These included functional motivations (for example, good value for money), emotional motivations (puts me in a better mood), and motivations related to self-image (for example, makes me feel more like the person I want to be, improves my social standing).

- *Self-discrepancy measure.*
  This consisted of respondents completing the sentence 'I am . . ., but I would like to be . . .' repeatedly, and rating the size and salience of each self-discrepancy.
- *Frequency of buying the same 9 types of goods as impulse purchases.*
  Impulse buying was defined as 'a "spur of the moment" decision in the shop'.
- *Buying motivations for impulse purchases.*
  These were the same as for planned purchases.
- *Materialism scale* (Richins and Dawson, 1992).
  This scale was used as a proxy measure for the extent to which an individual uses consumption as a compensation strategy. An example item is 'Some of the most important achievements in life include acquiring material possessions'.

Types of Goods and Motivations in Impulse Buying

To measure impulse buying, it is important to take into account how often a good is bought not only on impulse, but also as a planned purchase. For instance, if a good is purchased very frequently – but even more so as a planned than as an impulse purchase – taking only the raw impulse buying frequency would be misleading. We therefore constructed an 'impulsivity index', which compares impulse with planned buying frequencies for a particular type of consumer good. It can vary between -1 (indicating that the good is always bought in a planned fashion and never on impulse) and $+1$ (indicating that the good is exclusively bought on impulse and never planned). If a good is bought equally frequently on impulse and as a planned purchase, then the impulsivity index is zero, independently of the absolute buying frequencies. A more detailed explanation is given in Dittmar, Beattie and Friese, 1996.

Impulsivity index means for nine types of consumer goods are shown in Figure 7.2. All the means are negative, showing that goods are bought somewhat more as planned purchases than on impulse. However, some types of goods – such as jewellery, sports equipment and clothes – are bought significantly more on impulse than others – such as footwear or body care products. Goods in Figure 7.2 are ordered in terms of their proportional 'impulsivity', running from highest at the top to lowest at the bottom. Jewellery and clothes are more closely linked to self-image and appearance than shoes or kitchen items.

Figure 7.2   **Impulse Buying for Nine Types of Consumer Goods**

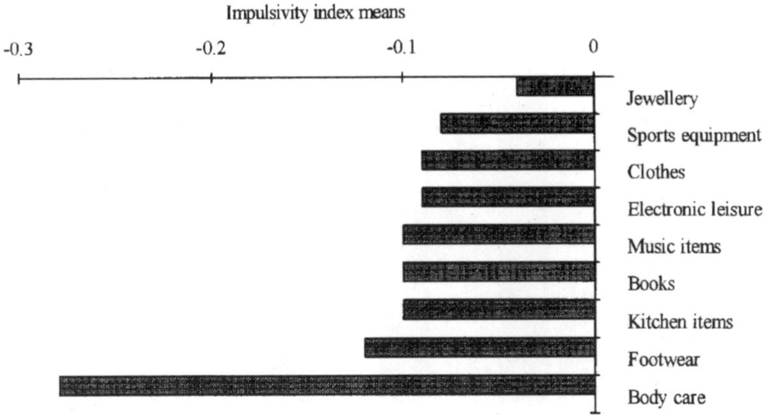

Impulsivity index means

-0.3	-0.2	-0.1	0

Jewellery
Sports equipment
Clothes
Electronic leisure
Music items
Books
Kitchen items
Footwear
Body care

In order to examine which buying motivations are important in impulse purchases, we averaged respondents' ratings of how important six different motivations are for them personally for two different kinds of consumer goods: the three types of goods most prominently bought on impulse (jewellery, sports equipment and clothes) and the three goods categories bought least often on impulse (kitchen items, footwear and body care products). Ratings were made on 6-point scales, ranging from 'not at all true of me' (1) to 'very true of me' (6). A comparison of mean ratings, shown in Figure 7.3 below, demonstrates that functional buying motivations, such as price and usefulness, are relatively less important for goods which are frequently bought on impulse, compared to goods less often bought on impulse. Conversely, emotional and self-image buying motivations become relatively more important for frequent impulse buy goods.

This suggests that improving their mood, thinking that buying the goods in question makes them feel closer to the person they want to be (their ideal self), and expressing their unique self are important underlying motivations when consumers buy on impulse. At the same time, concerns with the practical use of the goods and cost-benefit concerns in terms of value for money decrease in salience when making such purchase decisions. These findings support the proposition made at the beginning of the chapter that psychological and self-image concerns play a stronger role in impulse buying than planned purchases. However, differences are subtle, rather than

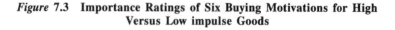

136   *Impulsive and Excessive Buying Behaviour*

Figure 7.3   **Importance Ratings of Six Buying Motivations for High Versus Low impulse Goods**

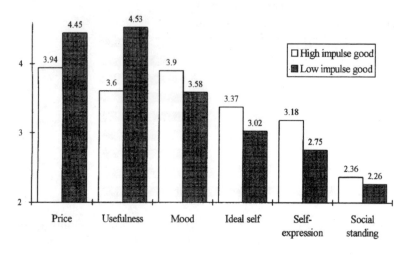

dramatic, which implies that non-functional buying considerations also play a role in planned buying, in purchase decisions which were deliberated and intended before entering the shopping environment.

These findings are consistent with recent social psychological work on individuals' balancing 'intuitive' with 'rational' decision-making strategies, which concludes that 'intuitive' processing – 'which operates in an automatic, holistic, associationist manner, is intimately associated with the experience of affect, ... derived from emotionally significant past experiences, and is able ... to construct relatively complex models for directing behaviour by the use of prototypes, metaphors, scripts and narratives' (Denes-Raj and Epstein, 1994) – can override rational considerations, even when people are fully aware that their resulting behaviour is 'irrational'.

Gender Differences

There is consistent evidence that women and men relate differently to their material possessions. A developmental American interview study (Kamptner, 1991), a cross-cultural investigation (Wallendorf and Arnould, 1988), and a sociological project

(Csikszentmihalyi and Rochberg-Halton, 1981) all show that, by comparison, women tend to value emotional and symbolic posses-sions, while men favour functional and leisure items. Moreover, they seem to value these possessions for different reasons: women gave more emotional and relationship-oriented reasons, while men's had a more functional, instrumental and activity-related focus (Dittmar, 1989). Reasons for valuing material goods owned may not correspond closely with purchase motivations, but a small-sample qualitative study on gender identity and impulsive buying provided evidence that men tend to buy instrumental and leisure items pro-jecting independence and activity impulsively, while women tend to buy symbolic and self-expressive goods concerned with appear-ance and emotional aspects of self (Dittmar, Beattie and Friese, 1995). Here, we consider whether similar gender differences emerge in the larger and more diverse survey sample.

Overall, we find that women buy significantly more frequently on impulse than men. This finding is particularly interesting with respect to claims made in the clinical literature that the great majority of consumers who engage in excessive or compulsive buying are women. In our survey, we found that a person classified as a 'com-pulsive shopper' according to the screener was over two-and-half-times as likely to be a woman rather than a man. There have been suggestions that the disproportionate number of women compul-sive shoppers may be in part a methodological artefact, on the grounds that women may be more likely to contact services or self-help organisations to ask for help with their spending or excessive buying problems. Yet, given the extreme difficulties we experienced on our project in contacting male compulsive shoppers – despite using diverse elicitation strategies, including appeals in radio pro-grammes, newspapers and flyers – it seems likely that there is a gender imbalance in excessive forms of impulse buying. It may be the case, that shopping still constitutes a more culturally available and socially acceptable activity for women than for men, and hence is more likely to be used as a compensation strategy. Other strat-egies, such as excessive sports or 'going out to the pub', may be more available and socially sanctioned for men.

Despite this overall difference in impulse buying, it is not simply a case of women buying 'more of everything'. The two types of goods which 'head the list' for women are jewellery and clothes, which seem linked to concerns with appearance, self-presentation and social interactions (see Figure 7.4). In contrast, the two most

Figure 7.4   **Impulse Buying by Women and Men**

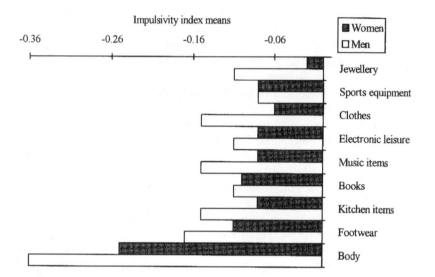

impulsive types of goods for men are sports equipment and electronic leisure items (such as videos or computer games). Such goods seem more instrumental, and linked to activities and leisure pursuits, and less concerned with social interactions. These findings thus corroborate our earlier study.

What is most striking in analysis of the six buying motivations identified in Figure 7.3 is that women and men hardly differ with respect to price and usefulness of consumer goods, although women are slightly less concerned with whether something is good value for money than men. In contrast, differences in the psychological buying considerations are more pronounced, where mood- and self image-related motivations were more salient for women's impulse buying. These findings are consistent with the greater frequency of impulse buying amongst female consumers.

Excessive Buying or 'Shopping Addiction'

Particularly in the last couple of years, there has been a good deal of media attention on excessive buying, often with buzz words such as 'shopping addiction' or 'shopaholism'. Empirical studies on 'shopping addiction' or 'compulsive buying' have been carried out

Figure 7.5   **Gender Differences in the Importance of Six Buying Motivations for Impulse Purchases**

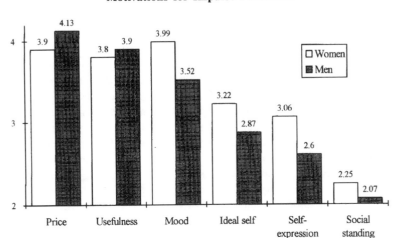

recently in the United States (Friese and Koenig, 1993; Hanley and Wilhelm, 1992; O'Guinn and Faber, 1989), Canada (Valence, d'Astous and Fortier, 1988), Germany (Scherhorn, Reisch and Raab, 1990) and the UK (Elliott, 1994). All suggest that such extreme buying is on the increase, affecting an estimated two to ten per cent of the adult population. Scherhorn *et al.* (1990) describe 25 per cent of German adults as showing some mild compulsive shopping tendencies. These statistics suggest that excessive non-planned, non-necessity purchases are rapidly becoming a sizeable and psychologically distressing problem, which needs research attention.

The term 'excessive' buying seems preferable to the term 'compulsive' buying, which is derived from the clinical psychological literature and makes an a priori assumption that consumers experience shopping episodes throughout as an activity over which they have no control and which is experienced subjectively as negative. More phenomenologically-oriented studies (for example, O'Guinn and Faber, 1989) report that consumers also experience an emotional 'high' while shopping, even if purchases are regretted later, suggesting both positive and negative dimensions. This has led some researchers to propose that excessive buying is better conceived of as an addiction, rather than a compulsion (for example, Scherhorn *et al.*, 1990). Such divergences over definitions are difficult to resolve and can be criticised for presenting excessive impulsive buying as a deviant activity that is radically distinct from ordinary impulse buying. In contrast, our project considers the possibility that a continuum may exist between excessive and impulsive buying, where similar underlying motivations influence both.

In our model we propose that excessive buying behaviour can be viewed – at least in part – as a strategy to compensate for perceived discrepancies in a person's self-concept, specifically between consumers' actual self (how they see themselves) and their ideal self (how they would ideally like to be). Moreover, this relationship between self-concept and excessive buying is moderated by individuals' value orientations with respect to consumption.

In terms of discrepancies in self-concepts, we used an open-ended approach to enable respondents to report on any aspect of their self they considered relevant. In order to be able to construct an overall quantitative measure for each respondent, they were also asked to indicate for each self-discrepancy on a rating scale how far they felt they were away from their ideal self (size of discrepancy) and how much they worry about it (psychological importance of discrepancy). Respondents were classified into compulsive versus ordinary shoppers on the basis of their score on the compulsive shopping scale, using a cut-off norm established in a previous UK study (Elliott, 1994). Results showed that compulsive shoppers report significantly greater and more psychologically worrying self-discrepancies overall than ordinary shoppers. At the same time, compulsive shoppers also have a stronger commitment to materialist values than ordinary consumers. Ordinary consumers on average fell below the mid-point of the materialism measure, while compulsive shoppers fell above the mid-point. Thus, it seems that compulsive shoppers believe much more strongly than normal shoppers that acquiring consumer goods is an important route to success, happiness and a sense of identity. These two findings demonstrate that there are systematic differences between compulsive and ordinary shoppers in the two main elements of our theoretical model.

A hierarchical multiple regression analysis was carried out in order to address the question of whether – for individual shoppers – extent of self-discrepancies and materialistic values predict tendency towards being a compulsive shopper. The dependent variable was the individual's score on the compulsive shopping scale. For this analysis, individuals were classified as either low or high in materialism, while self-discrepancy was treated as a continuous variable.

***Figure* 7.6   Self-Discrepancy and Compulsive Shopping Tendency as a Function of Materialist Values**

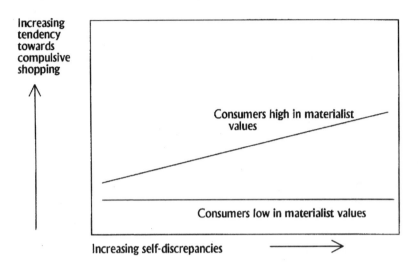

Self-discrepancy was multiplied with level of materialism to produce an interaction variable. The first step of this analysis consisted of a main-effects-only model, where level of materialism and self-discrepancy were entered as predictors. In the second step, the interaction term was added as a third predictor to assess the presence, strength and nature of any interaction between materialism and self-discrepancy. Our model predicts that a relationship between self-discrepancy and the dependent variable should be small or absent when materialism is low, and should be present when materialism is high. In other words, increasing self-discrepancy should be linked to a higher compulsive shopping tendency *only* when consumers make use of consumption as a compensatory strategy. The diagram shown in Figure 7.6 gives a schematic outline of this proposition.

The question of whether our model can predict the tendency of a person to become a compulsive shopper (operationalised through the score on the compulsive shopping scale) is a central concern of the current research. For compulsive shopping tendency, the expected interaction proved highly significant (t 1,305=3.15; p<.005), This means that – as expected – the inclusion of the interaction between level of materialism and self-discrepancies yields a superior explanatory model over using these two variables as independent predictors. The full regression model, including the interaction term, explains one third of the variance in individuals' compulsive shopping tendencies (R square = 0.33). With a significant interaction term, B and beta weights for the full model cannot be interpreted in a conventional fashion, and for this reason findings are presented separately for shoppers high and low in materialism in Table 7.2.

Self-discrepancies and compulsive shopping tendency are unrelated for those low in materialism, as shown by the non-significant correlation in Table 7.2. Only one per cent of the variation in their compulsive shopping tendency can be predicted from their self-discrepancies. It is likely that consumers with high self-discrepancies amongst this group use compensation strategies unrelated to consumption. In contrast, there is a strong relationship for those consumers high in materialism, among whom an increase in self-discrepancies is associated with an increase in compulsive shopping tendency. As the table shows, for those consumers who see consumption as an important route towards identity and success, almost a quarter of the variation in their compulsive shopping tendencies can be predicted from knowing the extent and gravity of their self-discrepancies. Thus, self-discrepancies – in conjunction with high materialism – are a reasonably strong predictor of compulsive buying tendencies.

Table 7.2   **Links Between Self-Discrepancy and Compulsive Shopping Tendencies**

Level of materialism	Constant	B	r	r square	p
High	26.12	1.0	0.10	0.01	n.s.
Low	24.79	0.24	0.49	0.24	<.001

CONCLUSIONS AND IMPLICATIONS

At its extreme, it appears that impulse purchasing can become a 'compulsion', leading to great personal debt and even bankruptcy. Our research suggests that there is a continuum between ordinary and excessive buying behaviour, rather than a qualitative disjuncture, because the relationship between self-discrepancies and compulsive shopping tendency is a continuous one for individuals who are high in materialism. We would not want to claim that shopping addicts are *only* or *mainly* excessive impulse purchasers, who are propelled by strong self-discrepancies, but it appears that they constitute at least one subpopulation of compulsive buyers. Self-discrepancies have not been previously hypothesised to play a role in compulsive buying. The psychiatric literature has tended to study patients who are hospitalised or in treatment for diverse clinical conditions, and it is therefore not surprising that they have found that individuals who suffer from excessive buying also present other psychiatric conditions, such as eating disorders or addiction to gambling. It appears that this literature has limited itself to a particular clinical population of individuals who present excessive buying amongst other conditions, who are therefore likely to show fairly generalised and extreme psychiatric disturbances. However it seems likely that other compulsive shoppers lead fairly 'normal' and reasonably successful lives, apart from their buying behaviour. It is probably safest to conclude at this stage that compulsive shoppers are not a homogeneous group, but a collection of subpopulations with different pathways into shopping addiction.

However, our model suggests a theoretical basis for therapeutic intervention, given that self-discrepancies have been identified as one important underlying motivation for compulsive buying. Self-help organisations for shopping addiction, or counselling services for debt management, tend to concentrate on aiding clients in developing realistic budget plans and strategies for long-term debt reduction. Their clients' concerns with self-image remain unaddressed. Current medical treatment for compulsive buying often entails the use of anti-depressant drugs, such as Prozac, or behavioural therapies. These forms of treatment can reduce the number of shopping episodes successfully, but buying tends to increase again after the end of treatment. This implies that treatment should focus on underlying motivations for compulsive shopping, rather than alleviating symptoms. Our research suggests that the issues of self-discrepancies and materialism need to be addressed therapeutically, either by aiding clients in changing aspects of their self-concept or finding different, more positive avenues for self-completion, which are less costly. Thus, treatment services for compulsive buyers may need to address fragile aspects of a person's self-concept in order to go beyond the mere alleviation of 'symptoms'. This suggests that debt counselling or clinical treatment – centred around psychotropic drugs, such as Prozac, or various behavioural therapies aimed at reducing the 'incidence of shopping episodes' – may be insufficient by themselves to provide true relief for the increasing number of sufferers.

Moreover, there are further theoretical and practical reasons why a better understanding of impulsive and excessive buying behaviour is of considerable importance to researchers and policy makers in the fields of economics, consumer behaviour, and psychology. Our aim is to complement existing rational choice models in economics and consumer research through predicting impulsive and excessive buying as based – at least in part – on the social psychological motivation of bolstering aspects of one's self-concept. Since impulse purchases represent a significant percentage of personal resource allocation decisions, reductions (increases) in impulse purchase rates should lead to greater (lower) aggregate savings rates (Thaler and Shefrin, 1981). Encouragement (discouragement) of impulse purchasing is realistic only when its basis is better understood. A predictive model of which products will tend to be bought on impulse, and by whom, can provide marketers with information to target in-store promotions.

The social psychological perspective on buying behaviour outlined in this chapter addresses the Programme's concern with the link between social-cultural norms and economic behaviour by focusing on the symbolic (non-functional) significance of material goods. This aspect of economic and consumer choice needs to be taken into account in order to overcome shortcomings of the still prevailing rational utility-maximising models of consumer decision-making.

8 Fair Pay and Pay Determination
Julie Dickinson and Lucia Sell-Trujillo

INTRODUCTION

Demands for 'fair pay' are a common feature of pay negotiations and human resource managers are careful to take 'felt fairness' into account when designing pay systems. However, wage theories hold that there is nothing inherently fair about pay differentials. In economic terms, pay is the price for labour, and the price is determined by market forces. Some economists, for example, Minford (1992) argue that the common preoccupation with the fairness of pay is an outcome of a poor understanding of how labour markets work. Nonetheless, most firms take concerns about fair pay seriously. Even if the scarcity of alternative jobs is such that there is little possibility of losing disgruntled employees, there is a strong risk of generating a climate of low trust and poor industrial relations if employees feel they are getting a raw deal.

The question of how people decide what is a just reward for labour is of considerable importance. The research discussed in this chapter sets out to explore the reasons underlying judgements of fairness. We were particularly interested in what criteria people think should be used as the basis for pay differentials.

Now is a particularly pertinent time to explore beliefs about fair pay. In the 1980s and 1990s, government policy towards wages has been driven by 'free market' theories which argue that the most efficient creation and distribution of wealth can be achieved if the laws of supply and demand are unimpeded by restrictive practices in the labour market (Fevre, 1992). It has also been driven by the battle against inflation; firms have been exhorted to make rates of pay more responsive to individual and company performance (Kessler and Bayliss, 1995). We investigated whether these new philosophies – that market forces and productivity should take precedence over the 'cost of living' – have spread to beliefs about fair pay.

There have also been changes in organisational structure and job design. Many companies have reorganised into smaller business units and introduced wage setting at the plant level. There has been a decline in collective bargaining and an increase in flexible employment contracts and performance related pay (Beaumont, 1993; Hartley and Stephenson, 1992; Millward *et al.*, 1992). Beliefs about fair pay may have an even greater impact on harmonious employment relations in smaller workplaces.

We interviewed 94 personnel managers, union representatives and employees from 11 private sector organisations about their perceptions of and judgements on the pay differentials in their organisations. The main aim was to discover what criteria people feel should determine pay differentials and the extent to which the three different groups – each with their different involvement in pay setting – share beliefs about the appropriate criteria. Industrial harmony, motivation and job satisfaction are all enhanced if employers and employees agree on the levels of pay for different jobs, but we know very little about what employers and employees think about pay differentials. There have been few previous attempts to measure beliefs about pay differentials in groups from different sides in industry and commerce.

The study had two further purposes: to investigate the influence of beliefs about fairness on pay determination, and to consider broader economic and sociological explanations of pay differentials.

ECONOMIC THEORIES OF PAY DETERMINATION

Many economists assume that the price of labour varies in response to market pressures like the price of any other commodity. In its most basic form, neo-classical economics predicts that pay for labour in demand rises when the supply of that labour is scarce and falls when the supply of labour exceeds demand, assuming, as a necessary pre-condition, that there is competition between employers for labour and competition between workers for jobs.

Market processes can be used to explain both fluctuation in rates of pay for particular skills and pay differentials between occupations. It is argued that pay differentials arise in response to demands for higher skills, the need to compensate for unpleasant working conditions or the need to persuade employees to take on additional responsibilities. Pay differentials act as an incentive to workers to invest in training or take on more arduous jobs. If it is assumed that people have equal opportunities and make free, informed career choices, it can be argued that market forces provide the most efficient way of matching talent and motivation to position (Rosen, 1982).

Few economists, however, would assume that perfect competition exists between employers or employees. Employees rarely move freely between jobs and organisations in a way that allows supply to equal demand in the labour market. Rising pay (in real terms) can co-exist with rising unemployment; low paid jobs tend to remain unfilled in conditions of considerable labour surplus.

Typically economists have looked to the operation of the labour market to try to explain why the price mechanism so often fails to adjust where wages are concerned (Fevre, 1992). One important approach is provided by human capital theory which holds that pay differentials reflect individual investment in training and skills rather than market demand for higher skills. Differences in human capital mean that workers cannot apply for jobs where demand exceeds supply because their skills do not match those required by the employers. Pay rates for unfilled jobs remain high to attract and reward the workers who have invested in the necessary skills despite an over-supply of labour generally. In effect, there is not one labour market but a multitude of non-interacting labour markets for different occupations. Another approach argues that work institutions such as trade unions, wages councils and unemployment benefits limit competition in the supply of labour by setting lower limits on pay. Consequently, it is argued, employers cannot afford to recruit the labour they require, so jobs remain unfilled and workers remain unemployed.

This approach has been promoted by 'free market economists', such as Hayek and Friedman, but has not gained wide support among labour economists. Its importance lies in its appeal to policy-makers in Britain in recent years. An important part of Government policy on wages has been to curb the power of trade unions and wage regulatory bodies, in order to remove what are termed 'restrictive practices' and allow pay to move more freely in response to market forces.

In general, economic approaches to pay determination have focused on price mechanisms within labour markets and the Hayek/Friedman theory has dominated Government policy towards wages. A number of economists and sociologists have criticised economic orthodoxy for neglecting to examine the process of wage determination within organisations (Brown and Nolan, 1988; Blanchflower and Oswald, 1990; Michie and Wilkinson, 1995; Thaler, 1989). The literature on pay in industrial relations points to the importance of political policies, collective bargaining, management strategies, and custom and convention in pay setting (see for example, Phelps Brown, 1977; Wootton, 1955).

The process of pay setting in organisations is heavily dominated by pay comparability arguments. Customary differentials and formal or informal job evaluation form a major source of legitimation for pay demands. We will now examine how beliefs about fairness can exert an influence on levels of pay.

NORMATIVE INFLUENCES ON PAY

Normative approaches claim that rates of pay reflect the social status of jobs and traditional beliefs about what labour is worth. The important forces are 'felt fairness' and beliefs about pay equity within organisations.

It is likely that beliefs about fairness serve more to maintain the existing structure of pay differentials than to introduce new standards for evaluating worth. In practice, employees tend to accept the traditional pattern of rewards as fair (Wootton, 1962) and feel cheated when expectations derived from customary differentials are not fulfilled (Brown, 1989). Consequently organisations risk demotivation or industrial action if they interfere with pay relativities.

Functionalist explanations interpret normative beliefs about pay differentials as a necessary support for the authority structure of organisations (Marsden, 1983). Thus supervisory and managerial jobs are seen to carry higher pay because they involve higher responsibility either for their span of control over subordinate jobs or for the importance of decisions at their level in the organisational hierarchy. However, whilst the criterion of 'responsibility' serves to justify pay differentials, the authority hierarchy theory holds that the 'real' cause of the pay differentials is the need to mark the social status of managerial jobs with higher pay. It is argued that if managers or supervisors do not receive an increment above the pay of the people they supervise, the basis of their authority will be seriously undermined. Marsden saw authority and pay in organisations as mutually reinforcing. In this way, normative beliefs about pay may be an important coordinating mechanism – part of the glue which holds organisations together.

Although beliefs about some criteria may be very stable, it seems likely that there is a highly subjective element in judgements of fair pay and that it is perennially a subject for negotiation and debate. Surprisingly little is known about what factors cause judgements of fairness to shift or what level of commonality might exist in the criteria for determining pay differentials. Agreement on what constitutes a fair wage can be hard to achieve and in industrial pay bargaining both sides usually claim legitimate grounds for their different positions. However, if every individual in an organisation believed in a different basis for determining pay then beliefs about fairness would not exert much pressure on pay negotiations.

The discipline most concerned with workers views on fair pay, industrial relations, has tended to neglect psychological research on beliefs about the basis for determining fair pay. The next section will discuss relevant findings from social psychology.

SOCIAL PSYCHOLOGICAL APPROACHES TO BELIEFS ABOUT FAIR PAY

There is some evidence that beliefs about pay are similar amongst groups of people from similar occupational and social strata. Managers tend to cite 'market forces on the price of labour' as an important criterion whilst employees tend to focus on 'qualifications', 'responsibility' and the 'importance' of the job (Dickinson, 1992). Dornstein's study in Israel (1985) found that more white collar than blue collar employees cited 'responsibility and authority' and 'indispensability' as important criteria for determining levels of pay; more blue collar than white collar employees cited 'difficult working conditions', 'inconvenient working hours' and 'family needs'. These findings do not imply that different explanations are exclusive to different groups, just that certain explanations tend to be preferred more by some groups than others. For instance, in Dornstein's study the criterion of 'responsibility and authority' was cited by 51 per cent of the white collar workers and 23 per cent of the blue collar workers.

Dornstein and Dickinson put forward different reasons to explain group differences. Dornstein attributed the differences between white and blue collar workers to group interests. For instance, the blue collar workers stood to gain more if their working conditions and hours of work were rewarded. Dickinson argued that the differences between managers and employees could reflect different social representations of the basis of pay (for more explanation see Dickinson 1992, Dickinson and Emler, 1992). The theory of social representations (Moscovici, 1984) holds that groups of people who regularly interact, converse and share media come to share explanations or theories about the nature and cause of events. Social representations are 'common sense theories and explanations' about the world. They constitute a shared reality.

There is no telling which is the best explanation for the group differences found by Dornstein and Dickinson – whether espoused beliefs reflect different representations of reality or rhetoric to further different interests. Consequently we will be open minded about the cause of individual and group differences in this research. Social psychologists have stressed the discursive nature of explanations provided by individuals (Potter and Wetherell, 1987). For instance, the accounts provided by respondents in interviews are each respondent's construction of reality as he or she sees it, *and* as he or she wants the interviewer to see it.

The purpose of our research was to explore the normative nature of espoused beliefs and opinions about fair pay. Unlike labour economists and industrial relations specialists, we were not aiming to discover the causes of pay differentials *per se*, but to contribute to a better understanding of the ideological grounding of pay setting in organisations.

THE INTERVIEWS

The 94 interviewees were drawn from 11 large organisations in the private sector. All were 'blue-chip' companies and several were market leaders. The interviewees were all full-time, skilled or professional employees in permanent jobs and included personnel managers, union representatives and employees, both in companies providing financial services (mainly white collar employees) and in companies engaged in manufacturing and engineering (mainly blue collar employees). All the companies recognised trade unions and determined pay by collective bargaining for the bulk of the workforce except for one financial services organisation and one engineering services organisation. In total, the sample contained 15 personnel managers (11 male, four female) from the 11 companies, 10 union representatives (all male) from six of the 11 companies, and 69 employees (50 per cent female in finance; 11 per cent female in engineering) from five of the 11 companies. Table 8.1 shows the split of the employees between finance and engineering and unionised and non-unionised companies. Tape-recorded interviews were carried out in two stages. First, the personnel manager or director was interviewed to gather background information about the company, information on pay setting arrangements, general criteria for setting pay differentials and future concerns about pay. The second stage interviews with the other respondents overlapped in content with the first and included more questions to explore views on the fairness of pay differentials and the criteria individuals felt should underpin the pay structure. A key component of the interview schedule, which helped to draw out beliefs about the criteria for determining the value of jobs, was a section where each respondent had to name three jobs in his or her company, estimate their rates of pay and discuss the reasons for the pay differentials between them. This interview was carried out with all the employees and most of the personnel managers and union officials. We did not carry out the second stage interview with some personnel managers and union representatives in companies where we were not able to interview employees.

THE FINDINGS

We will examine beliefs about fair pay in relation to economic theories of pay determination and changes in patterns of work which might influence attitudes towards pay. We will look firstly at whether the respondents drew on market forces and other labour market factors to explain and justify pay differentials, and secondly at whether they supported criteria such as performance and flexibility as a basis for pay differentials.

How can we assess whether such beliefs are 'normative'? Most respondents in the study drew on a large number of factors to explain pay differentials. Their arguments were often complex because of the 'dilemmatic' nature of their accounts (Billig, 1987). Most people have a more or less conscious internal debate about what they think and feel. For example, a respondent might begin an argument by attributing pay differentials to levels of skill and end it by blaming them on out-dated traditions about the worth of jobs. Sometimes the respondents attempted to resolve the contradictions,

Table **8.1   Sample Details for Employees**

	Unionised	Non-unionised
Financial services	11	12
Manufacturing/ engineering services	31	15

sometimes they seemed unaware of them. We shall try to assess the normative nature of beliefs by looking at how frequently they were mentioned by each group, but it is important to note that beliefs about pay are characterised by debate rather than conviction.

Before looking at how people explain and judge pay differentials it is important to examine how they perceive pay differentials.

PERCEPTIONS OF PAY DIFFERENTIALS

Although most people have a very accurate perception of the rank order of pay for jobs, their knowledge of what people *actually* get paid is poor (Goldthorpe and Hope (1972), Emler and Dickinson (1985) and Dickinson (1990). When the employees in this study were asked to estimate the pay of some jobs in their organisations, almost all of them made comments like, 'Its a mere guess' and 'Probably miles off with that, I'm just guessing'. They were not usually miles off, but the estimates were very variable. Eight employees in the non-unionised engineering services company who estimated the pay of 'branch administrator' provided estimates from £10,500 to £15,000. Fifteen employees in a unionised engineering company who estimated the pay of 'secretary' provided estimates from £9,000 to £15,500.

In contrast to the employees, the personnel managers and union representatives were much more knowledgeable about rates of pay, although the union officials were only confident of the rates for the people they represented. It is perhaps not surprising that the personnel managers and union representatives are well informed as pay is something that they *do*. Pay is something that *happens* to ordinary employees. Nevertheless, perceptions of the size of differentials are important for understanding judgements of fairness. The relative naiveté of employees may lead them to be more accepting of pay differentials if they assume the size of the differentials to be equitable.

EXPLANATIONS AND JUDGEMENTS OF PAY DIFFERENTIALS

Market Forces

Eighty-seven per cent of the personnel managers, 60 per cent of the union representatives and 38 per cent of the employees mentioned market forces as an influence on pay. Among the latter group, an emphasis on market forces was concentrated among the 15 employees who were also line managers, 11 of whom as against 19 of the 69 who were not cited market forces. There were no significant differences between the two sectors in the study.

The managers and union representatives who mentioned market forces tended to discuss them in quite an extensive way, relating levels of pay to the operation of the labour market and the need to recruit and retain personnel.

For example:

as far as the shop floor is concerned we are much better payers than the rest, because there isn't an awful lot of industry in this area to compare it with now.... certainly in terms of this local industrial area that we're in, there isn't much industry. What there is now is very, very small units that tend to be poor payers, so we really are the only large engineering company left in the local area, I think that's why people stay because the rates are quite good. (Personnel manager, engineering).

Of the 28 per cent of ordinary employees who mentioned market forces, more than half made only a passing reference to the 'going rate' for the job.

No mention of market forces does not imply no understanding of market forces. The term 'going rates' is commonly used though it was notable that it was mainly older and more experienced employees who referred to the 'going rates' in this study. It is more likely that certain explanations for pay differentials are more *salient* for certain groups in the workforce. The labour market is probably more salient for managers and union representatives than for employees for several reasons. They are more likely to be involved in setting budgets for recruiting employees, more likely to use salary surveys and more likely to learn about the labour market in management training or union seminars. Indeed, while all the personnel managers and union officials had used salary surveys, most employees were not aware of their existence.

It is important to note that those involved in fixing pay see pay, at least partly, as the price for labour. However, only one respondent felt that market forces were the predominant cause of pay differentials:

The pay is driven by external market forces – fairness is irrelevant. (Line manager, finance).

Most people talked about market forces as something that forced an occasional adjustment in the rate for the job.

For example:

we haven't got a blank piece of paper, we've already got a set of . . . existing scales and so what exists already, what's common sense with regard to those scales, what are the relative responsibilities of the job and how do they compare with what we've got already. But clearly we don't live in a vacuum either and there's an outside world so when we're creating new jobs or where we're bringing people in then we have to have a mind for market salaries as well. (Personnel manager, engineering).

This kind of argument would seem to support traditional values about the worth of jobs and relegate market forces to a secondary position, though economists would argue that wages eventually adjust to the ruling mechanism of supply and demand for suitable human capital. We will discuss the relationship between beliefs about fair pay and human capital in the next section, but first we will look at what support there was for market forces as a means of setting pay levels.

Nobody singled out market forces as a criterion that should be used to determine pay differentials. Most people saw them as a fact of life and a barometer to be heeded. Three or four employees argued that their companies should pay the going rate when they felt there was a danger some jobs were being paid less than the going rate. Some other employees were resigned to loosing out because they recognised rates of pay were falling. As one employee put it:

there's too many banks on the high street and also too many building societies all selling the same products, and there's not enough jobs and that drives the wages down unfortunately. (Employee, finance).

Most of the personnel managers and union representatives said their organisations kept a close eye on market rates when determining annual pay settlements and rates for new staff. This concern reflected fear of becoming uncompetitive, or losing or failing to recruit good staff, rather than support for market forces as a means of setting pay levels. The following quotation demonstrates how closely some organisations watched their competitors:

I think the other big, big pressure is . . . not being out of line with their competitors and, presumably, if they were to step out of line and pay a payment much higher than the others were doing, I would guess in whatever forum they meet, the others will be pulling them together and saying, 'What the bloody hell are you playing at? Why are you stepping out of line and making life difficult for us?' (Union representative, finance).

The picture presented by the personnel managers and union representatives was that market forces were a mixed blessing for organisations. In so far as companies can stay in line with their competitors, the market is effectively controlled. Pay rates remain fairly stable and employees' expectations of pay are not disrupted. The best of all worlds is achieved when competitors cooperate and most of them try to do so. However, labour markets are frequently and continually disrupted by factors other than competitors breaking ranks. In our sample the organisations suffered from a number of changes which had forced them to adjust their rates of pay in line with new market pressures (for example, the effects of new technology, mergers, increased competition and market deregulation). Perhaps the biggest single impact on pay in the finance sector was market deregulation which had allowed retail companies and building societies to compete with banks and insurance companies and produced the downward pressure on pay described above. Two of the companies in the finance sector had a stated policy of paying the market median and seeking to retain high performing staff by raising their pay with bonuses or performance related pay. They had adopted this strategy to try to curb wage costs.

It is easy to lose control of market forces and suffer the effects of rising or declining rates of pay. The volatility of market rates can also lead to anomalies in organisational pay structures, such as a situation where experienced employees are being paid less than new recruits. The following quotation describes the resulting dilemma:

The problem is with this company and any other big companies, somebody that joins the company 'x' years ago and starts on £16,000 a year, anybody else that joins after that, to get somebody to join, they have to pay them probably more than £16,000 a year, but what they don't do is bring the people that are here up to the same level. . . . That's unfortunate, yes, but from the company's point of view why would they want to hike everybody else's pay up just because they need somebody there to get them at the same level? I don't know. It's difficult. (Line manager, engineering).

In fact this company was taking steps to resolve such anomalies and most of the personnel managers described recent situations where they had raised the pay for a group of people who had fallen behind, usually in response to increased turnover or staff complaints.

Market forces would be less of a problem, of course, if it were not for two major assumptions about pay:

(1) that employees performing at the same level in the same job should receive the same pay, and
(2) that pay never falls (at least in monetary terms). Although no respondents explicitly stated these rules, they were implicit in the discourse of almost all the interviewees.

We will return to these assumptions below.

Given the problems created by market forces and the time and effort required to monitor them, it is perhaps not surprising that most of the nationwide companies in this study were wary of adopting local or regional rates of pay. The one company which did have regional rates, may have been helped by not being unionised and the nature of the business which operated from isolated branches and could draw on a ready supply of technical skills in the external market. The other companies tended only to use local market rates for clerical staff.

Government policy towards pay in the 1980s and 1990s was designed to make pay more responsive to market forces. However, none of the respondents in this study, employers or employees, were particularly welcoming of the impact of market forces on pay.

Equity and Human Capital

All the respondents used criteria such as 'responsibility', 'training', 'hours worked', 'experience', 'value to the company', 'working conditions' and 'skills' to explain pay differentials. These criteria are all dimensions of individual contribution or individual hardship, that is equity criteria. The assumed relationship between these criteria and pay is that greater contribution deserves greater reward and that pay is fair when the ratio of contribution to reward is held stable in the organisation. Equity is usually the crux of judgements of fair pay and most of the interviewees did judge the fairness of pay differentials in terms of whether people were over or under rewarded for their contribution.

Beliefs about equity were often formally built into the reward systems. Eight of the 11 organisations used job evaluation schemes quite extensively.

Each of the groups in the study explained and justified pay differentials in terms of equity, but there was a difference between the employees and the personnel managers and union representatives; the employees' judgements were almost entirely in terms of equity, whereas the personnel managers and union representatives also drew on labour market and pay negotiation arguments.

Some equity criteria fit with human capital theory in economics. If pay reflects investment in education and training, then people should recognise criteria such as 'qualifications', 'training', 'skills' and 'competencies' as a basis for pay differentials. We looked at whether the respondents did explain pay differentials in terms of these criteria. Approximately equal percentages (between 80 and 87 per cent) of the three groups interviewed (employees, personnel managers and union representatives) drew on qualifications, training, skills or competencies to explain the pay differentials in their companies. The percentages in the engineering groups were slightly, but not significantly, higher than those in the finance groups.

Human capital theory appears to form the implicit basis for popular explanation of pay differentials. Are differentials understood in this way seen as fair? High percentages in each group believed that skills, competence, training and education *should* attract a higher salary (employees: 80 per cent; line managers: 67 per cent; personnel managers: 80 per cent; union representatives: 60 per cent – no significant differences between finance and engineering), though sometimes, as the following quotation suggests, the employers had built these criteria into the pay system with some reluctance, in order to meet employee expectations.

We've trained people into it, and of course the pay consequence of that is that people expect more for it and that's been a feature. We have paid more. (Personnel manager, engineering).

It appears that beliefs about fairness support the division of the labour market into a large number of different occupational markets.

Another equity factor which received strong support was 'responsibility'. Eighty-seven to 96 per cent of each group of respondents drew on 'responsibility' to explain pay differentials in their organisations. It was often hard to define precisely what respondents understood by this notion, since the term can refer to the 'size' of the job (in terms of the range of tasks), the importance of the decision making involved or the responsibility for managing people. Consequently 'responsibility' tends to be used as a catch-all phrase to include both authority and the range and number of tasks.

There was clearly a widespread belief that managerial posts should carry more pay, though this was often implicit in what people said. For example:

One of the bugbears, certainly, on managerial pay each year was the problem of overlap – the top of the staff grade and the bottom of the managerial grade – which we've tried to address in claims and the bank has tried to do something about. (Union representative, finance).

Almost all the respondents who estimated and discussed the pay of a managerial or supervisory job felt managerial responsibility deserved more pay. For example:

that's an extra step up the ladder isn't it so that's what some people strive for, so therefore it would be pointless having a supervisor on the same pay 'cos why would you want to do that? (Employee, engineering).

These deeply held assumptions fit with the theory that normative beliefs about pay may help to preserve the authority structure of organisations. The second quotation also reveals the vested interest that many employees have in the organisational hierarchy. Marsden (1983) argued that employees support higher pay for senior posts because of the status attached to them and the opportunities provided by a career ladder. Several personnel managers spoke of the importance of some form of scale or rank order that allowed the employees to see the possibilities for progression. Some opportunity for progression was seen as contributing to employee motivation. The following comment illustrates the dilemma experienced by management when they decided to restructure the grade system:

in addition it took nine years... to get from the bottom to the top. Now there's no way it would take anyone nine years to learn a job, especially a clerical job. We argued, discussed, debated and in many ways I think I would actually have liked two years, but we actually wanted to keep in motivation of some kind. In the end the scheme that we introduced was designed round four years from minimum to maximum. (Personnel manager, finance).

If employees see 'responsibilities' as the main determinant of pay differentials and they desire opportunities for progression, what are the repercussions of changing patterns of work that encourage flexibility, flatter structures and pay based on performance rather than status?

Flexibility and Performance

A lot of management text books have claimed that bureaucracy is dead and successful organisations have fewer levels of hierarchy, more autonomous employees and performance management systems which steer all employees' efforts towards the achievement of company goals. The reality may differ, but 13 of the 15 personnel managers emphasised that their organisations were seeking to encourage and reward flexibility together with performance. We will look first at the impact of flexibility on employees beliefs about pay, and then at the impact of performance related pay. We will not discuss the views of union representatives in this section, because most of the results are broken down by sector and the sample of union representatives is too small for meaningful analysis in this way.

A move toward flexibility in working practices normally means a number of things. firstly, it usually involves restructuring from a large number of different jobs with separate pay scales towards a single salary scale with a small number of grades. Secondly, it sometimes entails a move away from job descriptions with lists of the roles and duties of incumbents to less bureaucratic 'job profiles'. The aim is to create broader, less closely defined jobs and encourage workers to learn different skills and take on different roles. The workforce becomes more flexible since employees can turn their hands to different tasks as required by the company.

The move is in part a response to the rigid demarcation of roles in British industry in the 1970s and 1980s, which was widely regarded as inefficient, and in part a response to the demand for small batch production which benefits from multi-skilled workers who can carry out a variety of tasks. All the engineering and manufacturing companies in this study had moved to a simpler grading structure in the early 1990s or were in the process of negotiating such a change. Four of the six companies (including one in which we interviewed employees) had started to broaden roles and train workers to cover a variety of jobs.

Fifty-five per cent of the personnel managers in engineering, emphasised the importance of achieving and rewarding flexibility. In contrast only 13 per cent of the employees suggested flexibility should be rewarded. This does not mean employees were opposed to flexible working patterns. Indeed, those experiencing the introduction of flexible working arrangements were fairly happy about them. The following quotation demonstrates the benefits perceived by one employee:

> I'm glad that they're doing this training programme and sending us on these courses, I really am.... it's got to benefit you outside work as well as inside work.... I mean the possibility is we might not be here for the rest of our lives, you know we could be at other places, and its going to stand you in good stead anyway, especially if you have to move to other companies.... I think its definitely the right way to go, yes. (Employee, manufacturing).

The two criteria most popularly supported by the employees in engineering were 'competencies' (46 per cent) and 'responsibility' (46 per cent). Sixty-five per cent of employees felt one or both of these criteria should be used to determine pay differentials. In so far as flexibility concerns encouraging employees to gain additional competencies and take on extra responsibilities, employees and personnel managers appear to be in agreement. However, there was an important difference. The employees wanted to be rewarded incrementally for what they were achieving in terms of extra skills and duties, while the managers wanted to move away from the notion of a list of abilities that each carry a price. The following comment illustrates the divergence:

We all feel, well, the majority of people feel, that it's the way that it's going to be going because of the way the world is moving. But. . . . I think the management would like us to take a load on and then get paid for it whereas we'd like to be paid for like every job we take on . . . just to show us that we were actually getting somewhere. A lot of times you get so far and then that's it. You're doing them jobs and not getting paid for it. (Employee, manufacturing).

We will discuss the issue of performance before trying to explain these differences between employees and managers.

Performance related pay usually means that each employee's annual pay increment depends on his or her performance rating. The increment is usually consolidated if it fits within the salary scale, but in some cases over-scale payments are made on a lump sum basis. Although performance related increments usually account for up to ten per cent of base pay and the average increment usually approximates to the rate of inflation, an employee regularly rated as a high performer can end up being paid substantially more than an average performer in the same grade. In our study, two of the finance companies, including one in which we interviewed employees, and the non-unionised engineering company operated this kind of performance related pay system.

Five out of nine personnel managers in engineering (55 per cent) and five out of six personnel managers in finance (83 per cent) felt pay should reflect performance. Thirty-three per cent of the employees in engineering and 61 per cent in finance also supported the measurement of performance, though the comments suggested that those employees with little or no experience of performance pay tended to equate 'performance' with 'competence'. Those with more experience showed stronger support for 'performance'. Employers, especially in the finance sector, appear to have a mandate from their employees for rewarding performance.

However, the most popular criterion for determining pay differentials among employees in the finance sector was 'responsibility', which was supported by 93 per cent of the group. This suggests there is still a strong desire for a clearly structured pay scale. Those employees with experience of performance related pay (usually less than two years) often pointed to the difficulty of measuring performance accurately.

In general, then, it appears that employers would like pay to be based on criteria that feed into company performance, for example flexibility and performance, and that employees are supportive of these criteria in so far as they recognise the need to earn money for the company. Employees would also like their contribution to be recognised in the more concrete and stable terms provided by competencies and responsibilities. It is a rational response for employees to want pay increments to mark the effort they have expended and the range of activities over which they exert control. Business performance does not always follow from employee performance as the following comment illustrates:

> The people had performed very well but the company hadn't because of the Yen and the Deutschmark, you know. (Union representative, engineering).

However, it is also a rational response for employers to say:

> In an ideal world I'd like to be able to reward these people for the contribution that they put in, but if we're not making the right money then we just can't do it. (Personnel manager, engineering).

CONCLUSIONS

In summary, we found little support for market forces as a means of determining pay differentials. Employers in the primary labour market would rather try to control market forces than respond to them. When they are unable to control them, they will try to adjust to market rates. We found that almost everyone supported fairness criteria and that human capital theory is strongly supported by employees' beliefs about equity. The desire of employees to see a return for their investment in training made them reluctant to support criteria such as flexibility. Finally, performance based pay was endorsed at the theoretical level even if the approach was not fully supported in practice.

Groups within organisations clearly use pay criteria as means to justify policies that serve their own ends. There are obvious reasons why it is in the interests of managers to relate pay to what the company can and cannot afford and in the interests of employees to relate pay to what they deserve. The interesting thing is that managers also talk about what employees deserve. There is a widespread belief that effort invested in learning new skills or taking on additional responsibilities deserves to be rewarded. Consequently beliefs about fair pay have a major influence on pay determination because both sides in the workforce are striving to reward people for their contributions in a fair manner.

The belief that effort should be rewarded is widespread, but three beliefs – employees performing at the same level in the same job should be equally rewarded, pay should never fall and higher positions in the authority structure deserve higher pay – are so strongly entrenched as norms that they probably count as basic assumptions about pay. These embedded assumptions mean that when companies try to restructure their working arrangements, there is almost always a time lag before salaries can adjust to the new practices. Several personnel managers said that even though they had moved from a system of several dozen jobs with different pay structures to a small number of grades, the grades currently contained a lot of rates to protect the employees' previous salaries.

This study is concerned with organisations in the primary labour market. Dore (1994) argued that such organisations operate like 'communities' in which the employees are stakeholders just as much as the managers and shareholders. Consequently all arguments surrounding pay revolve around notions of fairness. In comparison, he argues that secondary labour market employees, being low skilled and easily replaceable, can be treated with much less sensitivity and without appeals to fairness. Our findings support Dore's arguments and we would also speculate that the stability of primary sector organisations depends in part on their perceived integrity and that as a result they need to develop relationships with their employees which are based on trust.

This chapter shows the contributions that social psychology can make to a better understanding of the ideology of pay determination. Recent government pay policies have neglected that contribution.

9 Morals and Markets: Some Theoretical and Policy Implications of Ethical Investing

Alan Lewis, Paul Webley, Adrian Winnett and Craig Mackenzie

INTRODUCTION: ETHICS, MARKET AND POLICY

Margaret Thatcher was fond of retelling the parable of the Good Samaritan. In her version the main point was not only that the Good Samaritan was shown to be putting into practice neighbourly concern, but also that he had the money so to do. By implication, a government prepared to restrain public expenditure and reduce taxation is handing moral responsibility for the provision of welfare back to individuals. With a reduced tax burden, the government can be seen as empowering people to put their money where their morals are, which they may exhibit by giving to charity and making provision, through private insurance and savings schemes, for schooling, future health needs, and retirement.

Recent governments of both parties have taken the view that a large welfare state breeds dependency, where people look to the state to put things right rather than taking the appropriate actions themselves. Mrs Thatcher used statistical evidence to back her claim that, during her period of office and as a consequence of the fiscal policies of the Conservative government, charitable giving in the United Kingdom (a measure of individual moral action) was greater than ever before; although this claim has been contested (Jones, Cullis and Lewis, in press). The morality of individual financial responsibility can also be related to the rise of the ethical investment movement: the claim is that people do not want to make money at any moral cost, but would prefer to invest in ways that are ethically acceptable.

The notion of 'individualism' can be interpreted from two perspectives. The first implies that it is morally right for governments to return moral and financial responsibility to individuals on the grounds that this enlarges the scope for individual morality. Big government crowds out individual moral responsibility. The alternative argument is that a government which reduces spending on health and education is itself failing to take moral responsibility. Far from empowering individual moral responsibility, it encourages instead the worst kind of 'individualism' where people care only for themselves and have little notion of 'social' or 'civic' responsibility.

The positive perspective on individualism implies that governments should not intervene in questions of business ethics and that companies will ultimately stand or fall depending on their competitive ability to satisfy consumer demand. If consumers do not want to buy cosmetics tested on animals, or invest in companies which pollute the environment or employ child labour, then they will choose not to buy these products and not to invest in those companies, and the market will respond accordingly. The central idea is that the choices that consumers make can influence the development of the economy: responsibility lies with individual purchasers and investors, not solely with governments.

Ethical investment is the practice of investing in companies which pass a series of 'negative' ethical criteria and satisfy positive ones. This raises a number of questions. Do people believe that by investing ethically they can contribute to making a better world? How do they think people can do it? Are they prepared to take a financial loss in order to do so? Are they investing ethically because they believe that they should take up the regulatory slack, now that the 'nanny state' has withdrawn? Can ethical investment be expected to make a practical contribution by, for example, lobbying for reform of corporate practice, or does it serve merely to satisfy the consciences of investors?

The topic of ethical investing also provides a useful case study which may contribute to the continuing debate between socioeconomics and economic psychology on the one hand and mainstream neo-classical economics on the other (Hollis and Nell, 1975: Marr and Raj, 1983; Earl, 1983; Lewis, Webley and Furnham, 1995). Economists tend to prefer a deductive methodology, offering parsimonious explanations for aggregated economic changes and employing 'objective' economic variables. They offer accounts of economic changes which do not refer to the attitudes, beliefs and moral commitments of individuals (often lumped together in economic-speak as 'preferences'). Consequently, economic models are constructed as if the mental world of economic actors (apart from assumptions about self interest and related factors) mattered not at all. The case of ethical investing poses an interesting challenge to neoclassical economic explanation, since the question arises of whether such behaviour can be understood without recourse to mental states.

ETHICAL INVESTMENT: THE SELLERS

The Evolution and Structure of the UK Ethical Investment Industry

Ethical investment is a venerable idea, dating back as far as the ethical prohibitions on usury established by Jewish law in biblical times. Ethical investment in the form it is practised today can be dated to the 19th century when a number of Church organisations adopted ethical prohibitions on certain kinds of investment: 'sin stocks' included companies involved in alcohol and gambling. In the US, the Pioneer Fund, which deliberately screened investments on ethical grounds, was set up in 1928 (Harrington, 1992, p.6). In the UK, the Commissioners of the Church of England had been operating an ethical policy since 1948, but it was not until the late 1960s that discussion began about establishing ethical unit trusts. In 1984 'Stewardship' was launched by Friends Provident, a large mutually owned life insurance company, set up in the 1830s by Quakers.

Against expectations and despite some disdain from the City, Stewardship rapidly grew into a substantial fund. There are now three Stewardship unit trusts, and a Stewardship pension fund. The Stewardship funds together total around £710 million and dominate the ethical unit trust market in the UK. They have come to play a central role in Friends Provident, where they are among the largest single funds it manages. Since 1984 about 30 additional ethical unit trusts have been set up in the UK, managed by some 20 mainstream financial institutions. Collectively these funds have approaching 150,000 investors and £1.3 billion of funds under management. An important subset of the ethical unit trusts are the eight or so 'green' funds which concentrate less on ethical issues, and more on environmental concerns. Ethical unit trusts offer reasonably competitive financial performance. Some of the leading ethical funds, have over the years produced returns in the top half, and even the top quartile, of their unit trust sectors. Other ethical funds have performed poorly, but a spread of performance is typical of any sector in the unit trust market. It is now possible to buy a wide range of financial products by means of ethical unit trusts, including savings plans, personal equity plans, life and health insurance, endowment mortgages, and pensions.

While the ethical unit trusts get the most coverage in the media, they are not the only or even the largest forms of ethical investment in the UK. The biggest ethical funds in the UK are institutional ethically screened funds. The largest of these is managed by the Church Commissioners of the Church of England which manages over £2 billion of equity investment. Each of these institutions has its own ethical policy which, like the ethical unit trusts, screens out companies regarded as unethical. A number of charitable trusts, with combined assets of perhaps £6 billion (Sparkes, 1995, p. 179) have also adopted ethical policies. One cancer research charity was recently shamed into adopting such a policy when it was revealed in the press that it held shares in a tobacco company. In addition, the Co-operative Bank, with assets which exceed £3 billion, has adopted an ethical policy which debars it from doing business with companies regarded as unethical. A number of local authority pension funds, including those managed for Nottingham, Berkshire, Lothian, Lincolnshire, Merseyside, and Hampshire, are adopting ethical or environmental policies for at least part of their investments. Several institutional investment funds regularly join together to take shareholder action on issues such as director's pay and corporate governance more generally. Most of these retain the services of PIRC (Pension Investment Research Consultants), a consultancy on governance and shareholder activism.

These are the largest ethical funds, but they are not necessarily the ones which have the strongest impact. There are a number of far smaller 'alternative' ethical funds which direct their resources to support projects which are expected to have special social or environmental impact. 'Shared Interest', for example, is an industrial and provident society based in Newcastle with £10 million of assets which it lends at favourable rates to small, environmentally sustainable ventures in third world countries. It also provides finance to fair trade organisations such as Traidcraft. It currently pays two per cent interest to its depositors, though many depositors choose to waive their interest altogether. 'Triodos' is an ethical bank with branches in the Netherlands, Belgium and the UK and £110 million of assets. It lends to a wide range of socially and environmentally beneficial projects.

Ethical unit trust investment in the UK is still in its infancy. It accounts for about 0.1 per cent of the total money invested in the London Stock Exchange. However, ethical unit trusts are growing faster than most sectors of investment. For some time there has been debate about the legal position of trustees of charity and pension funds who adopt ethical policies. The law requires such trustees to seek the best interests of their beneficiaries, which has traditionally been interpreted in exclusively financial terms. While the legal position has not yet been clarified, ethical investment is achieving greater legitimacy. It is possible that substantial institutional funds may come under ethical management in the next few years.

The central concern of our research is with retail ethical unit trusts. We move on to consider in more detail how these funds operate.

Screening and Authenticity

Ethical unit trusts are in most respects identical to ordinary unit trusts. They pool the money of a large number of small investors in order to invest in stock market listed companies. Every unit trust has an investment policy which states its aims and limitations: growth or income, UK or international, general investment or sector specific. Ethical funds have these policies too. Most of them are general UK Growth funds but ethical funds are different in that they also have an ethical policy which limits their investment to an 'acceptable list' of companies which pass various negative and positive screening criteria. For example a negative criterion might commit an ethical fund to avoid investment in companies involved in the manufacture of armaments, and positive criteria typically commit ethical funds to investment in companies making a strong positive contribution to environmental improvement. Typical negative criteria areas include alcohol, animal welfare, armaments, gambling, human rights, pornography, tobacco and various kinds of pollution and environmental destruction. Typical positive criteria include involvement in providing 'basic necessities,' environmental sustainability, and progressive employment and community involvement policies. While the marketing material of ethical funds often emphasises the positive, the negative criteria have the most influence on the ultimate shape of the portfolio. Seventeen of the 27 ethical funds that have their own ethical policies use the screening services of EIRIS (Ethical Investment Research and Information Service), and consequently base their screening criteria on those available from this service. The EIRIS screening service is based on a large and sophisticated database of objective and uniform information on some 1,100 UK companies. Consequently when these funds claim that they do not invest in companies which manufacture armaments, they can be sure of considerable accuracy. The same can perhaps not be said of some of the funds which do not use EIRIS. However, sometimes precision can be sacrificed for subtlety: Jupiter Ecology for example employs a knowledgeable in-house research team which does its own more subjective but more holistic and personal research on corporate environmental practice.

THE BUYERS

How visible are ethical investments and how are they viewed by investors? Are ethical investors special people? Empirical information is available from structured surveys, qualitative interviews and simulation experiments, to which we have contributed.

The Survey Evidence

Two national sample surveys have been carried out recently, both with samples of 1,000 adults. One was conducted by National Opinion Polls (1995) for Friends Provident and one by Gallup (1995) for NPI. The NOP poll showed that approximately 20 per cent of respondents were aware of ethical investment, an awareness which was highest among middle aged professional males. The most familiar ethical funds were those offered by the Co-operative Bank (63 per cent), followed by Friends Provident (44 per cent) and NPI (also 44 per cent). For both the Gallup and NOP samples 'environmental concerns' were those most mentioned as relevant to investment decisions, followed by concern for the unnecessary exploitation of animals, employee welfare and trade with oppressive regimes (Gallup).

From the NOP sample the most popularly endorsed statements explaining respondents financial behaviour were: 'I would like to make a profit without anyone getting hurt in the process' (a mean of 3.7 agreement on a 4-point scale) and 'I want my investment to benefit companies which are helping rather than harming the world' (also 3.7).

These surveys and from further work by Mintel (1996) are useful but the findings are limited to a general population sample. It is unclear how many of those interviewed were ethical investors, or indeed investors at all. A study which collected information from 1146 ethical investors reported by Lewis and Mackenzie (1997) casts light on the views of those who were actively involved in investment choices. The results show that the majority of ethical investors perceive ethical investing as no more risky than other investments (57.9 per cent), with a similar number considering them more risky (18.3 per cent) as less so (18.8 per cent). Forty one per cent believed that ethical investments produced a slightly lower rate of return than ordinary investment funds in the long term, while 40.8 per cent thought the return was similar.

The survey also indicated that many investors are prepared to forego financial return in order to invest according to ethical principles. Eighty-one per cent said they would retain their ethical investment if the average annual return over five years was eight per cent for ethical funds and 10 per cent for 'ordinary' unit trusts; and 56.5 per cent said they would retain their ethical investment when the returns were five per cent and 10 per cent respectively. In this latter case 24.9 per cent would reduce their ethical investments.

The results are not directly comparable with those from an earlier study by to Lewis and Webley (1994) who asked investors how they would invest a one thousand pounds sterling windfall but it does suggest that the behaviour of ethical investors is relatively inelastic for losses and elastic for gains. In the Lewis and Webley (1994) study over 50 per cent of non-ethical investors chose to reduce their hypothetical ethical investments when the return on ordinary investments was ten per cent compared with eight per cent for ethical investments. In the Lewis and Mackenzie study which focused on real-life ethical investors only 5.2 per cent would reduce their ethical investments when the differential in return between different investments stood at this level.

The ethical investors interviewed were more likely to work in education or health related occupations compared with the general population. Over two-fifths were regular Guardian readers and much more likely to be members of the Labour and Liberal Democratic party than any other. This sample of ethical investors like others were often active participants in The National Trust, Amnesty International, Oxfam, Friends of the Earth and Greenpeace.

Qualitative Interviews

Twenty ethical investors were interviewed by telephone as part of the research project (for full details see Mackenzie and Lewis, 1998). Ten of these were investors in Shared Interest and ten others were users of EIRIS. Members from Shared Interest (SI) were selected as they are at the 'alternative end' of ethical investment. SI has the legal structure of a co-operative lending society, lending the bulk of its money to small, co-operative commercial projects in the Third World and currently pays its investors an interest rate of only two per cent. Users of EIRIS on the other hand are more likely to see themselves as mainstream investors and to expect a competitive financial return.

The study investigated investors' motives, how they integrated moral purposes with financial goals and how they resolved conflicts between different motives. Analysis of the responses showed that the trade-off between financial motives and ethics is complex and depends on whether the money is variously classified in investors 'mental accounts' as 'essential' or 'surplus' money.

> Many investors seem to have a certain core amount of money which they consider to be essential to their financial requirements, and an amount of money which was surplus to these requirements. Money was considered essential for a number of reasons – for retirement income, to bequeath to children. While a small amount of return on the core money could be traded off for ethics, this money must produce a reasonable return. The money considered to be surplus can be traded-off for ethics quite aggressively. Indeed, some investors claimed that they would find losing it altogether to be acceptable. (Mackenzie and Lewis, 1998)

Investors appear to have a portfolio attitude to ethics which fits with their portfolio approach to investment. It was common for investors to invest both ethically and relatively unethically at the same time justifying this by their need to provide for their essential financial requirements (in the latter case) or by an argument that the unethical investments were inherited and therefore the ownership (and guilt) was in some way not their own.

These findings conflict with conventional rational choice theory.

> While ethical investors were prepared to trade-off ethics for financial return, they did not appear to be maximising their financial return or their ethics for that matter. Instead they seemed to be accepting the hand of fate, adopting haphazard rules of thumb, and making satisficing accommodations with their consciences. (Mackenzie and Lewis, 1998).

Simulating Decisions

As well as the interview and survey evidence experimental approaches can be useful. Experiments (in this context often called games, simulations or role-plays) are particularly useful in untangling causal relationships and, since artificial environments are rather easier to manipulate than real-life situations, we can study private behaviour that ordinarily we cannot observe. Artificiality is, of course, a problem as well as a bonus, and one needs to ensure that participants are involved and take simulations seriously.

Investment has been investigated experimentally in the past: good examples are Andreassen's (1987) use of a simulated market to explore, among other things, the use of the 'representativeness heuristic' to estimate the future price of a stock, De Bondt's (1993) study of stock price forecasts and Lundberg's (1995) use of a multimedia experimental futures market to explore dynamic decision making. Similar approaches have been applied to the study of ethical investment. Webley (1992) and Lewis and Webley (1994) for example, report on a study in which students role-played (on a computer) the management of a portfolio of investments over an eighteen month period. Participants were required to invest £40,000 in unit trusts, one of which was an ethical trust. They were randomly allocated to one of three groups: ethical high, ethical average and ethical low, where the financial performance of the ethical trust reflected its name. After the simulation, participants completed a questionnaire which included a 'green' attitude scale. The results showed that those high on the green scale invested more in ethical trusts and good financial performance of ethical trusts was associated with more investment, but there was no significant interaction between green attitudes and trust performance.

We have carried out other (unpublished) studies of this type. However the problem with these approaches is that, for the most part, they have used non-investors (students or members of the general public) as participants, and they are all simulations of trading on the stock market. It is clear that most real individual investors in shares and trusts do not actively trade. Rather they take a single investment decision (after having, for example, inherited some money) and tend to maintain their portfolio unchanged for long periods. This suggests that a quite different type of simulation or role-play is required, one where the situation being simulated is not trading on the market but a consultation with a financial advisor. This changes the emphasis somewhat. In a trading-style experiment the participant focuses on the financial performance of his or her portfolio and the explicit or implicit aim is to maximise the financial outcome. In our current work, the aim of the participant is to provide accurate information to the advisor about his or her preferences and attitudes so as to receive helpful advice.

To date one exploratory study has been completed and another larger scale study is currently being carried out. In both of these studies participants took part in a role-play of a consultation with a 'virtual' financial advisor. This was set up on the World Wide Web. Participants use the *Netscape* browser to provide financial and other information to the financial advisor. In the exploratory study, the twenty participants were asked to imagine that they had been left £5,000 which they were required to invest for five years. They were asked about their marital status, political affiliation, income, amount of savings and completed an 'ethical' attitude scale. They were then presented with pairs of investment choices where the rate of return on an ethical unit trust was fixed and the return on a standard unit trust varied. For some pairs information on the returns was presented in cash terms, for others in terms of percentages. We found that participants were more willing to sacrifice financial return in order to invest ethically when the return was framed in percentage terms than in cash.

THEORETICAL IMPLICATIONS (RATIONALITY AND MORALITY)

Economic Models

Can conventional economic models cope with ethical investing? Analysis of how a portfolio of assets is selected can be viewed as a particular application of the general economic theory of choice under risk. Both the general theory and the particular application have been extensively developed and tested with a high level of technical sophistication. However, some fundamental issues remain unresolved. The decision to consider ethical objectives alongside financial return and risk adds more complexity to the model. Some of the ways in which this complexity can be introduced have been considered in more general attempts to discuss the relationship between economic decisions and ethical beliefs, but there has been little attempt to relate this explicitly to financial decision-making. The pursuit of ethical objectives also highlights certain issues which have arisen in the general discussion of financial decision-making, especially the apparent failure of at least some kinds of rationality in many financial decisions. Thus we need to consider two areas: ways in which ethical beliefs have been introduced into the theory of choice and attempts to model 'irrationality' in financial decision-making, since a proper understanding of (and also much of the interest in) the decisions of ethical investors requires us to consider how these factors interact. In both respects, the development of richer, psychologically-based accounts of economic decision-making has been influential. Further, this goes beyond simply considering individual (or institutional) decision-making: if investors really are making decisions which are unlike those described in the mainstream economics literature, then this may influence market outcomes. There is an important interaction here, since market outcomes partly define the sorts of constraints under which decision makers can expect to operate: the market offers feasible mixes of risk and return to investors.

One interpretation of ethical investment is that investors may be prepared to choose lower return for given risk, that is they are 'inefficient' investors in usual market terms. However we know that many or even most investors, not just ethical investors, are inefficient in this sense. It may be that the behaviour of ethical investors simply illustrates a more general kind of 'irrationality', but one that in their case is justified by drawing on distinctively ethical rationalisations, or there may be some interaction between these factors. Again, this may modify market outcomes, and one reason for this may therefore be the ethical beliefs held by investors (Thaler, 1993).

Two approaches to understanding the possible behaviour of ethical investors are relevant. One is concerned with the way in which preferences may be partly structured by ethical considerations and the other with the influence of context on decisions. In terms of the standard economic model of individual decision-making, the first may be thought of as highlighting complications to the objective function held by the decision-maker and the second as focusing on the constraints faced by the decision-maker. Most discussions of 'ethical preferences' have been concerned with reconciling either individual's selfish and altruistic motives or, more broadly, self- and other-directed actions. Probably the most favoured model, and certainly the one which most clearly bridges the economic and psychological approaches to decision-making, is that of the multiple self (Margolis, 1982). At its most simple, this involves dual selves, selfish and altruistic, with either some rule for adjudicating conflicts at the margin or some meta-self which establishes preferences over preferences.

Some ethical investment activity seems to be readily interpretable in these terms. Where there is a clear readiness to sacrifice return, we can ask 'how much?'. However some behaviour does not fit the model. Simple trade-offs may not be apparent: we may find that people hold predetermined proportions of ethical and other investments irrespective of return or they may use lack of return as itself an index of the ethical quality of the investment. It is possible to rationalise such behaviour by incorporating features such as transaction and information costs, respectively, but such emendations undermine the simplicity of the original theory.

Closely related to altruistic and selfish selves, are short-sighted, temptation driven selves and long-sighted, responsible selves (Shefrin and Thaler, 1988). Again, some ethical investment activity is interpretable in these terms, particularly that which invokes environmental concerns. Here the individual trades-off present returns against future returns, or against less future risk, or some composite of these and altruism. If the longer-lived self includes the interests of descendants, this becomes altruistic, and can be developed into the full-blown model of intergenerational altruism widely used in discussions of the possibility of sustainable development. There is, of course, an abiding suspicion that such multiple self models are essentially uninformative, and the proliferation of such selves to account for all sorts of apparently inconsistent behaviour lends weight to this view.

It is now widely understood that decisions are not independent of the context within which they are made: they are framed. There are a number of ways in which framing can influence financial decision-making. Perhaps the most important is the tendency of investors not to treat their wealth as fully fungible (interchangeable between different uses), and to apply different criteria in terms of, say, return, risk, and 'ethicalness' to different components of their wealth. The question is then to establish how these 'mental accounts, which regulate fungibility, are set up, and we should again be alert to the emptying of content which occurs if mental accounts proliferate to handle all kinds of apparent inconsistency. Possibilities include a reluctance to liquidate existing assets, a *status quo* effect which overvalues what we already hold, and the differential treatment of windfalls, and, more generally, of 'spare cash' (somehow defined). These factors can be combined, for example, in an inheritance. It may be that a lower return can be contemplated for windfalls, making them particularly eligible for ethical investment. An intriguing possibility is that ethical criteria can themselves contribute to the construction of mental accounts, rather than ethical investment simply tapping into already defined accounts: consider for example the duty imposed by inheriting certain kinds of assets, or, more generally, the notion of an inheritance being something 'passed on' which chimes particularly well with the emphasis on long term responsibility in much ethical investment promotion.

'Popular Models' and Social Representations

The introduction of concepts like the 'multiple self' and 'mental accounting' arguably makes economic theory richer and more realistic, but it is quite possible to take a much more radical view than this, drawing on contemporary themes in psychology and sociology relating to discourse, rhetoric, social representations and 'lay' explanations (McCloskey, 1986; Klamer, 1984; Lewis, Webley & Furnham, 1995; Evans, 1996). From this point of view economic models can be seen as just another kind of discourse about how markets work, a discourse which is not necessarily superior or inferior to other discourses and explanations. Explanations can be seen as competing with one another where the 'winning' explanations are not necessarily the ones with the greatest 'truth content' but the ones which are currently most persuasive to powerful elites (such as politicians and policy makers) or are the models currently held as being 'common-sense', what every 'reasonable' person would adhere to. The processes whereby elite or technical explanations become enculturated is of particular interest to 'social representation' researchers (for example Moscovici, 1984; Lewis, 1990) as is the analysis of how these representations are shared and the functions that they serve. 'Popular' economic models (which are, in part, versions of more technical ones) may therefore be the driving force behind economic decisions, including investment decisions, and could determine market outcomes.

One way of exploring these 'popular' models in the context of ethical investing is through a reading of the promotional material of the financial services industry and the financial press, publicity for ethical investment and also from less conventional sources, including charities, and political and religious organisations. The ethical financial industry is increasingly using the latter to promote its products, hoping to reach potential investors who have not hitherto had much sophisticated financial involvement. Some of these tactics have themselves prompted criticism of the commercial ethics of some ethical investment providers. We here focus on the coverage in the financial press, drawing on a detailed examination of the personal finance pages of the Sunday broadsheets (Winnett and Lewis, 1997). Compared to the size of the ethical investment market, the press coverage is quite extensive and is increasing.

The extent of the coverage partly reflects the novelty value of ethical investment and partly, also, the linkage to mainstream news stories of political repression, environmental catastrophe, and so on. Nearly all the substantial articles develop a few common themes, which enable us to build up a composite picture. This is of some interest, since ethical investment throws into sharp relief certain assumptions which are widely held by financial commentators and presumably by their readers. These assumptions constitute what might be called the popular model of financial markets: some of the claims made by proponents of ethical investment show these assumptions at work in a very clear way.

If ethical investments are authentic, this raises the possibility of conflict with more conventional financial objectives. These are typically resolved in one or more of three somewhat inconsistent ways: to recognise that there can be a trade-off between return and ethics, and to provide the information for a proper choice; to use performance data to show there is no trade-off; or to say that there is no trade-off in the long-run. Each of these exposes certain common assumptions of the popular model: the first often relies on the alleged restriction of portfolio choice as a depressant of returns, not recognising the relatively small range of assets necessary to achieve reasonably efficient diversification; the second tends to invoke a 'spot-the-winners' argument, either from simple extrapolation of past performance (which for *some* ethical investments has been good) or from claims that ethical investment providers have particularly keen insight into the way the world is going; the last is also a component of the long-term success argument.

This final argument fades into a more generalised play on the connotations of words such as 'long-term' and 'responsible'. Given the rather obvious lack of these virtues in much of the financial services industry, it is easy to portray ethical investment as financially as well as socially responsible. In some ways the most revealing comments are those which invoke the 'share boycott' argument. These commonly imply that in some sense selling or even refusing to buy existing shares is a denial of funds to the firm or firms targeted, or that buying or even holding shares is a provision of funds. These are clearly descriptions of how people interpret the morality of their individual financial decisions and they then believe these translate into market efficacy. Of such personifications of the market are economic metaphors made.

POLICY IMPLICATIONS: CAN ETHICAL INVESTMENT MAKE A DIFFERENCE?

Much of the growth of ethical investment products is based on attempts to tailor products to particular moral concerns. This is characteristic of the 'clean hands' approach to ethical investment, enabling individual investors to avoid investments which are linked to particular kinds of harm, such as tobacco or armaments. The question arises of whether ethical investment can have a further impact and lead firms to reduce the harm they cause or to promote positive goods. The view that it can involves a more contentious assertion in terms of both moral justification and practical efficacy. While the former claim is limited to matters of individual conscience, the latter involves an agenda for social morality and is thus more likely to conflict with some interpretations of the restricted (or non-existent) moral code of the market. Its efficacy is also debatable. In some respects it can be seen as an attempt to persuade investors that they can influence the outcomes of their investments, and not simply be passive recipients of the market effects of corporate decisions. This is clear in some 'alternative' investments, where investors are able to support projects with social or environmental merit directly, and more generally, where funds are only invested in particular ventures, especially those which might have difficulties raising finance from the usual sources. However in a more conventional financial market context, this 'connectedness' is more improbable.

The easiest way to achieve connectedness in conventional financial markets is through shareholder activism and more subtle forms of corporate lobbying (Mackenzie, 1997). Such an approach could even justify involvement in highly 'unethical' firms in order to reform them, although most providers of ethical investment are committed to avoiding unethical investment. The key belief is that connectedness may be achieved through the response of financial markets to the decisions of committed groups of investors to hold or not to hold particular investments. This approach is often justified by analogy with the efficacy of consumer boycotts of particular products, some of which have been financial products like bank deposits. In a stock market context and even with ethical investment on a very much larger scale than at present seems conceivable, this view is sharply at odds with most accepted views of how the market prices shares. With even limited market efficiency, the effects of 'share boycotts' or the converse would be rapidly arbitraged away and would be of no concern to the firm affected. There may, however, be more tenuous effects: firms may view ethical investors as having longer time horizons or as having political knowledge or influence, and thus as signalling appropriate corporate strategies; and investment analysts might take a lead from green funds with regard to identifying companies with potential environmental liabilities (Cullis, Lewis and Winnett, 1992).

There are questions as to whether ethical funds are appropriate agents for corporate reform. Many of them are owned by big financial services companies (one of which, incidentally, is owned by BAT, the large tobacco company). Most of them manage other non-ethical funds which invest in all the companies which their ethical funds avoid. While no doubt there are ethical motives which play a role in these companies, it seems plausible that their commitment to ethical investment is at least as much an attempt to exploit a particular niche market in the unit trust sector, as it is to promote more ethical business practice. This may not matter. One might think that as long as the ethical funds offer a good ethical service, then it does not matter what the actual ethical convictions of the

fund managers are. There are some doubts as to whether many of
the ethical funds are prepared to provide the financial resources
to pay for the expertise necessary to engage intelligently in the
attempt to change the policies of corporations. However, NPI Global Care, Friends Provident Stewardship and one or two other funds
stand as a counter example to this, and perhaps if the consumers
of ethical investment come to reward this approach it may gain
the resources it needs to in order to be an effective vehicle for
corporate reform (Mackenzie, 1997).

CONCLUSIONS

Ethical (and green) investing is growing rapidly. More and more
people now consider that ethical concerns need to be taken into
account when making financial decisions, even if they do not usually
rank as highly as financial ones. There is also an increasing likelihood that Independent Financial Advisors will mention them, and
even among 'hard-nosed' city analysts the younger ones at least
believe these issues are not going to go away or wax and wane like
preferences for flared trousers. Ethical investors cannot be dismissed
as cranks, they wish to satisfy both the demands of financial return
and of principle. To achieve this they make moral compromises
instead, neither trying to maximise their wealth nor their ethics.
Such satisficing or more generally compromising behaviour can have
market consequences, as long as it is sophisticated and widespread
enough to influence the culture of individual companies, or of
financial markets as a whole. While morality and finance may be
uncomfortable partners it is clear that certain aspects of moral
conduct are essential for markets to run smoothly. These include
such norms of behaviour as trust, fairness and reciprocity. The
question arises of whether other moral concerns may also play a
part. The answer may be that trust and fairness can have financial
advantages but other ethical considerations do not. However, the
excellent financial performance of some of the ethical funds indicate that ethical business might be good business.

   In general terms ethical investing is unlikely to cause mainstream
economists much trepidation as one can simply say that there has
been some change in preferences which may affect the prices of
some stocks and shares in the short term but will soon pass as
other investors with a different set of preferences (or fewer scruples

– whichever the reader prefers) will realise that these same stocks and shares are under-valued and snap them up. This however presupposes that the 'culture' of the market remains unchanged and that the actions and preferences of 'unethical' investors are unaffected by the actions and preferences of ethical investors. We believe that ethical and green investing is more than a fad and reflects a persistent change in values which can no longer be ignored even if the same views are not shared by all. In many parts of the USA and sections of the UK as well it is no longer appropriate to smoke in restaurants and public places even though one may still wish to smoke. Other people's preferences matter. One can imagine circumstances where one might wish to pick up under-valued unethical shares but that one might not do so because of the implicit and explicit disapproval of important others.

One can see however that ethical preferences can be incorporated in a utility function as some kind of 'psychological' gain which is the mirror image of any opportunity costs. Nevertheless if these persist and have market consequences the explanations of economists are merely *ex post*. If nothing else, economic psychology should concentrate on identifying persistent value shifts that can be separated from fads and fashion as well as making it clear that economic explanations, whether mainstream or not, are themselves influenced by changes in beliefs about how the world (including markets) works.

If, as we believe, ethical investment is here to stay, it raises interesting questions for policy making, and in particular for the question of whether companies should be regulated by the state or by their shareholders. In the 1840s when the legal idea of the limited liability company was established, the core assumption was that companies should be regulated by their shareholders, rather than the state (Mackenzie, 1993, p. 50). It was assumed that shareholders, as owners and recipients of dividends, would ensure for themselves that companies were well run, and acting in a responsible way. However, in the intervening 150 years companies have grown very large, and shareholdings have become highly fragmented. This has happened to the extent that arguably they can no longer do their regulatory job – particularly in the light of the scandals concerning the Maxwell Corporation, Polly Peck, BCCI and others.

Can ethical investment come to the rescue? In the US, where ethical investment is older and larger, activism on corporate governance, ethical and environmental issues is widespread and is increasingly effective. Each year various investor groups table several hundred governance and social responsibility resolutions at the AGMs of major corporations. Many of the organisations promoting activist agendas are large institutional investors with many billions of dollars in assets. While these rarely win a majority of votes, companies often change their practices in line with the resolution. If ethical investment in the UK continues to grow at a rapid rate among consumer and institutional investors, and if it can move from the idea of avoidance and share boycotting to that of effective corporate lobbying, it could contribute to significant corporate reform and so demonstrate that voluntary private action can reduce the need for public legislation.

10 Benefit Fraud and Citizenship

Hartley Dean

To commit fraud is to exercise an illicit choice. Nobody openly approves of fraud, and yet between 75 and 92 per cent of us may regularly add to our incomes in ways which are, strictly speaking, illegal (Mars, 1994, p. 1). That fraud by state welfare recipients seems to be regarded as a rather particular problem reflects perhaps, not so much moral concern, as political disquiet: in Britain it has lately become as much an issue for the Labour Party (*Guardian* 11.6.96) as it has been a preoccupation of Conservative governments throughout the 1980s and '90s (see Golding and Middleton, 1982; Smith, 1985; Deacon and Fairfoot, 1994; Sainsbury, 1996). Although the issues may be differently conceived, the disquiet which is shared across the political spectrum stems from common assumptions about the rationality of benefit recipients on the one hand, and about the changing nature of economic opportunities on the other. The concern is that people may choose to live by defrauding the benefit system at a time when labour markets are demanding greater flexibility and competitiveness.

It is a concern which speaks to several of the themes that run through this book. This particular chapter begins by considering the changing political context in which citizens of a welfare state must exercise economic choices. It then describes a study which has employed qualitative methods to investigate, not only the attitudes expressed by individuals who engage in benefit fraud, but also the underlying discourses on which they draw to explain their economic choices. It will be seen that the findings from the study demonstrate, among other things, that the choices which fraudulent claimants make do not necessarily depend on full and accurate information about benefit rules and entitlements; that they reflect claimants' substantive experiences of having restricted or uncongenial choices; and that they are often informed by a sense that the benefit system is unfair and has betrayed those whom it should protect. The chapter will also discuss the different strategies which different claimants seem to adopt in order to contend

183

with uncertainty and risk and the social context from which claimants' values and their expectations of citizenship are drawn. Finally, in this chapter, I shall return to the question of the political context in order tentatively to consider the policy implications of the study.

FRAUD IN THE CONTEXT OF A CHANGING WELFARE STATE

Jessop (1994) has argued that we may be witnessing a process of transition from a Keynesian Welfare State (KWS) to a Schumpeterian Workfare State (SWS) (see the discussion by Taylor-Gooby in chapter 1). The KWS was characterised by a commitment to full employment, social welfare and the management of aggregate demand. The SWS is characterised by a commitment to market opportunity, popular capitalism and supply-side management. This describes the contrast between the policies of British governments in the 1940s with those pursued in the 1980s. As Whiteside puts it, 'Whereas the former aimed to shape the international economy in accordance with broader social and political objectives, the latter accepted international economic forces as given and aimed to create a labour market that conformed to them' (1995, p. 69). The result, according to Jessop, is a more highly heterogeneous and unequal society, populated by a largely passive citizenry, closely ordered by a technocratic elite. Commentators of the radical Right have criticised the old KWS because it restricted legitimate choice, not only in the market place, but also through certain 'rules of the game' established by social policy. Murray, for example, claimed that state welfare provided perverse incentives which are corrosive of the morality of rational actors; rules which 'make it profitable for the poor to behave in the short term in ways which were destructive in the long term' (1984, p. 9). In this context, the social security 'scrounger' and the 'dole cheat' became especially potent symbols of all that had supposedly been wrong with the KWS. On the centre-Left, however, the concern is that the victims of the collapse of the old economic certainties of the KWS should not be lured into benefit fraud, which is wasteful of valuable resources, but that humane supply-side labour market policies should ensure their rapid reintegration into new kinds of work (Field and Owen, 1994; Labour Party, 1996).

The SWS, therefore, whether it is presided over by a government of the Right or of the centre-Left, is likely to link its concern to combat benefit fraud with attempts to moderate social security spending and to tighten control over benefits administration. In Britain, the former has already been achieved, in part at least, by a shift in favour of more means-testing and discretionary benefits; the latter by a more managerialist approach and an increase in centralised control (see Dean, 1993). This has coincided with a restructuring of labour markets and the emergence on a substantial scale of 'atypical' forms of work, especially part-time employment, temporary/casual employment and intermittent self-employment (Blackwell, 1994); or what has been called the 'hypercasualisation' of the labour market (Jordan and Redley, 1994). This has been accompanied, on the one hand by growing wage inequality with downward pressure on wage levels at the bottom of the earnings distribution (Goodman and Webb, 1994) and by a tendency for shrinking opportunities to be unequally distributed between 'work rich' and 'work poor' households (Pahl, 1984; Gregg and Wadsworth, 1995).

In as much, therefore, as choice has been extended within the emerging SWS, it has increased conspicuously more for those at the top than for those at the bottom of the income distribution. The choices available to groups such as unemployed people and lone-parents remain limited and by and large uncongenial. Recent research has demonstrated that people of working age who are dependent on social security benefits are no less likely than other citizens to aspire to 'proper' jobs, 'satisfying' family relationships and 'independence' from the state (Dean and Taylor-Gooby, 1992; Kempson, 1996). However, the choices available to people dependent on state benefits are incommensurate with such aspirations: such jobs as may be available are likely to be low paid, low status and impermanent; increased financial stress and inter-dependency within familes may undermine the quality of personal relationships; continued receipt of state benefits is stigmatising and involves unacceptable levels of official surveillance. Ironically, attempts by governments to clamp down on benefit fraud tend to increase the extent to which social assistance benefits are stigmatised (van Oorschot, 1995).

Firm evidence as to the extent of social security benefit fraud, in spite of attempts at official estimation, are difficult or impossible to obtain. A recent exercise carried out in Britain, not by independent researchers, but by official investigators, purported to confirm that 5.2 per cent of the income support claims reviewed were fraudulent, and in a further 4.6 per cent of cases fraud was 'suspected' (SSBA, 1995a). The basis for such statistics and the manner in which they were subsequently reported have been dismissed by some commentators as 'misleading' (for example, Sainsbury, 1996) and, certainly, a Permanent Secretary at the Department of Social Security once acknowledged to a Select Committee that accurate estimation of the incidence of *actual* fraud (as opposed to the estimation of financial losses arising from *detected* fraud) is not achievable (SSC, 1991, p. 25). Debate about the exact extent of benefit fraud tends therefore to be somewhat sterile in nature, but the question of how willing people might be to commit fraud remains important.

When asked hypothetically whether they would 'fiddle' their claims to get extra benefit (if they knew they could get away with it) more than half the claimants interviewed in one study said they would (Dean and Taylor-Gooby, 1992, p. 118). It was observed that willingness by claimants to defraud the benefit system appeared to correlate with feelings of unfairness about the way the system treated them, or with a belief that the welfare state was falling short of what claimants expected of it. There was a sense in which claimants were holding on to the expectations and values fostered by the 'old' social democratic KWS. The study that is reported in the remainder of this chapter builds on the latter finding and seeks to relate it to the findings of others (Jordan *et al*, 1992; Evason and Woods, 1995a and 1995b) who have argued that combining benefit fraud with informal economic activity is a rational household survival strategy for people trapped on low incomes. I shall first describe the research, before setting out its principal findings and then discussing the strategies of benefit fraudsters and reflecting on the relationship between choice and social citizenship. I shall conclude with some observations about the implications for public policy.

THE STUDY[1]

The study, conducted between August 1994 and October 1995, used qualitative methods and relied primarily on interviews with a sample of 35 individual social security recipients who had made fraudulent claims for social security benefits by concealing personal circumstances affecting their entitlement. The project was not concerned with 'organised' forms of fraud (such as counterfeiting or systematic multiple identity claims).[2] Contact with respondents, who were drawn mainly from Luton and London, was established through community 'gatekeepers', informal contacts and 'snowballing'. Interviews were conducted, subject to strict undertakings as to confidentiality, at venues of the respondents' own choosing and respondents were given, and frequently exercised, the option of remaining anonymous or of using pseudonyms. The interviews, which were semi-structured and in-depth, were all tape-recorded and transcribed and the resulting data were studied using conventional content coding and computer aided qualitative discourse analysis.

The nature of the topic rendered this what has been called 'sensitive' research (Lee, 1993; Renzetti and Lee, 1993) and establishing the sample proved quite difficult. In anticipation of such difficulty, all participants were offered 'expenses' of £10 and a further £5 finder's fee if they could put the project in touch with other fraudulent claimants willing to be interviewed: though nominal, these payments represented a small incentive for respondents to participate and also signalled to them that their participation was valued. The project's original intention had been to establish a core sample by way of referrals from local professional and community agencies, but levels of co-operation were poor and greater use than had been anticipated was made of less formal community contacts and of snowballing. The frauds committed by all but one of the resulting sample had not been detected by the authorities and this presented a unique opportunity to study benefit fraud from its hidden aspect.

This approach had potential drawbacks, most of which are endemic to the nature of the research topic. First, the sample was not necessarily representative of the population of fraudulent claimants as a whole (the composition of which is in any event unknown). Second, the clandestine nature of the interviewing process made it impossible to verify information given by respondents or to be sure they were telling the truth (although this applies to a great deal of field-based social scientific inquiry). Certainly, the sample will have included only those claimants who were sufficiently self-confident to agree to an interview. This is something which can to a certain extent be taken into account in the interpretation of the findings and it in fact makes the high levels of anxiety exhibited within the sample (see below) all the more striking. As to the probative value of the data it must be said that, having once decided to 'confess' in confidence to an interviewer, respondents had no more reason to lie than tell the truth and, in spite of the exhaustive scrutiny to which the transcripts were subject, it rarely appeared that respondents might be in any way deliberately dissembling.

The sampling method used represented the only practicable method in the circumstances, short of seeking the collaboration of the benefit authorities, an approach which could not have given access to undetected fraudulent claims and which would have made it difficult or impossible to establish a relationship of trust with respondents. The choice of qualitative interviewing and analysis techniques was in part dictated by the scale and terms on which the study was conducted but, more importantly, by the objective of the project which was to establish the meaning which social security fraud has for those engaged in it.

The achieved sample consisted of 21 men and 14 women and included six black (African-Carribean) respondents (but none from Asian communities). Most of the fraud committed by the sample involved 'working on the side' and related to undisclosed earnings from informal employment, although nearly a third of respondents were involved in more than one kind of fraud, including non-disclosure of cohabitation and certain kinds of invalidity and housing benefit fraud.

THE PRINCIPAL FINDINGS

What emerged from the study may be encapsulated in two principal findings. First, people in our sample who were claiming social security benefits fraudulently did not by and large seem to be exercising a conscious life-style choice. Second, their attachment to the social democratic values of the old KWS may have been weak, but it had not been replaced by any sense of duty commensurate with citizenship of a SWS.

A number of factors would seem clearly to refute the idea that benefit fraud represents a life-style choice by a selfish or irresponsible minority. Most respondents were on the one hand highly motivated to work and on the other anxious to maintain a reasonable standard of living: their behaviour did not signal any erosion of the work ethic or of their desire for conventional life-styles. An important factor for most respondents was a strong belief (informed as much by hearsay as experience) that benefit fraud is widespread: this, however, was not a reason for what they did, although it did make them feel more comfortable about it. This much is consistent with findings from other research (for example, Cook, 1989; Hessing *et al.*, 1993). Almost all the respondents cited economic deprivation or hardship as the primary reason for their behaviour and, although many of them were anxious about the risks involved, the worry of living on a low income had become a bigger worry than the prospect of getting caught for fraud.

What was perhaps less expected was that the claimants were not informed by a sophisticated understanding of the social security system and only seldom by any degree of systematic planning: they were by and large neither street-wise nor proficient in what they did. Their lack of knowledge about the benefits system appeared to arise because they felt inhibited from investigating their entitlements by the deterrent nature of the system. Similarly, they tended not to calculate or plan their involvement in undeclared employment, either because the small amounts of additional income obtained hardly justified elaborate planning, or else because the only consistently available employment was that offered by unscrupulous employers who expected workers to supplement paltry wages by 'signing on'.[3] The claimants in the study tended therefore to respond as opportunities presented themselves, often without significant premeditation. They had not chosen to live this way, it was simply that, like Mr Micawber (the character in Charles Dickens' novel, *David Copperfield*), they were biding their time in the hope that better choices would turn up. The only thing which would dissuade virtually all the respondents from fraudulent claiming would have been a 'proper' job: employment, that is, at reasonable pay and with reasonable status.

The second main finding stemmed from the project's attempts to investigate the respondents' perception of their citizenship. The ideal of the KWS is predicated on a concept of citizenship in which a balance is struck between political freedoms, civil obligations and social rights (Marshall, 1950, 1981). In practice, this requires a trade-off between legitimate expectations instigated through the development of a welfare state and the correlative obligations which constrain the citizen to pay such taxes and contributions as may be due, and to observe certain rules established by the state.

In the case of the study reported in this chapter, the claimants interviewed had ambivalent conceptions of citizenship. Although respondents might articulate beliefs about the rights of citizenship, the concept of citizenship was, for many, too vague or unfamiliar to enable them to address what the correlative obligations of citizenship should be – either confidently, or at all. Their conceptions of citizenship were more implicit than explicit and had to be explored, for example, through the way they talked about 'rights' and 'fairness'. Most believed they had a right to claim social security benefits, although this was not a right which was highly prized. They were generally uncomfortable with or felt stigmatised by their status as claimants: it was not the status from which they would voluntarily draw their subjective sense of identity. At the same time, members of this sample were unclear about their obligations as citizens. Some defined such obligations vaguely in terms of 'being a good person', or 'obeying the law', though others felt they had no particular obligations. Nor, as a group, were these claimants especially politically focused, though their discourse exhibited a relatively high incidence of general anti-government or anti-establishment sentiments.

Most respondents did not admit that what they were doing was dishonest, or else they distinguished between 'fiddling' (which they felt to be harmless) and more serious or organised forms of fraud (which they did not). This is consistent with other research findings suggesting that both social security and workplace 'fiddlers' generally impose their own moral limits or rules upon their behaviour (Jordan, *et al.* 1992, Mars, 1994), although such limits are not consistently drawn. However, in spite of their contentions that fiddling is not fundamentally dishonest, most claimants, as has been seen, still experienced some degree of anxiety or conflict about it (not least, for some, because of the risk of prosecution). Subscribing to some expedient formulation of what might be legitimate was not necessarily enough to put the respondents entirely at their ease.

This ambiguity in the moral stance of fraudulent claimants was probed in two ways: first, respondents were asked directly whom they thought was to blame for benefit fraud; second, the analysis of the interview transcripts was used to isolate and explore instances of a discourse of 'justified disobedience'. Of the respondents who ventured an opinion, most to some extent blamed the government for benefit fraud – either directly (because benefit levels are too low or because benefit rules are perverse), or indirectly (because of the government's supposed mismanagement of the economy). Only a quarter of the sample was prepared in any way to blame the individuals who commit benefit fraud. In 25 of the 35 main interviews respondents were observed to have engaged with discourses by which they justified their own disobedience as citizens. At its simplest, such discourse translated economic necessity into justification: 'It's impossible to live on that money without fraud'; 'I think the law makes us do it'. However, some respondents, because of the difficulties entailed in establishing their claims, were reacting to the way they had been 'messed about' or given 'a hard time' by the system. Elements of such discourses of justification could touch on issues of equity and justice. Feeling they had not received that to which they were entitled, respondents might justify their actions with reference to the taxes and contributions which they or their forbears had paid: 'we're getting back what we've put in all our lives'; 'my father's worked and he's paid in – so I'm getting back a bit'. Implicit here was the idea that the KWS had betrayed them; that the SWS was unfair.

It should be emphasised that respondents seldom endorsed the values of the KWS in any explicit sense. A few even openly subscribed to Thatcherite values and one such respondent acknowledged, with almost disarming candour, that he was not 'deserving' of the benefit he fraudulently claimed, adding 'I'm not proud to do it, but I'm greedy'. There was a sense in which at least some claimants apprehended that the very nature of citizenship within the emerging SWS has been somehow impoverished. This emerged most clearly from re-interviews conducted with a small sub-sample of ten respondents, of whom seven agreed that receiving social security benefits made them feel like 'second class citizens'.[4] Asked what 'first class citizenship' might consist of, five respondents (half the sub-sample) referred to issues of life-style, employment or educational status, or wealth. In so doing they were recounting what they perceived to be the currently prevailing conception of citizenship, rather than that to which they necessarily subscribed. As one respondent put it (with deliberate irony) – 'the first class citizen . . . would be someone who can support themselves, have their own house, have this supposedly "ideal" existence, yes? . . . [T]his is what you need to have in order to be a successful, happy, fulfilled sort of person'.

It is not possible to conclude from such evidence whether the discourse of social democratic citizenship had more meaning for social security claimants in the past, but it would appear that it has rather little purchase now among the fraudulent claimants interviewed in this study (especially, incidentally, for the younger claimants and some of the men). What would seem to be informing their behaviour is in part resentment, fuelled by values left over from the KWS, and in part a sense that the competitive world of the SWS is largely devoid of values, other than the value that is placed on consumer choice.

FRAUDULENT STRATEGIES

Fraud is one of the survival strategies open to households which find themselves dependent on an increasingly parsimonious benefits system, while they are at the same time marginalised within an increasingly polarised labour market (Jordan and Redley, 1994; Evason and Woods, 1995a). My argument, however, is not only that benefit fraud is seldom a strategy of optimum choice (a point to which I shall return), but also that it is never a simple strategy. It cannot be assumed that all fraudulent claimants are behaving in the same or in a consistent manner. One of the most striking things about the sample of claimants who participated in the study reported in this chapter was its diversity (for a full discussion of variations relating to age, gender and ethnicity see Dean and Melrose, 1996).

For the purposes of understanding the behaviour of this group of social security claimants, the most significant variations between them stemmed from the different ways in which they apprehended the opportunities and constraints to which they were subject. These differences related, on the one hand to the extent to which they were 'reflexive' (to which they reflected on and articulated the meaning of their fraudulent behaviour), and on the other the extent of their anxiety (their feelings of conflict and insecurity and/ or their fears about the consequences of that behaviour).

The concepts of reflexivity and anxiety which are being used here are drawn from recent sociological analyses of 'global' or 'late' modernity. Such analyses stress the *trust* which individual subjects must place in abstract systems and the *risks* associated with processes of social and economic transition (see particularly Giddens, 1990; 1991). Using these concepts as intersecting dimensions or axes, it was possible to assign each of the respondents to one of four 'ideal types' – see Figure 10.1. These types are not merely composite caricatures, nor do they necessarily represent fixed identities or statuses: they are analytical constructs that distinguish between the different moral and discursive repertoires on which respondents appeared to be drawing at a particular moment in time.

Figure **10.1 A Taxonomy of Fraudulent Benefit Claimants**

Type 2	*Type 4*
Self-confident philosophers	**Calculative worriers**
(7 respondents)	(13 respondents)
high reflexivity, low anxiety	high reflexivity, high anxiety
Type 1	*Type 3*
Macho survivors	**Unreflexive opportunitists**
(7 respondents)	(8 respondents)
Low reflexivity, low anxiety	Low reflexivity, high anxiety

Some respondents clearly did lack any sense of scruple, and there
was within the sample an unreflexive, self-confident, all-male group
of seven respondents (five of whom had previously been involved
in more 'serious' criminal activity), who could be called 'macho
survivors'. They had about them a certain hint of entrepreneurial
spirit and fraudulent claiming was for them a case of making the
best of an unsatisfactory situation. There was then a group of seven
relatively articulate respondents, who could be called 'self-confident
philosophers' for whom fraudulent claiming was, in one sense, a
self-consciously subversive activity and a reaction to a sense of
oppression. It should be stressed, however, that although members
of this group articulated a definite sense of anger, none of them
were especially radical figures: to the extent that benefit fraud may
be seen as a form of resistance, it is a rather conservative form of
resistance (see Dean and Melrose, 1997). Searching the transcripts
of the macho-survivors and the self-confident philosophers for a
discourse of risk and/or vulnerability revealed few instances for the
former group and none at all for the latter.

However, such discourse was universally evident within the repertoires of the other respondents. There was a group of eight respondents, who could be called 'unreflexive opportunists' for whom
fraudulent claiming seemed to be a sort of gamble; part and parcel
of the fatalism with which they engage with a life of uncertainty.
For all the other claimants in the sample fraudulent claiming was,

in essence, a rather poorly calculated act of desperation: the largest group (thirteen respondents) could be called 'calculative worriers', since they were on the one hand reflexive and rational, but on the other highly anxious about their 'fiddling'.

In so far that the project's sampling strategy was likely to have skewed the sample in favour of more confident or less anxious respondents it is probable that self-confident philosophers and macho-survivors were over-represented. When this is taken into account, the fact that calculative worriers and unreflexive opportunists should have outnumbered the self-confident philosophers and macho-survivors would seem to imply that most social security claimants who engage in individual benefit fraud are likely be experiencing some degree of ontological insecurity associated with their status as claimants, their fraudulent behaviour, or both.

Though the sample may have been unrepresentative, its particular composition did enable us to consider the diversity of the strategies by which fraudulent claimants are negotiating the maintenance of their own sense of self-identity and security. For none of the groups within the sample would fraudulent claiming have constituted an optimal choice. None the less, for the group here characterised as macho-survivors, fraudulent claiming is a 'smart' choice; for the self-confident philosophers, it is a justified choice; for the unreflexive opportunists, it is a blind choice; for the calculative worriers, it is a (particularly) reluctant choice. Understanding the circumscribed nature of the choices these claimants make provides important clues to the kind of alternative choices they might prefer.

CHOICE AND CITIZENSHIP

If freedom of choice represents the guiding axiom within what Jessop characterises as the SWS, it was security through citizenship which represented the axiom within the old KWS. The down-side of choice, as Taylor-Gooby points out in the first chapter is *risk*, while the down-side of security is *dependency* (but see Dean and Taylor-Gooby, 1992, ch. 6). The original ideal of the KWS had been, by insuring citizens against the risks of everyday life, to 'offer security for service and contribution', albeit on the basis that the state should not thereby 'stifle incentive, opportunity, responsibility' (Beveridge, 1942, para. 9). The KWS purported to guarantee independence and freedom of choice by securing a national minimum for all. However, the neo-liberal progenitors of the SWS have claimed that the processes of redistribution required to establish a national minimum inevitably violate the freedom of the individual (Nozick, 1974). The Thatcherite project of the 1980s, characterised by Gamble (1988) as the quest for a free market and a strong state, was consistent with Schumpeter's (1942) restricted definition of democracy and with the conviction that true freedom for the masses may be ensured only through the kind of choices made possible by market systems (Seldon 1990).

The relevance of this ideological contest to the doings of fraudulent social security benefit claimants can, up to a point, be traced through the discursive themes which figured in the interview transcripts from the study described in this chapter. The discourse which was used more extensively and intensively than any other was identified as a discourse of 'deprivation and hardship' (though it might just as well have been more archaically classified as a 'discourse of Want').[5] While some respondents would simply say 'The benefits just aren't enough' or 'I can't manage on the money', others would explain how it felt: 'I feel sad and depressed sometimes when I haven't got a penny' or 'Its not much fun living on the breadline'. Such discourse occurred most intensively among the unreflexive opportunists and least intensively among macho-survivors: for the former, the incentive required before they would run the risk of committing fraud had to be subjectively very high; the disposition of the latter will have made them feel it 'wimpish' to complain.

Often coinciding with the discourse of deprivation and hardship, was a discourse of 'materialism and consumption' (a discourse informed by the values of individual choice). Some respondents echoed the point made by Ignatieff, 'What we need to survive and what we need to flourish are two different things' (1984, p. 10). Thus one respondent said 'social security was going to give me money to survive and survival wasn't good enough for me: survival meant looking shabby'. For others, money itself was important: 'I prefer to have money in my pocket'. Such discourse featured in 20 interviews, but with much less intensity than the discourse of deprivation and hardship, and least extensively and with least intensity in the repertoires of calculative worriers.

The second most extensively used discourse (featuring in all but five interviews) was identified as a discourse of 'dependency and disempowerment'. Some respondents felt bad in themselves: 'you start to tire of yourself and you start to lose motivation and you start to feel a bit left out'. Other respondents blamed their powerlesness on external constraints: 'I'm in this position through no choice of my own'. Sometimes this stemmed from an explicit recognition of the disincentive effect of low wages: 'if you was to go out and look for work, there's no way its gonna make up for what you lose in benefits'. Such discourse was universally present in the repertoires of self-confident philosophers and unreflexive opportunists; in the case of the former, this reflects the fact that they were especially perceptive and articulate, but in the case of the latter it reflected the sense in which they felt they were at the mercy of forces beyond their calculation or control. The discourse occurred least extensively among macho-survivors, but those who did use it did so with considerable intensity: these respondents presented themselves as either contemptuously indifferent, or else as very resentful about their dependency on state benefits.

Closely associated with this discourse for some respondents was a loss of self-worth, either because of other people's perceptions ('When you're on the dole, people think you're a bum; . . . you're worth nothing') or because of their own ('You feel that you really haven't got much worth'). However, for a small number of respondents (six) the experience of claiming benefits was potentially liberating. As one self-confident philosopher said, 'Its been being on the dole that's enabled me to do other things . . . to work on your own thing and survive'. A more hedonistic version of this counter-discourse – identified by the project team as a discourse of 'liberation' – was put by one macho-survivor; 'I think its good. You know, I can go out whenever I want, I can stay up late at night, go out for meals'. Although the respondent who engaged with such discourse with the greatest intensity was the self-confident philosopher quoted above, it was a discourse used at moments by respondents in each of the other ideal type groups. Income support can, for example, be *relatively* liberating for women escaping from an oppressive partner: ' . . . they gave me a Giro that day and so I was independent from my husband for the first time in 13 years' (cf. Graham, 1987).

The overall picture therefore is a complex one, but what seems to emerge is that the demand for 'choice' manifested in the discourse of materialism and consumption (and the much less evident discourse of liberation), though by no means extinguished, is more or less eclipsed by the experience of 'Want' manifested through the dominant discourse of deprivation and hardship. At the same time, what underpinned the experiences of most fraudulent claimants was not any evident sense of security, but a generally pervasive discourse of dependency and disempowerment. Benefit fraud must be seen, not necessarily as the direct consequence, but within the context, of a denial of market choice and, additionally or alternatively, as a failure of security through citizenship.

THE POLICY IMPLICATIONS

To summarise, benefit fraud is therefore intelligible partly in terms of its economic rationality and partly in terms of an erosion of people's normative attachment to the ideals of social democratic citizenship. Assuming that policy makers are not prepared to tolerate benefit fraud there would appear to be three options:

1. To increase the risks which fraudulent claimants run by extending further the degree of surveillance to which claimants are subject, the likelihood of detection and prosecution, and/or the severity of the penalties associated with benefit fraud.
2. To decrease the incentives which claimants have to defraud the benefit system by increasing benefit levels and/or by changing rules of entitlement so as to make them more universal in character.
3. To extend the range of choices available to people currently excluded from the formal labour market through more effective training and labour market policies.

The first option is consistent with current government policy, but upon the basis of the evidence reported here is likely to be of limited effect. Increasing the risks associated with benefit fraud will certainly increase the anxiety experienced – particularly by unreflexive opportunists and calculative worriers – but it will probably have little impact on their actual behaviour. It will generally increase the stigma which attaches to the receipt of social security benefits and the uncongenial nature of the claiming experience and in so doing may deter the take up of benefits: this in itself could even have counterproductive consequences if it forces claimants to engage with the informal labour market without investigating their full entitlements.

The second option would almost certainly reduce benefit fraud if it restored claimants' confidence in the integrity of the benefits system. It is a strategy likely significantly to influence all but the least scrupulous macho survivors. However, it would constitute a wholesale return to the universalist principles of the KWS, a course which would appear to be widely politically discredited and one which is not now supported by either of the main political parties in Britain.

In the circumstances, it is the third option that is arguably the most likely to prove effective, depending upon just how it is pursued. There is a contradiction here. In one guise, such a policy might amount to a policy of full employment and to an alternative version of the KWS. In another, it might amount to a more sophisticated attempt to manipulate the supply side of the labour market and a more rigorous application of the principles of the SWS. Whichever version of the policy might be adopted, its impact on the incidence of social security fraud would depend on the extent to which it was successful in generating acceptable job choices for social security claimants, something which current training and labour market policies are clearly failing to do.

The tendency in Britain, particularly since the late 1980s, to tie training and employment initiatives increasingly closely to social security and unemployment relief has been taken as evidence of a shift towards 'workfare' on the United States model (see, for example, Ainley, 1993). However, as Whiteside (1995) points out, the origins of the 'workfare' principle may be traced, not to the USA, but to the Elizabethan Poor Laws: in its harshest form it may do no more than require unproductive forced labour or valueless 'training' in return for the payment of unemployment relief. Workfare in this 'pure' form has in fact rarely been implemented in the USA and the experimental work-welfare measures developed during the Reagan era sometimes involved high quality training initiatives, child care provision for lone parents, and resource intensive case management (Walker, 1991); precedents which the Conservative government in Britain was reluctant to emulate. Though it rejects the pejorative term 'workfare', Labour Party policy at the time of writing is informed by the recommendations of the Commission on Social Justice (1994, pp. 172–82) and the example of the Australian Jobs, Education and Training (JET) scheme. The 'welfare-to-work' programme outlined in Labour's 1997 Manifesto (Labour Party, 1997, p. 19) was targeted at young people, the long-term unemployed and lone-parents with children at school. Initiatives of this nature, while falling short of providing job guarantees or direct investment in employment creation, would involve 'active' re-employment services, training to improve 'employability', encouragement of self-employment; childcare initiatives, and various forms of selective employer subsidies. The success of this gentler form of workfare would ultimately be dependent on achieving real growth in the jobs market principally through domestic private sector and/or inward investment.

For the fraudulent claimants whom I have described as macho survivors, the effectiveness of a more developed workfare or work-welfare policy is likely to be limited and would depend on the extent to which the training and employment opportunities on offer could be construed as *smarter choices*; as options with greater credibility than those which they are currently exercising. For the claimants described as self-confident philosophers, the likelihood of their involvement in fraud would be reduced if the available training and employment opportunities were construed as *quality choices*; if the anticipated return would justify the effort involved. For the claimants described as unreflexive opportunists, improved training and employment opportunities would dissuade them from fraud provided such opportunities were transparent and could be construed as *certain bets*. For the claimants described as calculative worriers – the group that is probably dominant among fraudulent claimants – a new workfare strategy would alter their behaviour to the extent that it offered them *secure choices* and a lasting, 'bankable' alternative to benefit fraud.

Training and employment policy may therefore represent the most effective bulwark against social security benefit fraud, but, in the absence of the economic conditions and/or policies to guarantee substantive growth in formal employment, even a gentler, more sophisticated workfare state will almost certainly have to coexist with a flourishing informal economy and a high risk of benefit fraud. The evidence suggests that the people who commit benefit fraud are attempting (and failing) to reconcile freedom of choice with security through citizenship: they are neither innocent victims nor dangerous radicals, but their experiences do reflect the fundamental dilemma of a welfare state in transition.

The evidence presented therefore lends further support to three more general propositions with implications that reach beyond the specific preoccupations of this chapter. First, popular belief in the principles and moral underpinnings of the KWS is not yet dead. Second, although some people may be prepared to take risks –

even illegal ones – in their economic decision making, this need not imply that they do not value certainty and security. Third, there are inherent limits to the extent to which public policy mechanisms alone can prohibit the exercise of economic choice in certain directions through coercion, while promoting it in others through incentives.

Notes

1. The study was conducted at the University of Luton and funded by the Economic and Social Research Council under Award Ref: L122251010 as part of the Economic Beliefs and Behaviour Programme. The author is indebted to Margaret Melrose who assisted in the conduct of the research and commented helpfully on an earlier draft of this chapter. Full accounts of different aspects of the research may be found in Dean and Melrose (1996, 1997) and, for further discussion of the methodological considerations see Dean and Barrett (1996) and Melrose (1996).
2. According to official data, 83 per cent of the financial savings estimated to have been achieved in 1994/5 as a result of fraud detection work was attributed to some 392,000 cases of 'individual' benefit fraud, as compared with 17 per cent attributed to method of payment and 'organised' fraud (SSBA, 1995b). In themselves, however, these statistics have little if any probitive value in determining the relative extent of individual or organised fraud.
3. In the case of 15 of the 35 respondents employers appeared either to be indirectly colluding in the fraud being perpetrated, or to be actively encouraging it.
4. An identical proposition is put to a general sample of the population as part of the annual British Social Attitudes survey. In 1994, 49.8 per cent of the BSA sample agreed with it (Jowell *et al.*, 1995), though secondary analysis (see Dean and Melrose, 1996) reveals that a higher proportion of income support recipients were inclined to agree, namely 70.0 per cent – the same as the proportion for the sub-sample in this study.
5. The 'extent' of a discourse refers to the number of transcripts in which it was detected, while its 'intensity' refers to the frequency with which it occurred within individual transcripts.

11 Choice and the New Paradigm in Policy
Peter Taylor-Gooby

INTRODUCTION

Questions of economic choice have become central to public policy debates. However, we do not have a satisfactory theoretical account of choice. The approach that is currently most frequently used, which characterises choices as driven primarily by instrumental rationality, is open to question from a number of directions. The research discussed in this book does not provide the foundations of a general theory of economic choice. Its contribution lies in the critique it offers of the dominant theory which underlies current developments in public policy-making and in the insights it offers into the interplay between instrumental rationality and cultural and experiential factors in economic behaviour in a range of areas of current interest.

The main research approach used in the projects is the exploration of economic choices in concrete contexts rather than the testing of hypotheses derived from theoretical debate. The conclusions are therefore strongest in relation to practical policy issues. The most striking point to emerge is the strong contrast between the shift to the use of competitive markets in public policy, underpinned by the assumption that individual self-interest is the most consistent motivating force, and the evidence that social and cultural values play an important role in influencing behaviour in the areas studied. Closer attention by the policy community to social scientific accounts of behaviour is undoubtedly to be welcomed, but policy outcomes may differ from those anticipated if policy-makers do not consider a wider range of approaches.

THE IMPLICATIONS OF THE RESEARCH FINDINGS

The research uses a variety of methodological approaches, including quantitative survey through personal and postal interviews, discursive interview surveys, typically with sub-samples from a nationally or regionally representative structured interview survey, experiment, the tracing of particular choice processes over time, and primary and secondary analysis of behavioural data. It is thus possible to strengthen the conclusions by reinforcing findings produced through one technique by comparison with those derived from another. Most of the research teams were multidisciplinary and included economists, psychologists, sociologists and social policy analysts. The work is informed by theoretical perspectives from these different disciplines and reinforces from a variety of directions the point made in chapter 1, that it is difficult to explain economic choices and ideas about them simply in terms of instrumental rationality. The research also supports five additional themes of particular relevance to practical policy.

Coexistence of Self-Interest and Cultural Values

The work of several of the projects shows how different patterns of motives appear to coexist in relation to individual behaviour in a given field. This corresponds to the approach of Lea, Tarpy and Webley, who argue that economic behaviour can only be understood in terms of 'dual causation', reflecting both the individual's internal decision-making and the influence of external social factors (1987, pp. 538–9).

Expectations about the benefits to be derived from home-ownership are shaped by both political and social values (chapter 6). Any attempt to understand house purchase as a decision shaped by a rational analysis of costs and benefits is undermined by what one might see as a 'morality of house purchase' – housing is not simply a means of shelter and possibly an investment in bricks and mortar, but is also the context of home life and something that can be passed on to children. One outcome is that many people pursue home-ownership without necessarily regarding this strategy as the most rational investment available for their money. There is also an ambivalence in attitudes – many people strongly support home ownership, but at the same time support the expansion of social housing as insurance for those who are unsuccessful in the housing market. The range of values that interact in influencing choices thus depends on factors that are specific to the choice in question.

Ethical investors appear sometimes to trade off moral factors against investment return, but often behave as if their resources are divided between different mental accounts, which they treat in different ways (chapter 9). An important division lies between the core resources, retained for basic family needs and as a protection against insecurities where the over-riding concern is for security and a reasonable rate of return, and other resources where ethical issues may exert greater influence. While ethical considerations may make some impact on individual investment decisions, they do not appear to exert a strong influence on investment markets as a whole. Organised lobbying and publicity campaigns appear more likely to affect corporate behaviour than choices by particular individuals.

The Modification of Market Logic

The areas studied in the chapters vary in the extent to which the principles of market logic or of values associated with the development of citizenship and the welfare state are influential. The topics of wage determination, entrepreneurship and buying behaviour seems closest to the core of market philosophy. Even in these areas, other factors play an important role.

Research on beliefs about equity in relation to wage differentials shows that ideas about the fairness of the reward for the job are important, but that views on the wages appropriate for different individuals are also influenced by peoples' interests (chapter 8). These factors appeared to have a considerable influence on the way those most closely involved – personnel managers and union officials – approach wage negotiations, so that pure market factors of supply and demand for different kinds of labour do not exert an over-riding influence, despite the trend, particularly in the UK, to understand labour-markets in terms of flexibility in the face of stronger international competition.

The study of British Asian entrepreneurs provides perhaps the strongest example of the way in which cultural values influence the operation of rational considerations of self-interest (chapter 4). Self-employment is a rational response to the limitation of opportunities due to racism in the labour market and to the desire to achieve social mobility. Cultural factors which favour the family working together also play a part. However, the values of different cultures contribute to different understandings of what counts as success and of the factors that promote it. In many East Asian communities the fact of business involvement confers status, regardless of whether profits are larger than available wages. In Moslem cultures the view that the success of business is dependent on the will of God rather than the operation of the market may influence behaviour, so that irrational risks are taken and rates of return are erratic.

The work on GP-fundholding showed that the shift towards a quasi-market in the NHS has not led to the anticipated expansion of entrepreneurship in primary health care (chapter 3). Many GPs, irrespective of whether or not they have chosen to become fundholders, are simply disenchanted with the reforms and the perceived implication that clinical practice is to be driven by business rather than professional concerns. The majority of those who are fundholders tend to use the opportunities offered by the market to achieve efficiency savings but only a minority develop the innovations and improvements in the way the service is provided anticipated by policymakers. GPs who are not fund-holders are often able to develop comparable changes in their practice if they wish. Individuals who find themselves in a market context will not necessarily seize the opportunities available to them as market actors in the way intended. This project has implications for policies designed to enhance entrepreneurship in other areas of the NHS, in community care and more broadly in public services.

The study of compulsive buying focuses on self-identity and the contribution that market behaviour makes to an individual's sense of worth (chapter 7). It shows that a considerable proportion of shopping, varying between individual and individual and over time, is best understood in terms of the development and nourishment of a particular model of the self – 'self-completion' – rather than meeting the wants that a rational model of behaviour would attribute to the purchaser. The notions of ideal self that tend to be current among men and women lead to systematic gender-differences in the types of goods purchased on impulse.

Uncertainty and Cognitive Limitations

The importance of these factors has been pointed out by many writers on economic choice, as we noted in chapter 1. For example, the uncertainties surrounding the likelihood that an individual will need long-term social care, the terms on which it will be available and the future of public policy are seen as important factors in the discrepancy between approval for private insurance in this area and unwillingness to take out policies. Considerable uncertainties about price movements and future costs also influence attitudes to house purchase, and uncertainty about the impact of social welfare on a diffuse sense of social cohesion buttresses an individual's willingness to pay taxes for services she may not anticipate using herself.

The work on ethical investment supports the view that people adopt strategies which simplify the task of making decisions in the face of a limited human capacity to determine the appropriate actions in the complex and uncertain circumstances of real life. The pursuit of contradictory investment strategies with different portions of the available resources – pursuing green investment as well as standard return-maximising investment – may be understood in terms of the operation of 'mental accounts' (Shefrim and Thaler, 1988) concerned with safeguarding basic assets for possible future needs while allowing ethical considerations to influence the investment of additional resources, or in terms of 'satisficing' (Simon, 1978) competing needs rather than calculating the theoretical maximum return.

Spheres of Responsibility

Questions of whether government, family or the individual affected should be responsible for meeting a specific need arise most strongly in relation to areas where welfare state provision is on the agenda. The research carried out in the programme shows that awareness of the tax implications of service improvements tends to dampen enthusiasm for extra spending (chapter 5). However, in the most highly valued service areas – health and education – support for more spending remains very strong even when the tax implications are spelt out in concrete terms, and in the area of police and law and order tolerance of extra taxation also remains high. Users of non-state services, who are unlikely to benefit directly as individuals from service improvements, share these views, indicating that the widespread commitment to the core welfare state services is not based on immediate self-interest but is influenced by ideas about the proper scope for government provision.

In relation to social care, the picture is less clearly defined: many people do not see the need as a state responsibility, but seem unwilling to take responsibility for financing provision themselves. In part this is due to uncertainty about the incidence of the need for social care and the value of the various policies available, in part to uncertainties about the policy environment, and in part to strongly held social values about the importance of retaining assets built up over the life-time, so that they can be passed on to children (chapter 2). Housing is another area in which the state is seen to have a responsibility by those who do not themselves use government provision (chapter 6).

In relation to some areas of provision there is evidence of a sense of betrayal by service users, who feel that the promises implicit or explicit in policy have not been sustained in practice. This applies to perceptions of the inadequacy of social security benefits, the experience of negative equity in the housing market among those encouraged into home-ownership by the promise of a property-owning democracy or the assumption that government would take ultimate responsibility for social care. The research on social security fraud shows that there is considerable diversity in the views of petty dole-fiddlers, but that for the majority fraud is not a 'conscious life-style choice' but causal and opportunistic (chapter 10). 'Fiddlers' find it extremely difficult to survive on social security benefits. They would prefer not to be engaged in fraud but feel they have little realistic alternative. Their values remain those of the citizenship contract of the Keynesian Welfare State rather than the acceptance of low-waged employment or lower-level dole implied by the new market-oriented system.

Responses to Social Change

The research also highlights a further point concerning shifts in cultural values over time. Cultural values may develop in response to the demands of particular social contexts and require considerable periods to change. Instrumental rationality implies an immediate response to current opportunities and costs. Some recent policy measures require rapid changes in behaviour. GPs are expected to act as entrepreneurs (chapter 3), workers to adopt behaviour appropriate to a flexible labour market (chapter 8), citizens to extend private social welfare insurance cover (chapters 2 and 6). The research indicates that changes in values lag behind policy demands, leading to an observed – and experienced – disjunction between public values and the expectations of policy-makers. This is clearly seen in the study of tax-payers' attitudes, but also appears in the finding that many GPs do not seize the full opportunities of entrepreneurship in an entrepreneurial context, or that individuals do not pursue social care insurance as an immediate response to state withdrawal from provision in this area. The disjunction between observed values and the expectations of a new policy stance implies that policy changes may not yield the desired results because they do not correspond to expectations about the roles of government, individual and family.

These general points indicate that the relation between cultural values and rational choice in everyday life is complex. Further work and particularly work directed by common hypotheses across different areas is needed to clarify the relationship and its implications for the new directions in policy which stress the role of choice. We now turn to consider these implications in more detail.

PUBLIC POLICY AND MOTIVATION

Public policy is built on assumptions about the factors that influence people's behaviour. Policy-makers often wish to reinforce particular behaviour patterns – for example, those involved in the family or the work ethic, or in entrepreneurship, or in taking responsibility for one's own welfare and that of one's family, or in altruism – and to weaken others – for example, fraud or welfare dependency. Assumptions about motivation are sometimes implicit and often formulated at a vague and general level so that their relationship to social science theories is imprecise. However, ideas about motivation exert an important influence on the general direction of policy-making and policy change. A leading European sociologists argued in the early 1970s that the shortcomings of the modern political economy would ultimately lead to a legitimation crisis that is 'at root a crisis of motivation' (Habermas, 1976, p. 380), on the grounds that the cultural sphere would be unable to supply appropriate motives to balance private interests and render the market economy stable in the long term. Such a crisis has not occurred although the direction of public policy in the UK has undergone substantial change, reflected more recently in developments in other European countries. New theoretical approaches (for example Jordan, 1996) have stressed rational public choice in accounts of social exclusion and of the generation of poverty in rich market economies. The restructuring of the public sector has been accompanied by a radical shift in underlying ideas about why people behave as they do. The research of the programme indicates that the new paradigm in public policy is in important respects misleading.

The post-war welfare state was based on the principle of

tax-financed state provision. A range of services and benefits was made available, administered where appropriate by government officials and professionals, and it was supposed that these would meet needs efficiently and effectively. The key assumptions about motivation that buttressed the theory derived from the collectivism of social planners in the Fabian tradition and were rarely articulated – although Titmuss (1971, p. 243) does refer to a basic human motivation of altruism. The actors in the Keynesian Welfare State paradigm may be grouped into three categories: the makers and suppliers of policy – politicians, civil servants and the professionals and officials who actually ran the services – the tax-payers who financed most of social provision and the service users and clients, who were the consumers. Service providers were seen as motivated primarily by considerations of public service and pursuit of the common good and by professional ethics. The motivations of tax-payers were similar. It was assumed that altruism, or at least the desire for a secure safety-net, would motivate citizens to accept the increasing levels of progressive taxation necessary to finance collective services. Service users, however, were seen as essentially passive, content to accept bureaucratically-administered state provision designed by those who knew best and acted for the best. In an insightful analysis of the assumptions about behaviour built into recent social policy developments, Le Grand points to the disjunction between the roles of provider and tax-payer, where the primary motivation is active and altruistic, and that of recipient where behaviour is seen as passive and accepting. He dubs the former 'knights' and the latter 'pawns' in the traditional welfare state (1997, p. 154).

This model of welfare motivations corresponds to a central theme in the political science of the expansionist years of the post-war public sector. In particular the disjunction in motivation is reflected in Almond and Verba's influential account of the civic virtues appropriate to a modern democratic society as a 'mixed political culture' (1965, p. 29). As Verba put it: 'the model ... that required that all citizens be involved and active ... by itself ... could not sustain a stable democratic government. Only when combined ... with its opposites of passivity, trust and deference to authority and competence was a viable, stable, democracy possible' (Verba, 1989, p. 16). The civic culture of the welfare state assumed that activism and involvement were primarily the province of altruistic providers, while service users were required to trust and defer, confining their political involvement to voting when elections were called.

A number of commentators have pointed out that the assumptions underlying the altruistic/deference model of public policy in the UK were called into questions in the 1970s and 1980s and that new developments have replaced it by an approach which relies on a different account of motivation. As Lowe and others suggest (1995, pp. 300–303; see Timmins, 1995) the immediate challenge to the traditional welfare state was political and economic, but debates about motivation and behaviour led to the accusation that it was 'morally as well as politically bankrupt'.

CHALLENGES TO THE TRADITIONAL MODEL

Challenges to the altruism/deference model may be grouped in relation to the three categories of social actors defined by the welfare state.

Providers and Suppliers

In Western democracies, policy-making is ultimately based on the programmes of political parties. The work of Schumpeter, who argued that political contests were analogous to competition in an economic market-place (1944, p. 285), further refined by Downs in the claim that 'parties formulate policies to win elections, rather than win elections in order to formulate policies' (1957, p. 28), implies that policy-making is influenced as much by the desire to gain or retain office as by concern for the public good. The assumption that those who design and execute public policies are essentially altruistic came into conflict with new developments in the understanding of bureaucracy derived from rational choice theory and applied to the public sector. The central claim is that those responsible for directing and running public services will tend to follow private rather than public interest. The argument gives a sharper edge to ideas about 'x-inefficiency' or organisational slack (Liebenstein, 1966) and the general alienation of the citizen from an increasingly unresponsive and costly 'big government' (Rose, 1980).

One of the most influential exponents of rational choice theory in relation to bureaucracy, Niskanen, bases his arguments directly on claims about motivation. 'Among the several variables that enter the bureaucrat's motives are: salary, perquisites of the office, public reputation, power, patronage, output of the bureau . . all are a positive function of the total budget of the bureau during the bureaucrat's tenure' (1973, p. 22). Niskanen concludes that the primary goal of bureaucrats is the maximisation of the budget they control. The result, in the public sector, is a perennial risk of 'over-supply' of services, as those running individual departments seek expansion. More recent commentators have suggested different accounts of official motivation, more in keeping with the changes in agency organisation of the 1980s and 1990s. Dunleavy argues that 'rational officials do not want to head up heavily staffed, large budget but routine, conflictual and low-status agencies' (1991, p. 202). Instead they 'want to work in small elite, collegial bureaus close to political power centres' so that public bodies are responsive to politicians desire to retrench and decentralise, provided that these policies are carried out in ways that make their world more congenial and locate them firmly at the centre of decision-making. Corresponding theories about the role of professionals suggests that individuals may use autonomy and status to promote private rather than public interests so that they control the pace and nature of their work and can ration services to deter tedious or demanding cases (Glennerster, 1992, p. 37; Lees, 1996; Wilding, 1982).

Tax-payers

The available evidence from attitude surveys indicates strong enthusiasm for the core welfare state services – health care and education – and considerable support for other major welfare spending areas, as chapter 5 shows. It is noticeable that the levels of support for those services which meet the needs of particular minorities, who run the risk of being labelled undeserving is lower. The leading study is the annual Social Attitudes Survey (Jowell *et al.*, 1983 onwards) and a similar picture is presented in other work (Judge and Solomon, 1993, pp. 304–5; Dunleavy, 1985; Edgell and Duke, 1991). The pattern of support for the welfare is repeated throughout Europe (Ferrerra, 1993; Kaase and Newton, 1995, pp. 77–89; Svallfors, 1995).

Despite this evidence and indications that support for higher welfare spending grew in equal measure with the commitment to retrenchment expressed by the party of government, political parties associated with higher taxes lost four elections between 1979 and 1992. It is widely believed that the electorate is not willing to pay the taxes necessary to expand welfare and this view shapes the policies of the two largest parties. The disjunction between expressed opinion and electoral outcome can be explained by academic commentators as an intrinsic weakness of the survey method, a deficiency in representativeness of the first-past-the-post system or an artefact of questionnaire design – people may want more spent, but not be willing that extra should come from their own pockets (Brook, 1996, p. 188). Politicians and others who occupy central positions in the policy debate believe that a public sense of altruism which will support high and progressive taxation no longer exists, most clearly demonstrated in the fact that both major political parties are committed to tax restraint and compete in disparaging each other as 'the party of high taxation'.

Service Users

Counter-evidence to the assumption that service users display the patient virtues of passivity, trust and deference comes from two directions. First a large number of studies demonstrated that middle-class voters were defecting from state provision where they could to use private pensions, owner-occupied housing, and to a lesser extent, private medical care and schooling. Within the state sector, more influential groups (middle-class people and men) were able to deploy their social resources to gain access to preferential treatment within the NHS, better access to social care and to the most costly parts of the state education system and to use their financial power to enjoy the lion's share of the fiscal and other subsidies to private pensions, housing and transport. Social policy writers from Titmuss (1962) to Le Grand (1982) drew attention to the significance of the 'social division of welfare'. Dunleavy suggested that access to such services formed the basis of a new fundamental division into consumption sectors rather than social classes based on the division of labour (1980).

Secondly, a number of writers influenced by the work of Murray (1984) and Mead (1986) in the US argued that lower income groups also responded to the incentives built into social policy (see Dennis and Erdos, 1992 for a summary of the debate in the UK). Benefits for unemployed people and the provision of both benefits and services such as housing for one-parent families, it was argued, provided perverse incentives which undermined the work and family ethics seen as core elements in social cohesion. While the evidence for the construction of a 'dependency culture' as a result of welfare policy is weak (Dean and Taylor-Gooby, 1993, ch. 1; Walker, 1990), concerns about welfare dependency have coloured recent policy debates, perhaps most importantly through their vigorous promotion by the Social Security Minister of the 1997 Labour Government (Field, 1996, p. 11).

Other Factors

These shifts in intellectual debate chimed in tune with other developments to bring about radical changes in public policy-making. Lowe writes: 'after 1976 there was unquestionably an historic break in the development of Britain's postwar welfare state' (1993, p. 328). At the political level, the individualistic ideology of tax cuts and individual responsibility proved attractive to voters. Economic pressures led commentators to question the sustainability of traditional patterns of public policy (Bacon and Eltis, 1976). The emphasis on market individualism in analysis of welfare was further reinforced by new approaches to management which stress decentralisation and competition.

These approaches mount a sustained critique of the monolithic, large-scale, horizontally and vertically integrated organisation as appropriate to current conditions in either the private or the public sector (Handy, 1984, pp. 57–64; Kanter, 1985, pp. 42–58). The traditional firm endeavoured to control every aspect of its operation from procurement of raw materials through to marketing and after-sales service by incorporating all elements within a large bureaucratic structure. Similarly welfare agencies sought to encompass as wide a range as possible of elements relevant to the service. Approaches that developed in the private sector in the 1970s and 1980s point out that with modern information technology and communications it is no longer necessary to physically own elements in an operation in a order to control those aspects of them that are relevant, and that in a global market that may shift rapidly in unpredictable ways due to technological development or to international competition, large organisations may find it difficult to respond rapidly.

The outcome is a tendency for organisations to identify and focus on the core elements of their business and to make increased use of contractual relations to secure other goods and services in more flexible ways than were available to them under the previous structure. In government bureaucracies the trend has been to retain strategic planning, policy making, the setting of objectives and standards and the means of checking them, overall budgetary control and the co-ordination of the purchase of the services within state departments and to decentralise the provision of services to more or less independent bodies (state, private for profit, or private not-for-profit) which are typically in a contractual relationship with the centre, typically competing in an internal market (Taylor-Gooby and Lawson, 1993, p. 134; Hoggett, 1990). This is parallelled by an increased emphasis on individual responsibility for acquiring and managing a range of services to meet individual needs. Thus budgets are decentralised to schools, to NHS Trusts and GPs and within local authority social services departments.

APPROACHES TO MOTIVATION IN THE NEW PUBLIC POLICY

The central feature of the new paradigm is a reliance on the market rather than planned and bureaucratically delivered provision. The main change in the account of motivation is a shift from an approach that relies on assumptions about culture and behaviour to one that stresses the contribution of instrumental rationality and interprets rationality primarily in terms of the pursuit of self-interest.

The expansion of market provision has two aspects. First, individuals tend increasingly to purchase services and benefits in competitive markets as a result of constraint in state spending and of the increased targeting of state provision coupled with the expansion of subsidies for private provision and deregulation and other measures designed to broaden the range of providers. The clearest example of these processes is in the shift to private second-tier pension provision following the run down of the state earnings-related pension scheme after the 1986 Social Security Act. Use of the private market has also grown – in housing, following the sale of council houses and the ending of public sector subsidies, in mortgage protection, as benefits for mortgage repayment for unemployed people are cut back, in transport, as a result of the reduction in subsidies to and the deregulation of bus services and the denationalisation of rail, in social care, as a result of greater targeting of state provision and in health care, as tax subsidies for private medical insurance are increased and concern about standards in the NHS grows.

The second aspect of the market is internal to the public sector. The process of decentralisation of budgetary responsibility to provider units has created internal markets in education, where local authority and directly-financed schools, independent further education colleges and nursery schools and classes compete with each other to obtain resources provided effectively on a voucher basis, in health care where fundholding by GPs and District Authorities requires hospitals, clinics and other providers to compete with each other for contracts to treat the fundholders' patients, in social care, where services are again provided on a contractual basis and in the provision of a wide range of local government services. State sector provider agencies come into competition with private for-profit and not-for-profit providers (for a more detailed account, see Le Grand and Bartlett, 1993, ch. 1; Flynn, 1993, ch. 3).

The increased use of markets in public provision reflects greater emphasis on market competition in other areas of policy interest. The concern with enhanced labour market flexibility that led to legislation reducing the influence of trade unions, the abolition of wage councils, the weakening of employment protection legislation and the initial refusal to accept the social chapter of the Maastricht Treaty have been discussed in chapter 1. Changes in social security law leading to the abolition of unemployment benefit and its replacement by a shorter-term Jobseekers' Allowance in 1996 fit the logic of the shift from a Keynesian Welfare State towards a market-oriented Schumpeterian Workfare State.

The shift to the market is designed to overcome some of the problems associated with the traditional welfare state. In relation to providers and suppliers, competitive pressures require services to be oriented to consumer demand. Suppliers who do not follow this logic gain fewer resources and their importance dwindles. Competitive pressures also serve to reduce costs for taxpayers and empower the proactivity of users as consumers rather than passive clients. Since markets are, in principle, morally neutral in the sense that demand can be driven by any values held by the consumer, greater use of markets in welfare also requires more stringent regulation to prevent individuals acting in ways that undermine the ethics that those who design services wish to uphold.

This approach follows the arguments associated with Hirschman's influential book *Exit, Voice and Loyalty* (1970). Hirschman points out that in a number of contexts the traditional sanction available to those who are dissatisfied with a service – transferring from the unsatisfactory provider to a more acceptable one or, as he terms it, 'exit' – is difficult. This applies particularly in the state sector. Parents may be unwilling to disrupt a child's social networks by switching schools or to upset powerful professionals by switching GP. 'Voice' can only be exercised through the ballot box when welfare issues are entangled with a large number of other debates. In such cases, 'loyalty' is the only option. The implication is that opportunities for exit should be strengthened to allow individuals a greater element of choice and to bring the sanction of exit more effectively into play in the state sector, and this is the intention of the expansion in the role of the market.

RATIONAL BEHAVIOUR IN THE WELFARE STATE

The greater use of market systems implies a shift in the understanding of motivation implicit in policy-making. There are two aspects to this: the question of which motives are assumed to be most important in influencing actions and the social factors that sustain those patterns of motivation. The traditional welfare state was based on the assumption that altruism played an important part in the motivations of tax-payers and welfare state personnel, and also the clientele, so that perverse incentives were not seen as a problem, although a passive willingness to accept the services as they were offered was also seen as important. The new approach reflects Hume's view that in relation to public affairs 'every man ought to be supposed to be a knave and to have no other end in all his actions than private interest' (1875, p. 117, quoted by Le Grand, 1997, p. 149).

Market actors supply their own motives to overall patterns of demand. However, any attempt to pursue the kind of altruism presupposed by former models of public policy will impair the operation of the current system. Thus GPs are required to drive (on behalf of their practice) the hardest bargain they can to gain the most cost-efficient service from hospitals, individuals are assumed to press for and pursue the best for themselves, promoting high standards in provider agencies, and tax-payers are presumed to prefer low taxes above higher public spending so that individual responsibility for meeting need can expand via the private sector. Strict regulation of dependency is required and benefits for such groups as one-parent families and unemployed people of working age are strictly regulated. A flexible labour market will provide strong work incentives and deploy labour efficiently. Similarly the perverse incentives in the market require mechanisms to check that standards are maintained, and new mechanisms for inspection in education and social care have been introduced.

The new approach also tends to assume that the key actors who have budgetary responsibility under the new system will act to make the best use of the opportunities now available to them. GP fund-holders, social service budget-holders and school and college managers will develop innovatory ways of delivering services and attracting consumers. They will become more like entrepreneurs and less like state official or professionals directed by a service ethic.

The shift from altruism to self-interest as the assumed primary motivation is associated with a shift from a cultural to an instrumentally rational account of behaviour. In the former model, professional and public service ethics and a citizenship that included a willingness to finance services for the more needy members of the community were seen as guaranteeing the service of the common interest. The new public policy is based on the assumption that the rational pursuit of self-interest is the major motivating force. However, it is open to question whether market institutions can function effectively without a supporting cultural framework and such a framework is evident in the theoretical approach of the liberal tradition of political economy from Adam Smith to Frances Fukuyama. The shift in the direction of the market presupposes an appropriate cultural transition which is not explicit in the assumptions of its advocates.

Smith's *Theory of the Moral Sentiments* (1759; see especially, pp. 191–2) which underpins his political economy, was heavily influenced by Humes's *Treatise*, published 20 years earlier. Hume presents an account of 'volition' as originating in the passions, rather than in considerations of reason, but does not conclude that the egocentrism of the passions will lead to social institutions regulated entirely by self-interest (1739, pp. 460–3). In his discussion of government he argues that 'nothing is more certain than that men are, in great measure, governed by interest' but that 'tis no less certain that tis impossible for men to consult their interest in so effectual a manner, as by an universal and inflexible observance of the rules of justice' (pp. 585–6). The result is that social institutions naturally develop in society to restrain the short-run excesses of the passion of self-interest, and these institutions include those which will guarantee that market agreements are honoured, such as the social norm of trust – the example given is adherence to a contract between neighbours to bear the cost of draining a meadow, since no-one would be willing to initiate the work if they could not be confident that the others would play their part (p. 590).

Smith's celebrated account in *The Wealth of Nations* of the origin of the division of labour and its co-ordination through market institutions resting on self-interest nonetheless observes the important role of 'habit, custom and education' in maintaining the division (1776, p. 120). More recently Fukuyama whose millennialist claims for the global primacy of liberal market institutions provoked intense controversy (1992), has argued that 'there is a missing 20 per cent of human behaviour of which neoclassical' (elsewhere defined as free market) 'economics can give only a poor account' (1995, p. 13). 'Current economic discourse needs to recover some of the richness of classical ... economics, by taking account of how culture shapes all aspects of human behaviour, including economic behaviour, in critical ways' (1995, p. 18 – see also Hirsch, 1977, p. 137).

These arguments suggest that, for the transition to the market in public policy to succeed, individuals must accept a duty to take greater responsibility for meeting their own needs and that those involved in transactions require a degree of trust to ensure that costs of checking information supplied and service delivered are not damagingly high. Mechanisms to encourage the development of such a culture are contained in the inspection and regulation systems of the new public policy. However, the implication of the changes is a substantial shift in the cultural framework which provides the behavioural context for many people.

The research discussed in this book indicates that the ideas about economic motivation implicit in the new public policy are oversimple. Cultural values play an important role in influencing economic choices alongside instrumental rationality. It is striking that, as the developments in social science discussed in chapter 1 have called the instrumental rationality approach into question, it has strengthened its position as the dominant if frequently unacknowledged influence on policy debate. We move on to consider the practical impact of policies based on a partial account of why people make the choices they do.

THE IMPLICATIONS OF ECONOMIC CHOICE FOR POLICY-MAKING

The most striking theme in the findings of chapters 2 to 10 was that everyday choices could not be wholly understood in terms of instrumental rationality, since cultural values and experience also played an important role both in providing additional motivations and in defining the goals to which rational behaviour is directed. Research in those areas of social life in which decisions appear most likely to be determined by market rationality confirms the point. The expansion of green and ethical investment contradicts the assumption that investment behaviour is driven by considerations of return and security. Detailed analysis of investors' decisions shows that ethical and market factors operate in varying combinations in relation to decisions about different parts of individual portfolios. A considerable proportion of shopping choices are compulsive rather than rationally planned and appear often to be linked to ideas about self-identity which reflect social considerations associated with such factors as gender, rather than the utility of the item purchased. In the case of some groups of British Asian entrepreneurs, racism in the labour market pushes people towards self-employment, the employment of family members may be attractive for practical and cultural reasons and cultural values may lead to status being conferred on business people regardless of the financial return on the business. Thus the shift to small business rests partly on cultural factors which both reinforce and define the objectives for the operation of instrumental rationality.

In areas where choices are more obviously influenced by traditional welfare considerations, such as house-purchase, individuals understand their own buying as influenced by general factors of security and provision for the needs of children rather than the return on an investment, and wish also to see social housing provided. A similar pattern emerges in the balance of ideas about family and state responsibility in relation to social care. In the heart of the welfare state – willingness to pay tax for public services – self-interest reduces willingness to support provision in a number of fields, but in the core areas of health care and education, majorities still support public provision and this seems to be true even among those who are unlikely to benefit immediately from that provision because they have access to private alternatives. The implications for public policy-making are three.

Caution

First, policy-makers should be cautious, as Le Grand (1997, pp. 163–5) points out. If individuals behave as if they are influenced by a wide variety of possible motivations and combinations of motivations, it is important to ensure that policies do not presume a unitary and consistent account of actions. There is a strong risk of unanticipated consequences among some of those affected if brittle and unforgiving policy options are pursued. For example, GPs will not necessarily pursue the kind of innovative policies expected from entrepreneurs simply because they are presented with the opportunities of fundholding, and the same point applies to state sector professionals in other areas. Older people may be reluctant to arrange private social care insurance if a web of cultural beliefs about obligations on the part of the welfare state to care for frail elderly people and on their own part to pass assets on to their children constrain their actions. The situation is complicated by the uncertainty both about whether and how much social care individuals will need and about future government policies in this area. A flexible labour market may be difficult to achieve if beliefs about the fairness of wage differentials influence those involved in wage setting. Correspondingly, commitment to Keynesian citizenship values may undermine loyalty to a new welfare regime which sets benefits for unemployed people below the lowest available wages and may incline the disaffected to petty acts of fraud.

Cultural Change

Secondly, new developments presuppose cultural changes that have not yet taken place. The new public policy requires substantial shifts in behaviour and in sustaining cultural values away from the reliance on and acceptance of traditional welfare state provision towards a more entrepreneurial approach on the part of competing providers and an active consumerism coupled with an awareness of individual responsibility to arrange provision to meet needs on the part of recipients. In relation to work, individuals must be prepared to accept both the positive and the negative implications of labour market flexibility, to temper their expectations of wages and benefits when unemployed and be ready to undertake re-skilling appropriate to market circumstances.

Such cultural changes are strongly influenced by experience and take time. There is considerable evidence from the programme's attitude-studies in a wide range of areas, including tax and welfare spending, social care, home ownership, the fairness of wage differentials, entrepreneurship among state sector professionals and benefit fraud, that the cultural framework presumed by current directions in policy does not predominant among ordinary citizens. Many people still expect government rather than private citizens to take core responsibility for the improvement of the major welfare services through the enhancement of tax-financed public provision. Welfare state professionals do not automatically become entrepreneurs when confronted with the incentives of a market. Many claimers feel that government has a continuing responsibility to provide adequate benefits for those who become unemployed in an increasingly uncertain labour market. Ideas about desert and reward, as well as about incentives, exert an influence on attitudes to pay. These findings have strong implications for the pace of reform and for the institutions designed to encourage individuals to expand private provisions in areas like pensions, social care and home-ownership, to pursue opportunities as managers in welfare markets and to accept the implications of greater labour market flexibility.

In areas where private services are costly, the lead-in time for changes may be considerable. If many people believe that the government has a responsibility to provide in areas like social and health care, the withdrawal of government provision on the assumption that market alternatives already exist or will speedily emerge may prove disastrous.

Disenchantment

The third point is that the rapid shift in assumptions about motivation, incentives and responsibilities associated with the policy changes generates a strong sense of disenchantment among those involved. One of the most striking findings of the project on GP fundholding is the extent to which substantial numbers, both among those who had become fundholders and those who had not, reported strong disquiet at changes which seemed to treat them as responding to incentives in a way they saw as more appropriate to a business-person rather than a health-care professional. Allied with other concerns this led half of those interviewed to say that they would not choose GP practice if they had their medical careers over again (Whynes, 1966, p. 1). Similarly, unemployed benefit claimers report a sense of betrayal at the discovery that state benefits are inadequate, those interviewed about social care see such provision as a duty of government rather than the individual and the majority of home-owners insist that government should provide improved social housing services for those whose needs are not currently met. The sense of disenchantment resulting from collision between expectations about the role of citizen implicit in the new and old systems may damage the effectiveness of the changes as in the examples above. It may also contribute to the pressures inhibiting the cultural changes demanded by the new policy regime and to the sustenance of political forces which render that regime unstable.

CONCLUSIONS: ECONOMIC CHOICE AS A SOCIAL PROCESS

The intellectual position that underlies the new directions in public policy is based on a view of economic choice that sees behaviour as ultimately motivated by an instrumental rationality and argues that individuals in a market context will adopt the role of rational actor advancing their own interests and those of their enterprise. The research reported in this book shows that this approach is misleading. Behaviour in the context of markets and quasi-markets is strongly influenced by cultural factors. Ideas about obligations within the family, about equity and about the appropriate range of benefits that should be made available to welfare state citizens contribute to the choices that people make. The significance of these factors varies in different policy areas, influenced by the relevance of different cultural assumptions, the strength with which they are held, the way they interact with each other and with instrumental considerations and the uncertainty surrounding decisions. The practical outcome is that cultural changes which are likely to take a considerable time are necessary to make the new public policy work. In their absence, changes may yield unanticipated and unwelcome consequences.

At the theoretical level the approach underlying the new public policy is ultimately based on a simplified version of the economic psychology underlying traditional approaches in economics. This approach views the individual as 'essentially a rational bargain-hunter' (Hollis, 1987, p. 22) or inclined to 'maximise utility in a consistent way' (Becker, 1996, p. 22) and typically construes the goal of rational behaviour as the service of self-interest. As the first chapter suggested, these approaches are increasingly challenged by evidence of limitations in people's ability to make instrumentally rational choices and of the variety of social factors which influence the choices that are made. The uncritical acceptance of this approach to economic decision-making by the policy community will lead to new developments that fail to produce the anticipated outcomes. People cannot be understood simply as instrumentally rational actors. Their choices are influenced by cognitive limitations and by the cultural and experiential contexts of their lives. Ideas about the obligations and appropriate roles of state, private sector and kin, and about what is appropriate for their own social group influence their behaviour. The best way to give the users of welfare services more influence on provision is not to assume that competitive markets produce appropriately active consumers or responsive entrepreneurs, but to investigate the way people actually behave in marshalling the resources they require to meet the needs they perceive in different contexts.

Appendix: The 'Economic Beliefs and Behaviour' Programme–Projects, Researchers and Publications

Attitudes and Behaviour towards Financial Planning for Care in Old Age

Gillian Parker and Harriet Clarke with Jeremy Jones

Clarke, H. and Parker, G., 'Cost of Long-Term Care', *Insurance Trends*, ABI, London, October 1997.

Parker, G. and Clarke, H., 'The Development of Long-Term Care Insurance in Britain', Nuffield Community Care Studies Unit, University of Leicester, Working Paper: No. 42 September 1995.

Parker, G. and Clarke, H., 'Attitudes towards Long-Term Care for Elderly People: Evidence Submitted to the Health Committee', Nuffield Community Care Studies Unit, University of Leicester, Working Paper: No. 38, January 1996.

Parker, G. and Clarke, H., 'Attitudes and Behaviour towards Financial Planning for Care in Old Age: Results of a National Survey', in C. Roland-Lévy (ed.), *Social and Economic Representations*, 2, 1166–1175, proceedings of the International Association for Economic Psychology XXIst Annual Colloquium, Paris: Academie de Paris, Université de René Descartes, 1996.

Parker, G., Editorial – 'Can't Pay? Won't Pay? Finance for Long-Term Care', *Journal of Health Services Research and Policy*, July 1997.

Parker, G. and Clarke, H., 'Will you still need me? Will you still feed me? Attitudes towards long-term care', *Social Policy and Administration*, 31:2, 119–35, 1997.

Beliefs, Perceptions and Expectations in the UK Owner-Occupied Housing Market

Moira Munro, Kenneth Gibb, Duncan Maclennan, Ruth Madigan and Clodagh Memery

Madigan, R. and Munro, M., 'Housing Ladders and Household Strategies', University of Glasgow, mimeo, 1997.

Memery, C., 'Beliefs, Perceptions and Expectations of U.K. Homeowners', *Mortgage Weekly*, 10.11.95.

Munro, M., 'Rationality and Choice in House Purchase', in C. Roland-Lévy (ed.), *Social & Economic Representations*, 1, 473–486, proceedings of the International Association for Economic Psychology XXIst Annual Colloquium, Paris: Academie de Paris, Université de René Descartes, 1996.

British Asian Self-Employment: The Interaction of Culture and Economics

Tariq Modood, Satnam Virdee and Hilary Metcalf

Metcalf, H., Modood, T. and Virdee, S., *Asian Self-Employment: The Interaction of Culture and Economics in England*, London: Policy Studies Institute, 1996.

Modood, T. *et al.*, *Ethnic Minorities in Britain: Diversity and Disadvantage*, London: Policy Studies Institute, 1997.

A Distributed Artificial Intelligence Simulation of Budgetary Decision Making

Nigel Gilbert and Edmund Chattoe

Chattoe, E., 'The Use of Evolutionary Algorithms in Economics: Metaphors or Models for Social Interaction?', in E. Hillebrand and J. Stender (eds), *Many-agent Simulation and Artificial Life*, Amsterdam: IOS Press, 1994.

Chattoe, E., 'Why Are We Simulating Anyway? Some Answers from Economics', in K.G. Troitzsch, U.G. Müller, N. Gilbert and J.E. Doran (eds.), *Social Science Microsimulation*, ch.4, 67–68, Berlin: Springer-Verlag, 1996.

Chattoe, E., 'A Simulation of Budgetary Decision Making Based on Interviews with Pensioners', in C. Roland-Lévy (ed.), *Social & Economic Representations*, 2, 1114, proceedings of the International Association for Economic Psychology XXIst Annual Colloquium, Paris: Academie de Paris, Université de René Descartes, 1996.

Chattoe, E., 'Modelling Economic Interaction Using a Genetic Algorithm', in T. Bäck, D. Fogel and Z. Michalewicz (eds), *The Handbook of Evolutionary Computation*, New York: Oxford University Press/IOP Publishing, G7.1 1–5, 1997.

Chattoe, E. and Gilbert, N., 'A Simulation of Budgetary Decision-Making Based on Interview Data', in E. Chattoe and R. Conte (eds), *Evolving Societies: The Computer Simulation of Social Systems*, London: UCL Press, forthcoming.

Conte, R. and Chattoe, E., 'Introduction', in E. Chattoe and R. Conte (eds), *Evolving Societies: The Computer Simulation of Social Systems*, London: UCL Press, forthcoming.

Gilbert, N. and Doran, J. (eds), *Simulating Societies: The Computer Simulation of Social Phenomena*, London: UCL Press, 1994

Gilbert, N. and Conte, R. (eds), *Artificial Societies: The Computer Simulation of Social Life*, London: UCL Press, 1995.

Gilbert, N., 'Simulation as a Research Strategy', in K.G. Troitzsch, U.G. Müller, N. Gilbert and J.E. Doran (eds), *Social Science Microsimulation*, Berlin: Springer-Verlag, 1996.

Gilbert, N., 'Environments and Languages to Support Simulation', in K.G. Troitzsch, U.G. Müller, N. Gilbert and J.E. Doran (eds), *Social Science Microsimulation*, Berlin: Springer-Verlag, 1996.

Gilbert, N., 'Holism, Individualism and Emergent Properties: An Approach from the Perspective of Simulation', in R. Hegselmann *et al.* (eds), *Modelling and Simulation in the Social Sciences from the Philosophy of Science Point of View*, Dordrecht: Kluwer, 1996.

Gilbert, G.N., 'Computer Simulation and the Social Sciences', Report for ESRC, 16 October (17 pp.).

Gilbert, G.N., 'The Simulation of Social Processes', in T. Coppock (ed.), *Information Technology and Scholarly Disciplines*, London: British Academy, 1997.

Gilbert, N. and Troitzsch, K., *Simulation for the Social Sciences*, Milton Keynes: Open University Press, forthcoming.

Economic Learning and Social Evolution

Ken Binmore, Robin Dunbar, Henry Plotkin, Robin Seymour, David Ulph and Richard Vaughan

Binmore, K.G., 'Playing Fair', *Game Theory and the Social Contract I*, MIT Press, Cambridge, Mass., 1994.

Binmore, K.G., 'Rationality in the Centipede', in R. Fagin (ed.), *Theoretical Aspects of Reasoning about Knowledge: Proceedings of the fifth TARK conference*, Morgan Kaufmann, San Mateo, California, 1994.

Binmore, K.G. and Samuelson, L., 'An Economist's Perspective on the Evolution of Norms', *Journal of Institutional and Theoretical Economics*, 150, 45–71, 1994.

Binmore, K.G. and Samuelson, L., 'Drift', *European Economic Review*, 38, 851–867, 1994.

Binmore, K.G., Samuelson, L. and Vaughan, R., 'Musical Chairs: Modelling Noisy Evolution', *Games and Economic Behaviour*, 11, 1–35, 1995.

Binmore, K.G., Gale, J. and Samuelson, L., 'Learning to be Imperfect: the Ultimatum Game', *Games and Economic Behaviour*, 8, 56–90, 1995.

Dunbar, R. and Spoors, M., 'Social Networking, Support Cliques and Kinship', *Human Nature*, 6(3), 273–290, 1995.

Dunbar, R., Clark, A. and Hurst, N., 'Conflict and Co-operation among the Vikings: Contingent Behavioural Decisions', *Ethology and Sociology*, 16, 233–246, 1995.

Dunbar, R., 'The Mating System of Callitrichid Primates: I. Conditions for the Co-evolution of Pair Bonding and Twinning', *Animal Behaviour*, 50, 1057–1070, 1995.

Dunbar, R., 'The Mating System of Callitrichid Primates: II. The Impact of Helpers', *Animal Behaviour*, 50, 1071–89, 1995.

Dunbar, R., 'Neocortex Size and Group Size in Primates: A Test of the Hypothesis', *Journal of Human Evolution*, 28, 287–296, 1995.

Entrepreneurial Behaviour amongst General Practitioners

David Whynes, Christine Ennew and Teresa Feighan

Whynes, D. and Reed, G. 'Fundholders' Referral Patterns and Perceptions of Service Quality in Hospital Provision of Elective General Surgery', British Journal of General Practice, 44, 557–60, 1994.
Whynes, D., Baines, D. and Tolley, K., 'GP Fundholding and the Costs of Prescribing', *Journal of Public Health Medicine*, 17, 323–9, 1995.

Framing, Salience and Product Images

Michael Bacharach, Andrew Colman and Diego Gambetta

Bacharach, M. and Gambetta, D., 'Signalling Identity', mimeo, Institute of Economics and Statistics, Oxford, 1996.
Bacharach, M. and Gambetta, D., 'Elements of a Theory of Quality Signals', mimeo, Institute of Economics and Statistics, Oxford, 1996.
Bacharach, M., Jones, M. and Stahl, D., 'Measuring Saliences in an Oddity Task and a Memory Task', mimeo, Institute of Economics and Statistics, Oxford, 1996.
Bacharach, M. and Stahl, D., 'The Variable Frame Level-n Theory of Games', mimeo, Institute of Economics and Statistics, Oxford, 1996.
Bacharach, M. and Bernasconi, M., 'The Variable Frame Theory of Focal Points: An Experimental Study', *Games and Economic Behavior*, 19, 1–45, 1997.
Bacharach, M., 'Showing What You Are by Showing Who You Are', Russell Sage Foundation Research Report, mimeo, Institute of Economics and Statistics, Oxford, 1997.
Bacharach, M., Jones, M. and Stahl, D., 'Saliences of Objects in an Oddity Task and a Memory Task', mimeo, Institute of Economics and Statistics, Oxford, 1997.
Bacharah, M., (in press), 'Common Knowledge', *The New Palgrave Dictionary of Economics and the Law*, Macmillan: London, forthcoming.
Colman, A.M., Wober, J.M. and Norris, C.E., 'Sight Bites: A Study of Viewers' Impressions of Corporate Logos in the Communications Industry', *Journal of the Market Research Society*, 37, 405–15, 1995.
Colman, A.M., 'Prisoner's Dilemma, Chicken, and Mixed-Strategy Evolutionary Equilibria', *The Behavioral and Brain Sciences*, 18, 550–1, 1995.
Colman, A.M. and Stirk, J.A., 'Stackelberg Thinking in Mixed-Motive Games: An Experimental Investigation', in C. Roland-Lévy (ed.), *Social & Economic Representations*, 2, 1115–26, proceedings of the International Association for Economic Psychology XXIst Annual Colloquium, Paris: Academie de Paris, Université de René Descartes, 1996.
Colman, A.M., 'Singleton Bias in Multi-attribute Choice', mimeo, Department of Psychology, University of Leicester, 1996.
Colman, A.M. and Stirk, J.A., 'Singleton Bias in Multi-attribute Decision Making with Equally Valued Alternatives', mimeo, Department of Psychology, University of Leicester, 1996.

Colman, A.M., 'Focal Point Selection in Matching Games: Problems of Rational Justification', mimeo, Department of Psychology, University of Leicester, 1997.

Colman, A.M. and Bacharach, M., 'Payoff Dominance and the Stackelberg Heuristic', *Theory and Decision*, 43, 1–19, 1997.

Colman, A.M. and Wilson, J.C., 'Antisocial Personality Disorder: An Evolutionary Game Theory Analysis', *Legal and Criminology Psychology*, 2, 23–34, 1997.

Colman, A.M., 'Salience and Focusing in Pure Co-ordination Games', *Journal of Economic Methodology*, 4, 61–81, 1997.

Colman, A.M., 'Rationality Assumptions of Game Theory and the Backward Induction Paradox', in N. Chater and M. Oaksford (eds), *Rational Models of Cognition*, Oxford: Oxford University Press, forthcoming.

Colman, A.M., (in press), 'Salience and Focusing in Pure Co-ordination Games', *Journal of Economic Methodology*, forthcoming.

Colman, A.M. and Stirk, J.A., (in press), 'Stackelberg Reasoning in Mixed-Motive Games: An Experimental Investigation', *Journal of Economic Psychology*, forthcoming.

Gambetta, D., 'Model, Mimic and Dupe', Russell Sage Foundation Research Report, mimeo, Institute of Economics and Statistics, Oxford, 1997.

Pulford, B.D. and Colman, A.M., 'Overconfidence, Base Rates and Outcome Positivity/Negativity of Predicted Events', *British Journal of Psychology*, 87, 431–45, 1996.

Pulford, B.D. and Colman, A.M., 'Overconfidence: Feedback and Item Difficulty Effects', *Personality and Individual Differences*, 23, 125–33, 1997.

Morals and Money: Green and Ethical Investing

Alan Lewis, Paul Webley, Adrian Winnett and Craig MacKenzie

Lewis, A., 'Shared Economic Beliefs', in C. Fraser and G. Gaskell (eds), *The Social Psychological Study of Widespread Beliefs*, Oxford: Clarendon, 1990.

Mackenzie, C., 'The Stewardship Process: A Case Study of Friends Provident Stewardship', Discussion Paper, University of Bath, School of Social Sciences.

Mackenzie, C., 'Where are the Motives? Problems with evidence in the work of Richard Thaler', *Journal of Economic Psychology*, 18, 1, 123–37, 1997.

Mackenzie, C., 'Ethical Investment and the Challenge of Corporate Reform', PhD Thesis, University of Bath, 1997.

Mackenzie, C. and Lewis, A., 'Morals and Markets: The Case of Ethical Investing', in C. Roland-Lévy (ed.), *Social & Economic Representations*, 2, 1153–65, proceedings of the International Association for Economic Psychology XXIst Annual Colloquium, Paris: Academie de Paris, Université de René Descartes, 1996.

Mackenzie, C. and Lewis, A., 'Morals and Markets: The Case of Ethical Investors', *Business Ethics Quarterly*, 8, 1998.

Webley, P., 'Ethical Investing: The Willingness to Sacrifice Financial Return', in B. Rüggelambert *et al.* (eds), *Economic Psychology and Experimental Economics*, 49–51, Eschborn: Christian Reick Verlag, 1992.

Winnett, A., 'You'd have to be green to invest in this: journalism, finance and ethics', Discussion Paper, University of Bath, School of Social Sciences.

Public Attitudes to Taxation and Public Spending

Lindsay Brook, John Hall and Ian Preston

Besley, T., Hall, J. and Preston, I., 'Private Health Insurance and the State of the NHS', IFS Commentary No. 52, London: Institute for Fiscal Studies (1996).

Brook, L., Hall, J. and Preston, I., 'Attitudes to Taxation and Public Spending', in C. Roland-Lévy (ed.), *Social & Economic Representations*, 2, 1141–52, proceedings of the International Association for Economic Psychology XXIst Annual Colloquium, Paris: Academie de Paris, Université de René Descartes, 1996.

Brook, L., 'Attitudes to Spending on Welfare,' *Insurance Trends*, July 1997.

Hall, J., Ridge, M. and Preston, I., 'How Public Attitudes to Expenditure Differ', in D. Corry (ed.), *Public Expenditure: Effective Management and Control*, London: Institute for Public Policy Research, 1996.

Preston, I. and Ridge, M., 'Demand for Local Public Spending: Evidence from the British Social Attitudes survey', *Economic Journal*, 105, 644–60, (1995).

Preston, I., Hall, J. and Brook, L., 'Attitudes to Tax and Spending', in R. Jowell *et al.* (eds.), *British Social Attitudes: the 13th Report*, Dartmouth Publishing, 1996.

Symbolic Meanings of Goods as Determinants of Impulse Buying Behaviour

Helga Dittmar, Jane Beattie and Susanne Friese

Dittmar H., Beattie J. and Friese S., 'Gender Identity and Material Symbols: Objects and Decision Considerations in Impulse Purchases', *Journal of Economic Psychology*, 16, 491–511, (1995).

Dittmar, H., Beattie, J. and Friese, S., 'Objects, Decision Considerations and Self-Image in Men's and Women's Impulse Purchases', *Acta Psychologica*, 93, 187–206, 1996.

Dittmar, H., Beattie, J. and Friese, S., 'Objects, Decision Considerations and Self-Image in Men's and Women's Impulse Purchases', in P. Ayton, J. Beattie, R. Beyth-Marom and P. Koele (eds.), *Contributions in Decision Making: II*, North Holland, 1996.

Dittmar, H., Beattie, J. and Friese, S., 'The Role of Self-Discrepancies in Shopping Addiction', in C. Roland-Lévy (ed.), *Social & Economic Representations*, 2, 1140, proceedings of the International Association for Economic Psychology XXIst Annual Colloquium, Paris: Academie de Paris, Université de René Descartes, 1996.

Dittmar, H., Beattie, J. and Friese, S., 'The Role of Self-Discrepancies in Normal and Compulsive Shopping', *International Journal of Psychology*, 31, Special Issue Report of the 26th International Congress of Psychology, 1996.

Dittmar, H., 'Materialism', in P. Earl and S. Kemp (eds.), *The Elgar Companion to Consumer Research and Economic Psychology*, London & Brookfield, Vermont: Elgar, forthcoming.

Dittmar, H., 'Impulse Buying in ordinary and "compulsive" consumers' in J. Baron, G. Loomes and Weber (eds.), *Conflict in Decisions: Essays in Honour of Jane Beattie*, (forthcoming).

The Consistency or Inconsistency of Preferences under Risk and Over Time

Robert Sugden, Robin Cubitt, Graham Loomes and Chris Starmer

Beattie, J., Bullock, S. and Loomes, G., 'The Impact of Incentives upon Risky Choice Experiments', *Journal of Risk and Uncertainty*, 14, 149–62, 1997.

Cubitt, R.P. and Sugden, R., 'On Money Pumps', Economics Research Centre Discussion Paper No. 9509, University of East Anglia, 1995.

Cubitt, R.P., Starmer, C. and Sugden, R., 'Dynamic Choice and the Common Ratio Effect', Economics Research Centre Discussion Paper No. 9510, University of East Anglia, 1995.

Cubitt, R.P. and Sugden, R., 'The Selection of Preferences through Imitation', Economics Research Centre Discussion Paper No. 9510, University of East Anglia, 1995.

Cubitt, R.P., Starmer, C. and Sugden, R., 'On the validity of the Random Lottery Incentive System', Economies Research Centre Discussion Paper No. 9616, University of East Anglia.

Cubitt, R.P., 'Rational Dynamic Choice and Expected Utility Theory', *Oxford Economic Papers*, 48, 1–19, 1996.

Cubitt, R.P., Starmer, C. and Sugden, R., 'Some Tests of the Validity of the Random Lottery Incentive System', in C. Roland-Lévy (ed.), *Social & Economic Representations*, 2, 1176–1187, proceedings of the International Association for Economic Psychology XXIst Annual Colloquium, Paris: Academie de Paris, Université de René Descartes, 1996.

Loomes, G. and Sugden, R., 'Testing Different Stochastic Specifications for Risky Choice', Economics Research Centre Discussion Paper No. 9607, University of East Anglia, 1996.

Loomes G., 'Probabilities vs. Money: A Test of Some Fundamental Assumptions about Rational Decision-Making', *Economic Journal*, forthcoming.

Starmer, C., 'Explaining Risky Choices without Assuming Preferences', *Social Choice and Welfare*, 13, 201–13, 1996.

Starmer, C., 'The Economics of Risk', in P. Callow (ed.), *The Handbook of Environmental Risk Assessment*, Blackwell, 1997.

Starmer, C., 'Cycling with Rules of Thumb: An Experimental Test for a New Form of Non-Transitive Behaviour', *Theory and Decision*, forthcoming.

Starmer C., 'Experiments in Economics: Should We Trust the Dismal Scientists in White Coats?', *Journal of Economic Methodology*, forthcoming.

Starmer, C. and Sugden, R., 'Testing Alternative Explanations of Cyclical Choices', *Economica*, forthcoming.

Sugden, R., 'Alternatives to Expected Utility', in S. Barbera, P. Hammond and C. Seidl (eds.), *Handbook of Utility Theory*, Kluwer, 1997.

The Role of Beliefs about the Fairness of Wage Differentials in Wage Setting

Julie Dickinson and Lucia Sell-Trujillo

Dickinson, J., 'The Role of Beliefs about the Fairness of Wage Differentials in Wage Setting', *People Management*, November 1995.
Dickinson, J. and Sell-Trujillo, L., 'Explanations for Pay Differentials: Rhetoric or Social Representations?', in C. Roland-Lévy (ed.), *Social & Economic Representations*, 2, 1139, proceedings of the International Association for Economic Psychology XXIst Annual Colloquium, Paris: Academie de Paris, Université de René Descartes, 1996.

Welfare Citizenship and Economic Rationality

Hartley Dean and Margaret Melrose

Dean, H. and Melrose, M., 'Fiddling the Social: Understanding Benefit Fraud', *Benefits*, 14, 17–18, September 1995.
Dean, H. and Barrett, D., 'Unrespectable Research and Researching the Unrespectable', in H. Dean and D. Barrett (eds), *Ethics and Social Policy Research*, University of Luton and the Social Policy Association, 1996.
Dean, H., 'What sort of a problem?', *New Review of the Low Pay Unit*, No. 37, p. 16 (January/February), 1996.
Dean, H. and Melrose, M., 'Unravelling Citizenship: The Significance of Social Security Benefit Fraud', *Critical Social Policy*, 16, 3, 3–33, August 1996.
Dean, H., 'In Spite of Welfare: Understanding Social Security Benefit Fraud', in C. Roland-Lévy (ed.), *Social & Economic Representations*, 2, 1127–38, proceedings of the International Association for Economic Psychology XXIst Annual Colloquium, Paris: Academie de Paris, Université de René Descartes, 1996.
Dean, H. and Melrose, M., 'Manageable Discord: Fraud and Resistance in the Social Security System', *Social Policy Administration*, Vol. 31, 1997.
Dean, H., 'Underclassed or Undermined? Young People and Social Citizenship', in R. MacDonald (ed.), *Youth, the Underclass and Social Exclusion*, Routledge, 1997.
Melrose, M., 'Enticing subjects and disembodied objects', in H. Dean (ed.), *Ethics and Social Policy Research*, University of Luton Press/Social Policy Association, 1996.

References

Abratt, R. and Goodey, S.D. (1990) 'Unplanned buying and in-store stimuli in supermarkets', *Managerial and Decision Economics*, 11, 111–21.

Ainley, P. (1993) 'The legacy of the Manpower Services Commission: training in the 1980s' in Taylor-Gooby, P. and Lawson, R. (eds) *Markets and Managers: New issues in the delivery of welfare* (Open University Press, Milton Keynes).

Aldrich, H.E., J.C. Cater, T.P. Jones and D. McEvoy (1981) 'Business development and self-segregation: Asian enterprise in three British cities' in C. Peach, V. Robinson and S. Smith (eds) *Ethnic Segregation in Cities* (Croom Helm, London).

Allen G and Crow G (eds) (1989) *Home and Family: creating the domestic sphere* (Macmillan, London)

Almond, G. and Verba, S. (1965) *The Civic Culture* (Little, Brown & Company, Boston).

Almond, G. and Verba, S. (eds) (1989) *The Civic Culture Revisited* (Sage, Boston).

Andreasson, P. (1987) 'On the social psychology of the stock market', *Journal of Personality and Social Psychology*, 53, 490–96.

Audit Commission (1996) *What the Doctor Ordered: a study of GP fundholders in England and Wales* (Audit Commission, London).

Axelrod, R. (1984) *The Evolution of Cooperation* (Basic Books, New York).

Bacon, R. and Eltis, W. (1976) *Britain's Economic Problem: Too Few Producers* (Macmillan, London).

Bain, J. (1993) 'Budget holding: Here to stay?', *British Medical Journal*, 306, 1185–8.

Baldwin, S. (1994) 'The need for care in later life: social protection for older people and family caregivers', in S. Baldwin and J. Falkingham (eds), *Social Security and Social Change: New Challenges to the Beveridge Model* (Harvester Wheatsheaf, Hemel Hempstead).

Baron, J., Badgio, P. and Gaskins, I.W. (1986). 'Cognitive style and its improvement: a normative approach' in R.J. Sternberg (ed.), *Advances in the Psychology of Human Intelligence*, vol. 3 (Erlbaum, New Jersey).

Baumol, W (1968) 'Entrepreneurship in economic theory', *American Economic Review*, vol. 58, pp. 644–71.

Beattie, J. and Barlas, S. (1993) 'Predicting trade-off difficulty in multi-attribute decision making', *Journal of Experimental Psychology: Human Perception and Performance*.

Bechhofer, F. *et al.* (1974) 'The petits bourgeois in the class structure: the case of the small shopkeepers' in F. Parkin (ed.) *The Social Analysis of Class Structure* (Tavistock Publications, London).

Beck, U., Giddens, A. and Lash, S. (1994) *Reflexive Modernisation* (Polity Press, Cambridge).

Becker, G. (1981) *A Treatise on the Family* (Harvard University Press, Cambridge, Massachusetts).

Becker, G. (1996) *Accounting for Tastes* (Harvard University Press, Cambridge, Massachusetts).

Begg, I. and Nectoux, F. (1995) 'Social protection and European Union', *Journal of European Social Policy*, 5, 4, pp. 285–302.

Belk, R.W. (1988), 'Possessions and the extended self', *Journal of Consumer Research*, 15, 139–68.

Bellenger, D.N., Robertson, D.H., and Hirschman, E.C. (1978), 'Impulse buying varies by product', *Journal of Advertising Research*, 18, 15–18.

Benjamin, D. (ed.) (1995) *The Home: words, interpretations, meanings and environments* (Avebury, Aldershot).

Beresford, P. and Merchant, K (1997) 'The Eastern Eye Britain's Richest Asian 100', *Eastern Eye* (London).

Beresford, P. with S. Boyd (1997) 'The Sunday Times Rich List 1997', *The Sunday Times*, London.

Bernard, S. and Parker, G. (1995) 'The Determinants of Residential Care in Northern Ireland: Report on Secondary Data Analysis', *NCSSU Working Paper 35*, Nuffield Community Care Studies Unit, Leicester.

Besley, T., J.D. Hall and I.P. Preston (1966) *Private Health Insurance and the State of the NHS*, IFS Commentary No. 52, London.

Bethwaite, J. and Thomkinson, P. (1996) 'The ultimatum game and non-selfish utility functions', *Journal of Economic Psychology*, 17, 259–71.

Beveridge, W. (1942) *Social Insurance and Allied Services*, Cmd. 6404, HMSO, London.

Blackwell, J. (1994) 'Changing work patterns and their implications for social protection' in Baldwin, S. and Falkingham, J. (eds) *Social Security and Social Change: new challenges to the Beveridge model* (Harvester Wheatsheaf, Hemel Hempstead).

Bland, R., B. Elliot, and F. Bechhofer (1978) 'Social mobility in the petite bourgeoisie', *Acta Sociologica*, 21, 3, 229–48.

Bloch, P.H., Ridgway, N.M. and Dawson, S.A. (1994) 'The shopping mall as consumer habitat', *Journal of Retailing*, 70, 23–42.

Boleat, M. (1997) 'The politics of home ownership' in Williams, P. (ed.) *Directions in housing policy* (PCP, London), 54–67.

Bone, M. (1996) *Dependency in Later Life* (HMSO, London).

Boyett, I. and Finlay, D. (1993) 'The emergence of the educational entrepreneur', *Long Range Planning*, 26(3), 114–22.

Boyett, I. and Finlay, D. (1995) 'The quasi-market, the entrepreneur and the effectiveness of the NHS business manager', *Public Administration*, 73 (3) 393–411.

Braun, O.L. and Wicklund, R.A. (1989) 'Psychological antecedents of conspicuous consumption', *Journal of Economic Psychology*, 10, 161–87.

Brook, L., J.D. Hall and I.P. Preston (1996) 'Public spending and taxation' in Jowell, Curtice, Park, Brook and Thomson (eds).

Brook, L., J.D. Hall and I.P. Preston (1996) 'What drives support for higher public spending?', *EBB Discussion Paper no. 16*, Social Policy Department, University of Kent or EBB Web pages at http://www.ukc.ac.uk/ESRC/.

Bull, I. and Willard, G.E. (1993) 'Towards a theory of entrepreneurship', *Journal of Business Venturing*, 8, 183–95.

Burgoyne, C. (1995) 'Financial organisation and decision-making within Western households', *Journal of Economic Psychology*, 16, 3, 421–30.

Burrows, R. and Loader, B. (eds, 1994) *Towards a Post-Fordist Welfare State?* (Routledge, London).

Calnan, M., S. Cant and J. Gabe, (1993) *Going private: why people pay for their health care* (Oxford University Press, Oxford).

Camerer, C. and Thaler, R. (1995) 'Anomalies – ultimatums, dictators and manners', *Journal of Economic Perspectives*, 9, 202–19.

Carnoy, M., Castells, M., Cohen, S. and Cardoso, F. (1993) *The Global Economy in the Information Age* (Penn State University, Pennsylvania).

Casson, M.C. (1982) *The Entrepreneur: An Economic Theory* (Oxford, Martin Robertson).

Central Statistical Office (CSO: 1954) *Annual Abstract of Statistics*, 1954 (HMSO, London).

Central Statistical Office (CSO: 1995) *Annual Abstract of Statistics*, 1995 (HMSO, London).

Central Statistical Office (CSO: 1995b) *Social Trends no. 25* (HMSO, London).

Chambers, R. and Belcher, J. (1993) 'Work patterns of General Practitioners before and after the introduction of the 1990 Contract', *British Journal of General Practice*, 43, 410–12.

Cheah, H.B. (1990) 'Schumpeterian and Austrian entrepreneurship: unity within duality', *Journal of Business Venturing*, 5(6), 341–7.

Chell, E., Haworth, J.M. and Brearly, S.A. (1991) *The Entrepreneurial Personality: Concepts, Cases and Categories* (Routledge, London).

Christenson, G.A., Faber, R.J., de Zwaan, M. and Raymond, N.C. (1994), 'Compulsive buying: Descriptive characteristics and psychiatric comorbidity', *Journal of Clinical Psychiatry*, 55, 5–11.

Coles, I. and Furbey, R. (1994) *The Eclipse of Council Housing* (Routledge, London).

Commission on Social Justice (1994) *Social Justice: Strategies for national renewal* (Vintage, London).

Cook, D. (1989) *Rich Law, Poor Law: different responses to tax and supplementary benefit fraud* (Open University Press, Milton Keynes).

Coughlin, R. (ed. 1991) *Morality, Rationality and Efficiency: New Perspectives on Socio-Economics* (M.E. Sharpe, New York).

Csikszentmihalyi, M. & Rochberg-Halton, E. (1981), *The Meaning of Things: Domestic Symbols and the Self* (Cambridge: Cambridge University Press).

Cullis, J. Lewis, A. and Winnett, A. (1992), 'Paying to be good? UK ethical investments', *Kyklos*, 45, 3–24.

Daniel, W.W. (1968) *Racial Discrimination in England* (Penguin, Harmondsworth).

Darke, J. (1996) 'The English woman's castle . . .' pp. 61–71 in Booth, C., Darke, J. and Yeadle, S. (eds) *Changing Places* (PCP, London).

Darton, R. (1996) 'Length of stay of residents and patients in residential and nursing homes: statistical report', cited in Joseph Rowntree Foundation (1996).

d'Astous, A., Maltais, J. and Roberge, C. (1990) 'Compulsive buying tendencies of adolescent consumers', *Advances in Consumer Research*, 17, 306–13.

Davidsson, P. (1988) 'Type of man and type of company revisited: a confirmatory cluster analysis approach', in Kirchoff, B.A., Long, W.A., McMullan, W.E., Vesper, K.H. and Wetzel, W. (ed.) *Frontiers of Entrepreneurship Research* (Babson College, Wellesley, MA).

De Bondt, W.F.M. (1993) 'Betting on trends: intuitive forecasts of financial risk and return' *International Journal of Forecasting*, 9, 355–71.

De Bondt, W.F.M. (1993) 'Betting on trends: intuitive forecasts of financial risk and return', *International Journal of Forecasting*, 9, 355–71.

Deacon, A. and Fairfoot, P. (1994) 'Investigating fraud', *Poverty*, No. 87 (Spring).

Deakins, D., G. Hussain and M. Ram (1994) 'Ethnic entrepreneurs and commercial banks: untapped potential', *Regional Studies* 29(11) 95–100.

Dean, H. (1993) 'Social security: the income maintenance business' in Taylor-Gooby, P. and Lawson, R. (eds) *Markets and Managers: new issues in the delivery of welfare* (Open University Press, Milton Keynes).

Dean, H. and Barrett, D. (1996) 'Unrespectable research and researching the unrespectable', in Dean, H. (ed.) *Ethics and Social Policy Research* (University of Luton Press/Social Policy Association, Luton).

Dean, H. and Melrose, M. (1996) 'Unravelling citizenship: the significance of social security benefit fraud', *Critical Social Policy*, Issue 48 (16, 3).

Dean, H. and Melrose, M. (1997) 'Manageable discord: fraud and resistance in the social security system', *Social Policy and Administration'*, 31, 2.

Dean, H. and Taylor-Gooby, P. (1992) *Dependency Culture: the explosion of a myth* (Harvester Wheatsheaf, Hemel Hempstead).

Denes, R.V. and Epstein, S. (1994) 'Conflict between intuitive and rational processing: when people behave against their better judgement', *Journal of Personality and Social Psychology*, 66, 819–29.

Dennis, N. and Erdos, G. (1992) *Families without Fatherhood* (Institute of Economic Affairs, London).

Department of Employment (1995) *DoE Gazette*, 103, 10.

Department of Health (1996) *A New Partnership for Care in Old Age: a Discussion Document*, Cm 3242 (HMSO, London).

Department of Health (1997) *A New Partnership for Care in Old Age: A Policy Statement*, Cm 3563 (HMSO, London).

Department of Health and Social Security (DHSS: 1985) *The Reform of Social Security*, cmnd 9517 (HMSO, London).

Department of Health and Social Security (DHSS: 1989) *Working for Patients*, Cmd 555 (HMSO, London).

Dittmar, H. (1989). 'Gender identity-related meanings of personal possessions', *British Journal of Social Psychology*, 28, 159–71.

Dittmar, H. (1991) 'Meanings of material possessions as reflections of identity: gender and social-material position in society', in F.W. Rudmin (ed.), *To Have Possessions: A Handbook on Ownership and Property*. Special issue of *Journal of Social Behaviour and Personality*, 6, 165–86.

Dittmar, H. (1992a). *The Social Psychology of Material Possessions: to have is to be* (Harvester Wheatsheaf, Hemel Hempstead).

Dittmar, H. (1992b) 'Perceived material wealth and first impressions', *British Journal of Social Psychology*, 31, 379–92.

Dittmar, H. (1994) 'Material possessions as stereotypes: material images of different socio-economic groups', *Journal of Economic Psychology*, 15, 561–85.

Dittmar, H. (1996). The social psychology of economic and consumer behaviour', in G.R. Semin and K. Fiedler (eds), *Applied Social Psychology*, 145–72 (London: Sage).

Dittmar, H., Beattie, J. and Friese, S. (1995) 'Gender identity and material symbols: objects and decision considerations in impulse purchases', *Journal of Economic Psychology*, 15, 491–511. Special issue on Personal and Household Finance.

Dittmar, H., Beattie, J. and Friese, S. (1996) 'Objects, decision considerations and self-image in men's and women's impulse purchases', *Acta Psychologica*, 93, 187–206.

Dolan, L., (1995) 'When the state becomes a burden on the elderly', *The Times*, 13 May 1995, Weekend Money.

Dunkleberg, W.C. and Cooper, A.C. (1982) 'Entrepreneurial typologies: an empirical study', in Vesper, K.H. (ed.) *Frontiers of Entrepreneurship Research* (Babson College, Wellesley, MA).

Dunleavy, P. and Husbands, C. (1985) *British Democracy at the Cross-Roads* (George, Allen and Unwin, London).

Dunleavy, P. (1980) 'The political implications of sectoral cleavages and the growth of state employment, parts I and II', *Political Studies*, 28, 3, 364–83, 527–49.

Dunleavy, P. (1991) *Democracy, Bureaucracy and Public Choice* (Harvester Wheatsheaf, Hemel Hempstead).

Earl, P. (1983). *The Economic Imagination* (Brighton, Wheatsheaf).

Edgell, S. and Duke, V. (1991) *A Measure of Thatcherism* (HarperCollins, Hammersmith).

Elliott, R. (1994) 'Addictive consumption: function and fragmentation in postmodernity', *Journal of Consumer Policy*, 17, 159–79.

Employment Department Group (1995) *Government Expenditure Policies 1995/96–97/98*, cmnd 2805 (HMSO, London).

Ennew, C.T., Feighan, T. and Whynes, D.K. (1997) 'Entrepreneurial Beliefs and Behaviour Among GPs', *EBB Discussion Paper*.

Ennew, C.T., Jolleys, J., Robinson, P. and Whynes, D. (1994) 'Entrepreneurship and innovation among GP Fundholders: some preliminary evidence', *School of Management and Finance, Discussion Paper no. 94:7*, University of Nottingham.

Ennew, C.T., Robbie, K., Wright, M. and Thompson, S. (1992) 'Management buy-ins as a new organisational form: entrepreneurial characteristics and performance', *Frontiers of Entrepreneurship Research*, 628–44

Etzioni, A. (1988), *The Moral Dimension: toward a new economics* (New York, Free Press).

Etzioni, A. (1988) 'Normative-affective factors: toward a new decision-making model' *Journal of Economic Psychology*, 9, 125–50.

Etzioni, A. (1993) *The Spirit of Community: Rights, Responsibilities and the Communitarian Agenda* (Crown Publishers, New York).

EU (1995) *The Major Issues of European Demography* (European Commission, Luxembourg).

EU (1996) *Social Protection in Europe: 1995* (European Commission, Luxembourg).

Evans, R. (1996). 'Econometrics and expertise: a sociological investigation of macroeconomic modelling' PhD Thesis, University of Bath.

Evason, E. and Woods, R. (1995a) 'Poverty, de-regulation of the labour market and benefit fraud', *Social Policy and Administration*, 29, 1.

Evason, E. and Woods, R. (1995b) *Poverty, Charity and 'Doing the Double'* (Avebury, Aldershot).

Extel (1994), *City Analysts and the Environment* (London, Extel Ltd).

Faber, R.J., O'Guinn, T.C. and Krych, R. (1987), 'Compulsive consumption', Advances in Consumer Research, 14, 132–5.

Fallis, G. (1986) *Housing Economics* (Butterworth, Toronto).

Ferlie, E. (1992) 'The creation and evolution of quasi markets in the public sector: a problem for strategic management', *Strategic Management Journal*, 13 (special), 79–97

Ferrerra, M. (1993) *European Community Citizens and Social Protection* (Commission of the EU, Luxembourg).

Field, F. and Owen, M. (1994) *Beyond Punishment: hard choices on the road to full employability* (Institute of Community Studies, London).

Field, F. (1996) *Stakeholder Welfare* (Institute of Economic Affairs, London).

Finch, J. and Mason, J. (1993) *Negotiating Family Responsibilities* (Routledge, London).

Flynn, N. (1993) *Public Sector Management* (Harvester Wheatsheaf, Harlow).

Ford, J. (1994) *Problematic Home Ownership* (Joseph Rowntree Foundation, York).

Forrest, R. and Murie, A. (1994) 'Home ownership in recession', *Housing Studies*, 9, 55–74

Forrest, R; Murie, A. and Williams, P. (1990) *Home Ownership: Differentiation and Fragmentation* (Unwin Hyman, London).

Foxall, G. (1990) *Consumer Psychology in Behavioural Perspective* (London and New York, Routledge).

Friese, S. and Koenig, H. (1993) 'Shopping for trouble', *Advancing the Consumer Interest*, 5, 24–29.

Fukuyama, F. (1989) 'The end of history', *The National Interest*, 16 (summer), 3–18.

Fukuyama, F. (1995) *Trust* (Penguin Books, London).

Gamble, A. (1988) *The Free Economy and the Strong State* (Macmillan, Basingstoke).

Gartner, W.B. (1990) 'What are we talking about when we talk about entrepreneurship?', *Journal of Business Venturing*, 5, 15–28.

Gellner, E. (1992) *Postmodernism, Reason and Religion* (Routledge, London).

Gentle, G.; Dorling, D. and Cornford, J. (1994) 'Negative equity and British housing in the 1990s: Cause and effect' Urban Studies 31, 181–99.

Giddens, A. (1990) *Consequences of Modernity* (Polity Press, Cambridge).

Giddens, A. (1991) *Modernity and Self-Identity: self and society in the late modern age* (Polity Press, Cambridge).

Giddens, A. (1994) *Beyond Left and Right?* (Polity Press, Cambridge).

Giddens, A. (1976) *New Rules of Sociological Method* (Hutchinson, London).

Glennerster, H. (1992) *Paying for Welfare: the 1990s* (Harvester Wheatsheaf, Hemel Hempstead).

Golding, P. and Middleton, S. (1982) *Images of Welfare: press and public attitudes to poverty* (Martin Robertson, Oxford).

Goodman, A. and Webb, S. (1994) *For Richer, for Poorer: the changing distribution of income in the United Kingdom, 1961–91* (Institute of Fiscal Studies, London).

Gordon, C. (1988) *The Myth of Family Care? The Elderly in the Early 1930s*, Welfare State Programme Discussion Paper WSP/29, Suntory Toyota International Centre for Economics and Related Disciplines, LSE, London.

Graham, H. (1987) 'Being poor: perceptions of coping strategies of lone mothers' in Brannen, J. and Wilson, G. (eds) *Give and Take in Families* (Allen & Unwin, London).

Green,' D., K.Jacowitz, D. Kahneman and D. McFadden (1995) 'Referendum Contingent Valuation, Anchoring and Willingness to Pay for Public Goods', paper presented at *Econometric Society 7th World Congress*, Tokyo.

Gregg, P. and Wadsworth, J. (1995) *More Work in Fewer Households?* (National Institute for Social Work, London).

Griffiths, R. (1988) *An Agenda for Action on Community Care* (HMSO, London).

Guth, W. and Tiertz, R., (1990) 'Ultimatum bargaining behaviour', *Journal of Economic Psychology*, 11, 417–49.

Habermas, J. (1976) *Legitimation Crisis* (Heineman, London).

Hakim, C. (1988) 'Self-employment in Britain: recent trends and current issues', *Work, Employment and Society*, 2, 4 pp. 421–50.

Hamnett, C., Harmer, M. and Williams, P. (1992) *Safe as houses* (PCP, London).

Hamnett, C. (1989) 'The owner occupied market in Britain: A North-South divide?' in Lewis, J. and Townsend, A. (eds) *The North–South divide* (Paul Chapman Publishing, London).

Handy, C. (1984) *The Future of Work* (Blackwell, Oxford).

Hanley, A. and Wilhelm, M.S. (1992) 'Compulsive buying: an exploration into self-esteem and money attitudes', *Journal of Economic Psychology*, 13, 5–18.

Hargreaves-Heap, S., Hollis, M., Lyons, B., Sugden, R. and Weale, A. (1992) *The Theory of Choice* (Blackwells, Oxford).

Harrington, J. (1992), *Investing with your Conscience* (John Wiley & Sons, New York).

Heath, A. and J. Ridge (1983) 'Social mobility of ethnic minorities', *Journal of Biosocial Science Supplement*, 8, pp. 169–84.

Heidrich, S.M., Forsthoff, C.A. and Ward, S.E. (1994) 'Psychological adjustment in adults with cancer: the self as mediator', *Health Psychology*, 13, 346–53.

Hessing, D., Elffers, H., Robben, H. and Webley, P. (1993) 'Needy or greedy? The social psychology of individuals who fraudulently claim unemployment benefits', *Journal of Applied Social Psychology*, 23, 3.

Higgins, T. (1987) 'Self-discrepancy: a theory relating self to affect', *Psychological Review*, 94, 319–40.

Hirsch, H. (1977) *The Social Limits to Growth* (Routledge & Kegan Paul, London).

Hirschman, A. (1970) *Exit Voice and Loyalty* (Harvard University Press, Cambridge, Massachusetts).

HM Treasury (1996) *Public Expenditure, Statistical Supplement to the Financial Statement and Budget, 1996/97*, Cm 3201 (HMSO, London).

Hoch, S.J. and Loewenstein, G.F. (1991) 'Time-inconsistent preferences and consumer self-control', *Journal of Consumer Research*, 17, 1–16.

Hoffman, E., McCabe, K., Schavhat, K. and Smith, V. (1994) 'Preferences, property rights and anonymity in bargaining games', *Games and Economic Behaviour*.

Hollis, M. and Nell, E. (1975) *Rational Economic Man* (Cambridge University Press.

Hollis, M. (1987) *The Cunning of Reason* (Cambridge University Press).

Holmans, A. (1995) 'What has happened to the North-South divide in house prices and the housing market?' in Wilcox, S., *Housing Finance Review*, 1995/6 (JRF, York).

House of Commons Health Committee (1996) *Long-Term Care: NHS Responsibilities for Meeting Continuing Care Needs*; volume 1, session 1995–6, First Report (HMSO, London).

Howard, J.A. and Sheth, J.N. (1969) *The Theory of Buyer Behavior* (New York, Wiley.)

Hume, D. (1739) *A Treatise of Human Nature* (Penguin, 1985, Harmondsworth).

Hume, D. (1875) 'On the independency of parliament' in T.H. Green and T.H. Gross (eds) *Essays, Moral, Political and Literary*, vol. 1 (Longmans, London).

Hutton, W. (1996) *The State We're In* (revised edition) (Vintage, London).

Iganski, P. and G. Payne (1996) 'Declining racial disadvantage in the British labour market', *Ethnic and Racial Studies* 19(1) (Routledge, London).

Ignatieff, M. (1984) *The Needs of Strangers* (Chatto & Windus, London).

Jessop, B. (1994) 'The transition to post-Fordism and the Schumpeterian workfare state' in Burrows, R. and Loader, B. (eds) *Towards a Post-Fordist Welfare State?* (Routledge, London).

Jones, P. Cullis, J. and Lewis, A. (in press), 'Public versus private provision of altruism: can fiscal policy make individuals "better" people?'.

Jones, T. (1993) *Britain's Ethnic Minorities* (Policy Studies Institute, London).

Jones, T.P., D. McEvoy, and G. Barrett (1994) 'Labour intensive practices in the ethnic minority firm', in Atkinson, J. and D. Storey (eds) *Employment, the small firm and the labour market* (Routledge, London).

Jones, B. *et al*. (1991) *Politics UK* (Philip Allan, London).

Jordan, B. and Redley, P. (1994) 'Polarisation, underclass and the welfare state', *Work, Employment and Society*, 8, 2.

Jordan, B., James, S., Kay, H. and Redley, P. (1992) *Trapped in Poverty? Labour market decisions in low income households* (Routledge, London).

Jordan, B. (1997) *A Theory of Poverty and Social Exclusion* (Polity Press, Cambridge).

Joseph Rowntree Foundation, (1996) *Meeting the Costs of Continuing Care: Report and Recommendations* (Joseph Rowntree Foundation, York).

Jowell, R., Brook, L. and Taylor, B. (eds) (1991) *British Social Attitudes: the 8th Report* (Gower, Aldershot).

Jowell, R., J. Curtice, A. Park, L. Brook and K. Thomson (eds) (1996) *British Social Attitudes: The 13th Report* (Dartmouth, Aldershot).

Jowell, R. *et al.* (1983–96 annual) *British Social Attitudes* (SCPR/Dartmouth, London).

Judge, K. and Solomon, M. (1993) 'Public opinion and the NHS', *Journal of Social Policy*, 22, 299–328.

Kaase, M. and Newton, K. (1995) *Beliefs in Government* (Oxford University Press, Oxford).

Kahneman, D. and Tversky, A. (1979) 'Prospect theory: an analysis of decision under risk', *Econometrica*, 47, 263–91.

Kamptner, N.L. (1991), 'Personal possessions and their meanings: a life-span perspective', in F. Rudmin (ed.), *To Have Possessions: A Handbook on Ownership and Property*. Special issue of the *Journal of Social Behaviour and Personality*, 6.

Kanter, R., 1985, *The Change Masters* (Unwin, London).

Kempson, E. (1996) *Life on a Low Income* (Joseph Rowntree Foundation, York).

Kirzner, I.M. (1973) *Competition and Entrepreneurship* (University of Chicago Press, Chicago).

Klamer, A. (1984). *The New Classical Macroeconomics: Conversations with the neo classical economists and their opponents* (Brighton: Wheatsheaf).

Klein, R., and Millar, J. (1995) 'Do-it yourself social policy: searching for a new paradigm?', *Social Policy and Administration*, 29, 4, 303–16.

Kollat, D.T. and Willet, R.P. (1969) 'Is impulse purchasing really a useful concept for marketing decisions?', *Journal of Marketing*, 33, 79–83.

Krueger, D.W. (1988) 'On compulsive shopping and spending', *American Journal of Psychotherapy*, 42, 574–84.

Kuran, T. (1995) 'Islamic economics and the Islamic subeconomy', *Journal of Economic Perspectives,* 9(4) 155–73.

Labour Party (1996) *New Labour, New Britain: the road to the manifesto* (The Labour Party, London).

Labour Party (1997) *New Labour: because Britain deserves better*, Election Manifesto (The Labour Party, London).

Lafuente, A. and Salas, V. (1989) 'Types of entrepreneurs and firms: the case of new Spanish firms', *Strategic Management Journal*, 10 17–30.

Laing and Buisson, (1993) *Care of Elderly People: Market Survey 1992/3* (Laing & Buisson Publications, London).

Le Grand, J. (1991), 'Quasi-markets and social policy', *Economic Journal*, 101 (September) pp. 1256–67.

Le Grand, J. and Bartlett, W. (eds) (1993) *Quasi-Markets and Social Policy* (Macmillan, Basingstoke).

Le Grand, J. (1967) 'Knights, knaves or pawns? Human behaviour and social policy', *Journal of Social Policy*, 26, 2, 149–70.

Le Grand, J. (1982) *The Strategy of Equality* (Allen & Unwin, London).

Lea, S., Tarpy, R. and Webley, P. (1987) *The Individual in the Economy* (Cambridge University Press, Cambridge).

Lee, R. (1993) *Doing Research on Sensitive Topics* (Sage, London).

Lees, D. (1996) *Economic Consequences of the Professions* (Institute of Economic Affairs, London).

Leibenstein, H. (1968) Entrepreneurship and Development', *American Economic Review*, 58, 72–83.

Leibfried, S. and Pierson, P. (eds) (1995) *European Social Policy* (Brookings Institute, Washington).

Lewis, A. (1990), 'Shared economic beliefs', in *The Social Psychological Study of Widespread Beliefs* (C. Fraser and G. Gaskell (eds) (Clarendon, Oxford).

Lewis, A. and Mackenzie, C. (1997) 'Money and morals: a quantitative study of ethical/social investors', *Procedings of 9th International Conference on Socio-Economics* (University of Montreal).

Lewis, A. and Webley, P. (1994) 'Social and ethical investing: beliefs, preferences and the willingness to sacrifice financial return', in *Ethics and Economic Affairs*, A. Lewis and K-E Wärneryd (eds) 171–82 (Routledge, London).

Lewis, A., Webley, P. and Furnham, A. (1995), *The New Economic Mind: the social psychology of economic behaviour* (Harvester Wheatsheaf, New York).

Liebenstein, H. (1966) 'Allocative efficiency or x-efficiency?' *American Economic Review*.

Loomes, G. and Sugden, R. (1982) 'Regret theory: an alternative theory of rational choice under uncertainty', *Economic Journal*, 92, 805–24.

Lowe, R. (1993) *The Welfare State in Britain since 1945* (Macmillan, London).

Lundberg, C.G. (1995), 'Learning and doing in a multimedia-based experimental market', in *Frontiers in Economic Psychology*, Nyhus, E. and Troye, S. (eds) (NHH, Bergen) 472–85.

Lunt, P.K. and Livingstone, S.M. (1992), *Mass Consumption and Personal Identity* (Open University Press, Milton Keynes).

Lunt, P. (1996) 'Rethinking the relationship between economics and psychology', *Journal of Economic Psychology*, 17, 2, 275–88.

Mackenzie, C. (1993), *The Shareholder Action Handbook* (New Consumer, Newcastle).

Mackenzie, C. (1997) 'Ethical Investment and the Challenge of Corporate Reform' (PhD Thesis University of Bath).

Mackenzie, C. and Lewis, A. (1998), 'Morals and markets: the case of ethical investors', *Business Ethics Quarterly*, 8.

Maclennan, D. (1982, *Housing Economics* (Longman, London).

Marginson, P. (1994) 'Multinational Britain: employment and work in an internationalised economy', *Human Resource Management Journal*, 4, 4, 63–80.

Margolis, H. (1982), *Selfishness, Altruism and Rationality* (Cambridge University Press, Cambridge).

Marr, W. and Raj, B. (1983). *How Economists Explain* (University Press of America, Lanham).

Mars, G. (1994), *Cheats at Work: an anthropology of workplace crime*, new edition (Dartmouth, Aldershot).

Marsh, D. (1992) 'Industrial relations' in March, D. and Rhodes, R. (eds) *Implementing Thatcherite Policies* (Open University Press, Milton Keynes).

Marshall, T.H. (1950) 'Citizenship and social class', reprinted in Marshall, T.H. and Bottomore, T. (1992) *Citizenship and Social Class* (Pluto, London).

Marshall, T.H. (1981) *The Right to Welfare and Other Essays* (Heinemann, London).

McAvoy, R. (1993) 'Heartsink Hotel revisited', *British Medical Journal*, 306, 694–5.

McCloskey, D. (1986), *The Rhetoric of Economics* (Wheatsheaf, Brighton).

McCracken, G. (1990), *Culture and Consumption* (Indiana University Press, Indianapolis).

McElroy, S.L., Keck, P.E., Harrison, G., Pope, M.D., Smith, M.R. and Strakowski, S.M. (1994), 'Compulsive buying: a report of 20 cases', *Journal of Clinical Psychiatry*, 55, 242–8.

McEvoy, D., T.P. Jones, J. Cater and H. Aldrich (1982), 'Asian immigrant businesses in British cities', Paper presented to *The British Association for the Advancement of Science, Annual Meeting*, September.

McNeil, B., Parker, S., Sox, H. and Tversky, A. (1982), 'On the elicitation of preferences for alternative therapies', *New England Journal of Medicine*, 306, 1259–62.

Mead, L. (1986) *Beyond Entitlement: the social obligations of citizenship* (Free Press, New York).

Melrose, M. (1996) 'Enticing subjects and disembodied objects', in Dean, H. (ed.), *The Ethics of Social Policy Research* (University of Luton Press/ Social Policy Association, Luton).

Merrill, J. (1992) 'A test of our society: how and for whom we finance long-term care', *Inquiry* 29, 2, 176–87.

Metcalf, H., T. Modood and S. Virdee (1996) *Asian Self-Employment: The Interaction of Culture and Economics in England* (Policy Studies Institute, London).

Michie, J. (1994), *Managing the Global Economy* (Oxford University Press, Oxford).

Michie, J. and Wilkinson, F. (1995), 'Wages, government policy and unemployment', *Review of Political Economy*, 7 (2), 133–49.

Miles, D. (1994), *Housing, Financial Markets and the Wider Economy* (Wiley, Chichester).

Mintel (1996), *Green Consumers* (Mintel International, London).

Mischel. W. (1961) 'Preference for delayed reinforcement and social responsibility', *Journal of Abnormal and Social Psychology*, 62, 1–7.

Modood, T., Berthoud, R., Lakey, J. Nazroo, J., Smith, P., Virdee, S., Beishon, S. (1997), 'Ethnic Minorities in Britain: Diversity and Disadvantage', *The Fourth National Survey on Ethnic Minorities* (Policy Studies Institute, London).

Modood, T., S. Beishon and S. Virdee (1994) *Changing Ethnic Identities* (Policy Studies Institute).

Moscovici, S. (1984), 'The phenomenon of social representation', in R. Farr and S. Moscovicic (eds), *Social Representations* (Cambridge University Press, Cambridge).

Munro, M. and Tu, Y. (1996), 'The dynamics of UK national and regional house prices', *Review of Urban and Regional Development Studies* 8, 186–201.

Murray, G. (1984), *Losing Ground: American social policy 1950–1980* (Basic Books, New York).

Muthoo, A. (1996), 'Rationality, learning and social norms', *Economic Journal*, 106, 1357–59.

NOP (1995). *Ethical Investment: a report for Friends Provident.* NOP/43618 (NOP Consumer Market Research, London).

NOP(1995) *Ethical Investment: a report for Friends Provident*, NOP/43618 (NOP Consumer Market Research, London).

NPI (1995), *The Environmental Investors Briefing* (NPI, London).

National Institute of Economic and Social Research (NIESR: 1995) *National Institute Economic Review*, 4/95.

Newton, J., Fraser, M., Robinson, J. and Wainwright, D. (1993), 'Fundholding in Northern Region: the first year', *British Medical Journal*, 306, 375–8.

Niskanen, W. (1973) 'Bureaucracy – Servant or Master?' (Institute of Economic Affairs, London).

Nozick, R. (1974) *Anarchy, State and Utopia* (Blackwell, Oxford).

Nuttal, S., Blackwood, R., Bussell, B., Cliff, J., Cornall, M., Cowley, A., Gatenby, P., and Webber, J. (1993) *Financing Long-Term Care in Great Britain* (Institute of Actuaries, London).

OECD (1994) 'Labour standards and economic integration', *Employment Outlook*, July (OECD, Paris) 137–64.

OECD (1996) *Economic Outlook*, 62, December (OECD, Paris).

Office of National Statistics (ONS, annual) *Social Trends* (HMSO, London).

O'Guinn, T.C. and Faber, R.J. (1989) 'Compulsive buying: a phenomenological exploration', *Journal of Consumer Research*, 16, 147–57.

Oorschot, W. van (1995) 'Multi-level influences on non take-up: clarifying the responsibility of policymakers and administrators for the non-take-up of means-tested benefits', paper to CROP/IISL seminar, *Law, Power and Poverty*, Oñati, Spain, 11–13 May.

Oxley, H. and Martin, J. (1991) 'Controlling government spending and deficits – prospects for the 1990s', *OECD Economic Studies*, 17, Autumn, 145–89.

Pahl, R (1975) *Whose City?* (Penguin, Harmondsworth).

Pahl, R. (1984) *Divisions of Labour* (Blackwell, Oxford).

Parker, G. and Clarke, H. (1997) 'Will you still need me? Will you still feed me? Paying for care in old age', *Social Policy and Administration*, 31, 2.

Parker, G., and Clarke, H. (1996), *Attitudes Towards Long-Term Care for Elderly People: Evidence Submitted to the House of Commons Health Committe* NCCSU Working Paper 38 (Nuffield Community Care Studies Unit, Leicester).

Peach, C. (ed.) (1996) *Ethnicity in the 1991 Census. Volume Two: The ethnic minority populations of Great Britain* (Office for National Statistics, London).

Pierson, P. (1996) *Dismantling the Welfare State* (Cambridge University Press, Cambridge).

Pinch, S. (1994) 'Labour flexibility and the changing welfare state' in R. Burrows and B. Loader (eds) *Towards a Post-Fordist Welfare State?* (Routledge, London).

Piore, M. and Sabel', C. (1984) *The Second Industrial Divide* (Basic Books, New York).

Preston, I.P. and Ridge, M. (1995), 'Demand for local public spending: evidence from the British Social Attitudes Survey', *Economic Journal*.

Ram, M. (1992) 'Coping with racism: Asian employers in the inner-city', *Work, Employment and Society*, 6, 4, December, 601–18.

Renzetti, C. and Lee, R. (eds) (1993) *Researching Sensitive Topics* (Pluto, London).

Richards, E. (1996) *Paying for Long-Term Care* (Institute for Public Policy Research, London).

Richins, M. and Dawson, S. (1992) 'Materialism as a consumer value: measure development and validation', *Journal of Consumer Research*, 19, 303–316.

Rook, D.W. and Fisher, R.J. (1995) 'Normative influence on impulsive buying behaviour', *Journal of Consumer Research*, 22, 305–13.

Rook, D.W. (1987) 'The buying impulse', *Journal of Consumer Research*, 14, 189–99.

Rose, R. (ed.) (1980) *Challenge to Governance* (Sage, New York).

Rowlingson, K. and Kempson, E. (1994), *Paying with Plastic: A Study of Credit Card Debt* (Policy Studies Institute, London).

Sainsbury, R. (1996) 'Rooting out fraud – innocent until proven fraudulent', *Poverty*, 93, 17–20.

Sanders, J. and Nee, V. (1996) 'Immigrant self-employment: the family as social capital and the value of human capital', *American Sociological Review*, 61, April, 231–49.

Saunders, P. (1990) *A Nation of Home Owners* (Unwin Hyman, London).

Savage, L. (1954) *The Foundations of Statistics* (Wiley, New York).

Savage, S., Atkinson, R. and Robins, L. (1994) *Public Policy in Britain* (Macmillan, London).

Scherhorn, G., Reisch, L.A. and Raab, L.A. (1990) 'Addictive buying in West Germany: an empirical investigation', *Journal of Consumer Policy*, 13, 155–89.

Schlosser, S., Black, D.W., Repertinger, S. and Freet, D. (1994) 'Compulsive buying: demography, phenomenology, and comorbidity in 46 subjects', *General Hospital Psychiatry*, 16, 205–12.

Schultz, T.W. (1975) 'The value of the ability to deal with disequilibria', *Journal of Economic Literature*, 13, 827–47.

Schultz, T.W. (1980) 'Investment in entrepreneurial ability', *Scandinavian Journal of Economics*, 82, 437–48.

Schumpeter, J. (1934) *The Theory of Economic Development* (Harvard University Press, Cambridge, Massachusetts).

Schumpeter, J. (1942) *Capitalism, Socialism and Democracy*, 1976 edition (Allen & Unwin, London).

Scott, L. and O'Hara, M.W. (1993), 'Self-discrepancies in clinically anxious and depressed university students', *Journal of Abnormal Psychology*, 102, 282–7.

Seldon, A. (1990) *Capitalism* (Blackwell, Oxford).

Shafir, E., Tversky, A. and Diamond, P. (1994), *On Money Illusion*, MIT Working Paper, August.

Shefrin, H. and Thaler, R. (1988), 'The behavioural life cycle hypothesis', *Economic Enquiry*, 26, 609–43.

244

References

Simon, H. (1978), 'Rationality as process and as product of thought', *American Economic Review*, 68, 2, 1–16.

Smith, D.J. (1977), *Racial Disadvantage in Britain* (Penguin, Harmondsworth).

Smith, R. (1985) 'Who's fiddling? Fraud and abuse' in Ward, S. (ed.), *DHSS in Crisis: social security under pressure and under review* (Child Poverty Action Group, London).

Smith, A. (1759) *The Theory of Moral Sentiments* (Kelley, New York, 1966).

Smith, A. (1776) *The Wealth of Nations* (Penguin, 1986, Harmondsworth).

Social Security Benefits Agency (SSBA)(1995a) *Benefit Review (Income Support and Unemployment Benefit): Report on Methodology and Findings*, BA Security (Benefit Review Team, Leeds).

Social Security Benefits Agency (SSBA)(1995b) *Press Release*, 10 July.

Social Security Committee (SSC) (1991) *The Organisation and Administration of the Department of Social Security, Minutes of Evidence*, 25 June, HC 1990–91, 550-i (HMSO, London).

Sparkes, R. (1995). *The Ethical Investor* (HarperCollins, London).

Srinivasan, S. (1992), 'The class position of the Asian petty bourgeoisie', *New Community*, 19, 1, October, pp. 61–74.

Srinivasan, S. (1995), *The South Asian Petty Bourgeoisie in Britain* (Avebury, Aldershot).

Stephens, M. (1993), 'Housing finance deregulation: Britain's experience', *Netherlands Journal of Housing and the Built Environment*, 8, 159–75.

Stern, A. (1962), 'The significance of impulse buying today', *Journal of Marketing*, 26, 59–62.

Stewart, J. and Walsh, K. (1992), 'Change in the management of public services', *Public Administration*, 70 (Winter), 499–518.

Streeck, W. (1995) 'From market-making to state-building' in S. Leibfried and P. Pierson (eds), *European Social Policy* (Brookings Institute, Washington).

Strotz, R.H. (1956), 'Myopia and inconsistency in dynamic utility maximization,' *Review of Economic Studies*, 23, 165–80.

Sugden, R. (1991) 'Rational choice: a survey of contributions from economics and philosophy', *Economic Journal*, 101, 751–85.

Svallfors, S. (ed.) (1995) *In the Eye of the Beholder* (Impello Sajsupport, Umea).

Tajfel, H. (ed.) (1984) *The Social Dimension*, vols 1 and 2 (Cambridge University Press, Cambridge).

Tawney, R. (1926) *Religion and the Rise of Capitalism: A Historical Study* (John Murray, London).

Taylor-Gooby, P. (1991) Attachment to the Welfare State', in Jowell, Brook and Taylor (eds).

Taylor-Gooby, P. and Lawson, R. (1993) *Markets and Managers* (Open University Press, Milton Keynes).

Thaler, R. (ed.) (1993), *Advances in Behavioural Finance* (Russell Sage, New York).

Thaler, R.H. and Shefrin, H.M. (1981) 'An economic theory of self-control', *Journal of Political Economy*, 89, 392–410.

Thaler, R. (1990) 'Anomalies: saving, fungibility and mental accounts', *Journal of Economic Perspectives* 4, 1, 193–205.

Thaler, R. (1980) 'Towards a positive theory of consumer choice', *Journal of Economic Behaviour and Organisation*, 1, 39–60.

Thaler, R. (1992) *The Winner's Curse* (Free Press, New York).

The Economist (1995) 'Rational economic man', 24 December to 6 January, pp. 96–8.

Timmins, N. (1995) *The Five Giants* (HarperCollins, London).

Titmuss, R. (1962) *Income Distribution and Social Change* (Allen & Unwin, London).

Titmuss, R. (1971) *The Gift Relationship* (Allen & Unwin, London).

Tversky, A. and Kahneman, D. (1974) 'Judgement under uncertainty: heuristics and biases', *Science*, 185, 1124–31.

Tversky, A. and Kahneman, D. (1981) 'The framing of decisions and the psychology of choice', *Science*, 211, 453–8.

United Nations (UN) (1994) *World Economic and Social Survey* (UN Secretariat, New York).

Valence, G., d'Astous, A. and Fortier, L. (1988) 'Compulsive buying: concept and measurement', *Journal of Consumer Policy*, 11, 419–33.

Waldinger, R., H. Aldrich, and R. Ward (1990) *Ethnic Entrepreneurs* (Sage, London).

Walker, R. (1991) *Thinking about Workfare: Evidence from the USA* (HMSO, London).

Walker, A. (1990) 'Blaming victims in C. Murray (ed.) *The Emerging British Underclass* (Institute of Economic Affairs, London).

Wallendorf, M. and Arnould, E.J. (1988) 'My favourite things: a cross-cultural inquiry into object attachment, possessiveness and social linkage', *Journal of Consumer Research*, 14, 531–47.

Warde, A. (1994) 'Consumers, consumption and post-Fordism' in R. Burrows and B. Loader (eds) *Towards a Post-Fordist Welfare State?* (Routledge, London).

Weber, M. (1930) *The Protestant Ethic and the Spirit of Capitalism* (tr. T. Parsons), (Allen & Unwin, London).

Weber, M. (1922) *Economy and Society* (Bedminster Press, New York).

Weber, M. (1930) *The Sociology of Religion* (Beacon Books, Boston).

Webley, P. (1992) 'Ethical investing: the willingness to sacrifice financial return', in B. Rüggelambert *et al.*, *Economic Psychology and Experimental Economics*, pp. 49–51 (Christian Reick Verlag, Eschborn).

Webley, P., Robben, H.S.J., Elffers, H., and Hessing, D.J. (1991). *Tax Evasion: an experimental approach* (Cambridge University Press, Cambridge).

Werbner, P. (1990a) *The Migration Process* (Berg, London).

Werbner, P. (1990b) 'Renewing an industrial past: British Pakistani entrepreneurship in Manchester', *Migration*, 8.

Whiteside, N. (1995) 'Employment policy: a chronicle of decline' in Gladstone, D. (ed.) *British Social Welfare: Past, present and future*, (UCL Press, London).

Whynes, D. (1996) 'Can the NHS reforms make GPs into entrepreneurs?' *EBB Briefing Paper no. 3*, EBB Programme, Social Policy Department, University of Kent.

Wicklund, R.A. and Gollwitzer, P.M. (1982). *Symbolic Self-Completion* (Erlbaum, New Jersey).

Wilcox, S. (1996) *Housing Finance Review 1996/7* (Joseph Rowntree Foundation, York).

Wilding, P. (1982), *Professional Power and Social Welfare* (Routledge, London).

Winnett, A. and Lewis, L. (in preparation.) 'You have to be green to invest in this', *Journalism, Finance and Ethics*.

Winston, G.C. (1980) 'Addiction and backsliding: a theory of compulsive consumption' *Journal of Economic Behaviour and Organization*, 1, 295–324.

Woo, C.Y., Cooper, A.C. and Dunkelberg, W.C. (1991) 'The development and interpretation of entrepreneurial typologies', *Journal of Business Venturing*, 6(2) 93–114.

Wood, A. (1994) 'North–South trade', *Employment and Inequality* (Oxford University Press, Oxford).

Index

Notes: Chapter headings (in **bold** type) have been given against an entry where the subject matter is covered entirely, or almost entirely, within that chapter; these entries include references from the summary Chapter 11.

Page numbers in **bold** type refer to illustrative figures or tables.